CHINA AND THE MIDDLE EAST

HEARING

BEFORE THE

U.S.-CHINA ECONOMIC AND SECURITY REVIEW COMMISSION

ONE HUNDRED THIRTEENTH CONGRESS
FIRST SESSION

THURSDAY, JUNE 6, 2013

Printed for use of the
United States-China Economic and Security Review Commission
Available via the World Wide Web: www.uscc.gov

UNITED STATES-CHINA ECONOMIC AND SECURITY REVIEW
COMMISSION

WASHINGTON: 2013

U.S.-CHINA ECONOMIC AND SECURITY REVIEW COMMISSION

Hon. WILLIAM A. REINSCH, *Chairman*
Hon. DENNIS C. SHEA, Vice *Chairman*

Commissioners:

CAROLYN BARTHOLOMEW	DANIEL M. SLANE
PETER BROOKES	SEN. JAMES TALENT
ROBIN CLEVELAND	DR. KATHERINE C. TOBIN
JEFFREY L. FIEDLER	MICHAEL R. WESSEL
SEN. CARTE P. GOODWIN	DR. LARRY M. WORTZEL

MICHAEL R. DANIS, *Executive Director*

The Commission was created on October 30, 2000 by the Floyd D. Spence National Defense Authorization Act for 2001 § 1238, Public Law No. 106-398, 114 STAT. 1654A-334 (2000) (codified at 22 U.S.C. § 7002 (2001), as amended by the Treasury and General Government Appropriations Act for 2002 § 645 (regarding employment status of staff) & § 648 (regarding changing annual report due date from March to June), Public Law No. 107-67, 115 STAT. 514 (Nov. 12, 2001); as amended by Division P of the "Consolidated Appropriations Resolution, 2003," Pub L. No. 108-7 (Feb. 20, 2003) (regarding Commission name change, terms of Commissioners, and responsibilities of the Commission); as amended by Public Law No. 109-108 (H.R. 2862) (Nov. 22, 2005) (regarding responsibilities of Commission and applicability of FACA); as amended by Division J of the "Consolidated Appropriations Act, 2008," Public Law Nol. 110-161 (December 26, 2007) (regarding responsibilities of the Commission, and changing the Annual Report due date from June to December).

The Commission's full charter is available at www.uscc.gov.

June 10, 2013

The Honorable Patrick J. Leahy
President Pro Tempore of the Senate, Washington, D.C. 20510
The Honorable John A. Boehner
Speaker of the House of Representatives, Washington, D.C. 20515

DEAR SENATOR LEAHY AND SPEAKER BOEHNER:

We are pleased to notify you of the Commission's June 6, 2013 public hearing on "China and the Middle East." The Floyd D. Spence National Defense Authorization Act (amended by Pub. L. No. 109-108, section 635(a)) provides the basis for this hearing.

At the hearing, the Commissioners received testimony from the following witnesses: Dr. Dawn Murphy, Postdoctoral Research Fellow, Princeton-Harvard China in the World Program; Dr. Yitzhak Shichor, Professor Emeritus, the Hebrew University of Jerusalem and the University of Haifa; Dr. Erica Down, Fellow, John L. Thornton China Center, Brookings Institution; Mr. Bryant Edwards, Partner, Latham & Watkins LLP, Hong Kong; Dr. Jon B. Alterman, Director, Middle East Program, Center for Strategic and International Studies; Dr. Joel Wuthnow, Research Analyst, China Studies, CNA; and Dr. Andrew Erickson, Associate Professor and founding member, China Maritime Studies Institute, U.S. Naval War College. This hearing examined China's policies and perspectives related to the Middle East, including on energy security, trade and investment, regional conflicts and instability in countries like Syria and Iran. In addition, this hearing assessed how China's Middle East policies impact U.S. interests in the region and beyond.

We note that prepared statements for the hearing, the hearing transcript, and supporting documents submitted by the witnesses will soon be available on the Commission's website at www.USCC.gov. Members and the staff of the Commission are available to provide more detailed briefings. We hope these materials will be helpful to the Congress as it continues its assessment of U.S.-China relations and their impact on U.S. security.

The Commission will examine in greater depth these issues, and the other issues enumerated in its statutory mandate, in its 2013 Annual Report that will be submitted to Congress in November 2013. Should you have any questions regarding this hearing or any other issue related to China, please do not hesitate to have your staff contact our Congressional Liaison, Reed Eckhold, at (202) 624-1496 or via email at reckhold@uscc.gov.

Sincerely yours,

Hon. William A. Reinsch
Chairman

Hon. Dennis C. Shea
Vice Chairman

CONTENTS

THURSDAY, JUNE 6, 2013

CHINA AND THE MIDDLE EAST

Panel I: China's Perspectives and Policy in the Middle East

Panel II: China's Energy and Other Economic Interests in the Middle East

Panel III: China's Political and Security Challenges in the Middle East

CHINA AND THE MIDDLE EAST

THURSDAY, JUNE 6, 2013

———————

U.S.-CHINA ECONOMIC AND SECURITY REVIEW COMMISSION

Washington, D.C.

The Commission met in Dirksen Senate Office Building, Room 608, Washington, D.C. at 9:00 a.m., Commissioners Jeffrey Fiedler and James Talent (Hearing Co-Chairs), presiding.

OPENING STATEMENT OF JEFFREY FIEDLER
HEARING CO-CHAIR

HEARING CO-CHAIR FIEDLER: Good morning and thank you for joining us. Today's hearing on "China and the Middle East" is the sixth hearing of the Commission's 2013 Annual Report cycle. We appreciate your attendance and we encourage you to come to our other public events throughout the year. Our next hearing will be on June 27, and will focus on Macau and Hong Kong. Details will be forthcoming on the Commission's web site at www.uscc.gov.

Today's hearing will examine China's relations with the Middle East. Our first panel will assess the motivations behind Beijing's engagement with the region and explore how Chinese policymakers perceive the Middle East in the context of China's broader economic and strategic objectives.

While China's engagement in the region pales in comparison to that of the United States, there are indications that Beijing may take a more forward-leaning approach to the Middle East. For instance, some Chinese scholars have advised that Beijing adopt a new foreign policy emphasizing its political and economic ties to countries in the Middle East and Central Asia.

This policy, referred to as "March West," appears to be under consideration by policymakers in Beijing. In addition to discussing evolving strategic thinking about the region, this panel will also examine China's engagement with Middle Eastern countries which range from strategic partnerships to military exchanges to free trade agreements.

In our second panel, we'll call on witnesses to describe China's economic interests in the region. For centuries, China had robust ties with this part of the world by virtue of the Silk Road. Today, China's economic ties to the region are strong and growing. Foremost among China's economic interests is energy. China must increasingly rely on imported oil and gas to fuel its economy, and over one-half of China's oil imports come from the Middle East. According to the International Energy Agency, by 2035, 90 percent of Middle Eastern oil will be exported to Asia. Most of that oil will go to China.

But energy is not Beijing's only economic interest in the region. China seeks markets for its exports and investment opportunities, and despite political risks throughout the region, Chinese companies, many of them state-owned, are indeed "marching West" to the Middle East.

Our third panel will examine China's approaches to political and security challenges. Beijing was caught off guard by the changes wrought during the Arab Spring. In Egypt and Libya, China struggled to come to terms with regime change and scrambled to protect its citizens and investments abroad. In Syria, Beijing's refusal to punish the Assad regime has hindered international efforts to address the conflict.

Similarly, with Iran, China has worked to soften U.S. and international sanctions on Tehran. This has frustrated not only the United States but also Middle Eastern countries concerned about Iran's nuclear capabilities and its generally threatening posture. Finally, this panel will look at China's approach to maritime security in the region.

Before I turn the microphone over to my colleague, Senator Talent, I would like to thank the Senate Budget Committee Chairwoman Patty Murray and the entire staff of the Senate Budget Committee for helping to provide today's hearing venue.

PREPARED STATEMENT OF JEFFREY FIEDLER
HEARING CO-CHAIR

U.S.-China Economic and Security
Review Commission

Hearing on China and the Middle East

Opening Statement of Commissioner Jeffrey Fiedler
June 6, 2013
Washington, DC

Good morning and thank you for joining us. Today's hearing on "China and the Middle East" is the sixth hearing of the 2013 Annual Report cycle. We appreciate your attendance and we encourage you to come to our other public events throughout the year. Our next hearing will be on June 27, on Macau and Hong Kong. Details will be forthcoming on the Commission's website, uscc.gov.

Today's hearing will examine China's relations with the Middle East. Our first panel will assess the motivations behind Beijing's engagement with the region, and explore how Chinese policymakers perceive the Middle East in the context of China's broader economic and strategic objectives. While China's engagement in the region pales in comparison to that of the United States, there are indications that Beijing may take a more forward-leaning approach to the Middle East. For instance, some Chinese scholars have advised that Beijing adopt a new foreign policy emphasizing its political and economic ties to countries in the Middle East and Central Asia. This policy, referred to as "March West," appears to be under consideration by policymakers in Beijing. In addition to discussing Beijing's evolving strategic thinking about the region, this panel will also examine China's engagement in the region, which ranges from strategic partnerships, to military exchanges, to free trade agreement talks.

In our second panel, we'll call on witnesses to describe China's economic interests in the region. For centuries, China had robust ties with this part of the world by virtue of the Silk Road. Today, China's economic ties to the region are strong and growing. Foremost among China's economic interests in the Middle East is energy. China must increasingly rely on imported oil and gas to fuel its economy, and over one-half of China's oil imports come from the Middle East. According to the International Energy Agency, by 2035, 90 percent of Middle Eastern oil will be exported to Asia. Most of that oil will go to China. But energy is not Beijing's only economic interest in the Middle East. China seeks markets for its exports, and investment opportunities. And despite political risks throughout the region, Chinese companies, many of them state-owned, are indeed "marching west" to the Middle East.

Our third panel will examine China's approaches to political and security challenges in the Middle East. Beijing was caught off guard by the changes wrought during the Arab Spring. In Egypt and Libya, China struggled to come to terms with regime change and scrambled to protect its citizens and investments abroad. In Syria, Beijing's refusal to punish the Assad regime has hindered international efforts to address the conflict. Similarly, with Iran, China has worked to soften U.S. and international sanctions on Tehran. This has frustrated not only the United States, but also Middle Eastern countries concerned about Iran's nuclear capabilities and its generally threatening posture. Finally, this panel will look at China's approach to maritime security in the Middle East.

Before I turn the microphone over to my colleague Senator Talent, I would like to thank Senate Budget Committee Chairwoman Patty Murray and the entire staff of the Senate Budget Committee for helping to provide today's hearing venue.

\#   \#

OPENING STATEMENT OF JAMES TALENT
HEARING CO-CHAIR

HEARING CO-CHAIR TALENT: Thank you, Commissioner Fiedler, and welcome to our panelists and guests.

China's engagement with the Middle East is of particular importance to the United States given our country's multifaceted interests and investments in that part of the world. China is expanding its economic, diplomatic, political and security presence in and around the Middle East. The better America understands China's approach to the region, the better prepared we will be to respond in a way that promotes peace and prosperity. In light of China's growing footprint in the Middle East, we ask the following questions:

Will China contribute to political stability and economic growth in the Middle East?

Will China seek to match or challenge U.S. influence in the region?

What impact will China's massive appetite for Middle Eastern oil have on global energy security?

Will China's continued friendship with Iran undermine U.S. national security?

The answers to these questions are complex, and so far China's relationship with the Middle East has resulted in a range of outcomes, some of which complement U.S. interests and some of which undermine them.

For example, Chinese investments are underwriting key development projects in the Middle East, from highways and railways to power stations, irrigation systems, and housing. Chinese investments in Iraq's energy sector may enable post-war growth while bringing substantial new oil supplies on-line. Such engagement has the potential to contribute to stability and economic productivity in the region.

On the other hand, however, Beijing's support of regimes in Syria and Iran has undermined international efforts to stem violence and human rights abuses in the former and to stop the development of nuclear weapons in the latter. In these and other cases, China's activities detract from peace and security in the region.

We have a number of highly qualified expert panelists today to help us assess these issues and suggest how the United States might appropriately respond. I would like to remind the members of our audience that all the written statements submitted for the record are available on our web site at www.uscc.gov. The testimony at this and other hearings will help to inform our Annual Report to Congress, which will be published in mid-November.

Finally, we ask that the panelists limit their opening remarks to seven minutes each in order to leave plenty of time for questions and answers.

PREPARED STATEMENT OF JAMES TALENT
HEARING CO-CHAIR

U.S.- China Economic and Security
Review Commission

Opening Statement of Senator James Talent
June 6, 2013
Washington, DC

Thank you, Commissioner Fiedler, and welcome to our panelists and guests.

China's engagement with the Middle East is of particular importance to the United States given our country's multifaceted interests and investments in that part of the world.   China is expanding its economic, diplomatic, political, and security presence in and around the Middle East. The better America understands China's approach to the region, the better prepared we will be able to respond in a way that promotes peace and prosperity.

In light of China's growing footprint in the Middle East, we ask the following questions: Will China contribute to political stability and economic growth in the Middle East? Will China seek to match or challenge U.S. influence in the region? What impact will China's massive appetite for Middle Eastern oil have on global energy security? Will China's continued friendship with Iran undermine U.S. national security?

The answers to these questions are complex, and so far, China's relationship with the Middle East has resulted in a range of outcomes, some of which complement U.S. interests, and some of which undermine them. For example, Chinese investments are underwriting key development projects in the Middle East, from highways and railways to power stations, irrigation systems, and housing. Chinese investments in Iraq's energy sector may enable enormous post-war growth while bringing substantial new oil supplies online. Such engagement has the potential to contribute to stability and economic productivity in the region. On the other hand, however, Beijing's support of regimes in Syria and Iran have undermined international efforts to stem violence and human rights abuses in the former, and to stop the development of nuclear weapons in the latter. In these and other cases, China's activities detract from peace and security in the region.

We have a number of highly qualified expert panelists today to help us assess these issues and suggest how the United States might appropriately respond.

I would like to remind the members of our audience that all of the written statements submitted for the record are available on our website, uscc.gov. A transcript of today's hearing also will be published on our website at a later date. And the testimony at this and other hearings will help to inform our Annual Report to Congress, which will be published in mid-November.

We ask that the panelists limit their opening remarks to seven minutes each in order to leave plenty of time for questions and answers.

#   #

PANEL I INTRODUCTION BY COMMISSIONER JEFFREY FIEDLER
HEARING CO-CHAIR

HEARING CO-CHAIR FIEDLER: Thank you, Senator Talent.
The first panel explores Chinese perspectives and policies related to the Middle East. Our two expert witnesses for this panel are Dr. Dawn Murphy and Dr. Yitzhak Shichor.

Dr. Murphy is a postdoctoral research fellow at the Princeton-Harvard China and the World Program. Her current research analyzes China's interests and behavior as a rising global power, and she's working on a book about China's relations with the Middle East and Africa. Dr. Murphy received her Bachelor of Science degree from Cornell University, a Master's from Columbia, and a Ph.D. from George Washington University.

Dr. Shichor is a Professor Emeritus at the Hebrew University of Jerusalem and the University of Haifa. Dr. Shichor has written widely on Chinese domestic and foreign policy issues. His main research interests include China's Middle East policy, international energy relations, and Sino-Uyghur relations, among other things. Dr. Shichor received his Ph.D. in international relations from the London School of Economics.

Dr. Murphy, please start.

**OPENING STATEMENT OF DR. DAWN MURPHY
POSTDOCTORAL RESEARCH FELLOW
PRINCETON-HARVARD CHINA IN THE WORLD PROGRAM**

DR. MURPHY: I thank the Commission for the opportunity to testify before it on the topic of China and the Middle East. During my testimony, when I refer to the Middle East, I utilize the Commission's regional definition plus Algeria, Morocco, the Palestinian territories, and Turkey.

The first question posed by the Commission was: what drives Chinese policies, activities and interests in the Middle East? China's most important interest in the Middle East is promoting its own economic development. Natural resource supply and export markets for Chinese goods and services are at the heart of this interest. China became a net oil importer in 1993, and today it's the world's second-largest importer at 5.5 million barrels per day.

China's imports from the Middle East, primarily composed of petroleum and gas, grew rapidly from US$4 billion in 1999 to US$160 billion in 2012. As of 2011, the Middle East accounted for 55 percent of China's crude oil imports. China also views the region as an immense economic opportunity for Chinese firms. China's product exports to the region grew from US$6 billion in 1999 to US$121 billion in 2012. China's primary exports to this region are light industrial products, including consumer electronics and appliances, textiles, machinery, and automobiles.

The Middle East is also a huge service export market for China's construction, telecommunication, and finance industries. For example, in 2011, China's construction services in the Middle East were US$21 billion.

Related to China's economic interests are its concerns about economic security and regional stability in the Middle East. The region is viewed as a turbulent U.S.-dominated area, which is a hotbed of great power competition. To protect its economic interests, China wants stability between countries and within countries.

After promoting its own economic growth, China's second-most important interest in the Middle East is fostering international support in an emerging multipolar world. It envisions developing countries, including those in the Middle East, as playing an increasingly important role in this new order.

China's third-most important interest is ensuring its own domestic stability. In particular, Muslim support for insurgency activities in Xinjiang is a key concern. To maintain domestic stability, China seeks support from Middle Eastern governments for its suppression of its insurgency activities. After the beginning of the Arab Spring, China's concern regarding domestic stability has shifted from issues related to Xinjiang to a concern over preventing the spread of Arab Spring-style upheaval from the Middle East to China.

Finally, China also has a strong interest in advocating for

developing country causes. In the post-Cold War era, China has consistently called for the establishment of a just and equitable new international and economic and political order. Middle Eastern states are seen as key partners in South-South cooperation and pursuing that new order.

Now that I've discussed China's interests, I will briefly describe its engagement with the region. Since 2000, China's relations with Middle Eastern countries have rapidly expanded to include a vast array of political, economic, cultural and military interactions.

China has established two cooperation forums that include Middle Eastern countries: the Forum on China-Africa Cooperation, FOCAC, and the China-Arab States Cooperation Forum. FOCAC was established in 2000 and includes the entire continent of Africa, including North Africa. The Arab States Cooperation Forum was established in 2004. The League of Arab States represents its 21 members in the forum.

The foundations of political cooperation in these forums are China's Five Principles of Peaceful Coexistence, South-South Cooperation, the One China Principle, and support for Arab political causes, especially the Arab-Israeli conflict.

China's Five Principles of Peaceful Coexistence are: mutual respect for territory and sovereignty; mutual nonaggression; mutual non-interference in internal affairs; equality and mutual benefit; and peaceful coexistence.

The main areas of economic cooperation in these forums are trade, investment, infrastructure, and economic security. Military cooperation is not a major component of either forum.

Another important foreign policy tool is China's Middle East Issues Special Envoy. Established in 2002, the Envoy is focused on the Middle East peace process and other issues of concern in the region. It was established due to the urging of Arab states for China to become more involved in the issue.

Many Arab states perceive China to be a more balanced player in the Middle East peace process than other great powers, especially the U.S., due to China's historical support for Palestine.

China has also built political relations with countries in the region through strategic partnerships and top leader visits. China established a strategic partnership with the African continent in 2006 via FOCAC and with the League of Arab States via the Arab States Cooperation Forum in 2010. To date, China has initiated strategic partnerships with Egypt, Saudi Arabia, Algeria, Turkey, and the UAE. From 2003 to 2012, the Hu Jintao administration conducted top leader visits to Egypt, Saudi Arabia, Morocco, the UAE, Qatar and Turkey.

Yet another political tool utilized by China is the United Nations Security Council voting. In general, China votes in alignment with the other Permanent Five members of the United Nations Security Council. The vast majority of China's abstentions and all of China's vetoes have been over issues of territorial integrity, particularly sanctions and the jurisdiction of criminal courts.

China's yes votes that differ from the U.S. and the Security Council tend to involve Chinese support for the Palestinians in the Arab-Israeli conflict. Before 2011, China rarely utilized its veto power, but instead often employed abstention to voice disapproval without directly confronting the U.S. and other P5 members. That pattern changed with the beginning of the Arab Spring. From 2011 to 2012, China cast three vetoes on resolutions about Syria.

To build economic relations with the Middle East, in addition to economic activity in its cooperation forums, China has promoted economic engagement by launching free trade agreement negotiations with the Gulf Cooperation Council, provided extensive government support to Chinese companies operating in the region, and established special economic zones in Egypt and Algeria.

China also actively engages in cultural diplomacy with the Middle East. It has established Confucius Institutes in Egypt, Turkey, the UAE, Iran, Israel, Jordan, Lebanon, and Morocco.

Another area of engagement is China's military relations. To date, China has participated in four United Nations Peacekeeping Operations (UNPKO) in the Middle East: the U.N. Truce Supervision Organization, the U.N. Iraq-Kuwait Observer Mission, the U.N. Interim Force in Lebanon, and the U.N. Supervision Mission in Syria. Also in coordination with the international community since 2008, China has engaged in antipiracy operations in the Gulf of Aden.

China's bilateral military interactions with the region include conventional arms sales and military exchanges. Since the end of the Cold War, China's conventional arms sales to countries in the Middle East have consistently been limited. In 2012, sales to the entire regional totaled a mere US$45 million.

Finally, between 2001 and 2010, China performed high-level military exchanges with every Middle Eastern country except Iraq. China's highest volume of military exchanges in the Middle East were with Egypt, Turkey, Syria, Jordan and Tunisia.

Now that I've discussed China's interests and behavior in the Middle East, I will respond to a few additional questions posed by the Commission. First, how do Middle Eastern states view China? How do they view China's engagement in the region, especially vis-a-vis the U.S.?

In general, Middle Eastern government officials I have interviewed are quite positive about the impact of China in the Middle East. They view China as a formidable economic partner and a country that shares many of their world views as developing countries.

China is also seen as a relatively balanced power in relation to the Arab-Israeli conflict, which is positively received by Arab states and the Arab League. Generally, Middle Eastern officials do not want relations with China to endanger their existing close relations with the U.S.

It is important to note that China's vetoes in the Security Council regarding Syria did, at least temporarily, negatively impact China's relations with some members of the Arab League.

Although it is limited, public opinion polling from the region indicates that the broader public also views China favorably. For example, in recent Pew Global Attitudes Project polling, every Middle Eastern Country polled except for Israel had higher favorability scores for China than for the U.S. Even the Turkish population, many of whom have deep concerns about China's treatment of Uyghurs, have a higher favorability rating for China than the U.S.

Another question posed was: historically China has been perceived as reluctant to challenge the U.S. interests and influence in the Middle East. Assess whether this is true today.

Yes, in general, China still appears to be reluctant to challenge U.S. interests and influence in the Middle East. China's relative cooperation with the U.S. on various actions against Iran targeted at limiting Tehran's nuclear program is an example of China's attempts to avoid confrontation in the Middle East over an issue that is vital to the U.S.

That said, in recent years, China has been more willing to challenge the U.S. in the region. For example, despite heavy pressure from the U.S., China has cast three vetoes regarding the Syria issue.

Finally, I have some very broad policy recommendations. China and the U.S. share common interests in the Middle East, including a desire for energy security, regional stability, and economic and social development in the region. As a result, I would suggest that joint initiatives in the following areas be pursued to foster cooperation between the U.S. and China: energy source exploration; alternative energy research and development; further antipiracy initiatives; joint economic policy guidance to emerging markets in the region; and water security projects.

In light of perception in the Middle East that China is a relatively balanced actor in the Arab-Israeli conflict, the U.S. could also more actively involve China in the Middle East peace process efforts.

Thank you again for inviting me to testify today. I look forward to your questions.

**PREPARED STATEMENT OF DR. DAWN MURPHY
POSTDOCTORAL RESEARCH FELLOW
PRINCETON-HARVARD CHINA IN THE WORLD PROGRAM**

Testimony before the U.S.-China Economic and Security Review Commission

Dr. Dawn C. Murphy
Postdoctoral Research Fellow
Princeton University

Hearing on "China and the Middle East"

June 6, 2013

Introduction

I thank the Commission for the opportunity to testify before it on the topic of China and the Middle East. My comments below directly respond to the eight questions posed by the Committee.

The following comments focus on China's post-Cold War relations with the Middle East (1990-2012). In all of the below discussion, the Middle East is defined as including Algeria, Bahrain, Egypt, Iran, Iraq, Israel, Jordan, Kuwait, Lebanon, Libya, Morocco, Oman, the Palestinian Territories, Qatar, Saudi Arabia, Syria, Tunisia, Turkey, the United Arab Emirates, and Yemen.

My comments are heavily influenced by fifteen months of fieldwork conducted in China and Egypt from 2009 through 2013, including over 120 interviews. While a Visiting Scholar at the Chinese Academy of Social Sciences, Institute of World Economics and Politics, in Beijing, China, (September 2009 through May 2010), I conducted intensive research regarding Chinese academic work on this topic; collected data; and interviewed Chinese scholars, government officials, and economic actors as well as a number of Middle Eastern embassy officials. As a Visiting Research Fellow at the American University in Cairo, Egypt, (September 2010 through December 2010), I interviewed relevant scholars and government officials and identified pertinent scholarly work produced within the Arab world. Finally, in 2013 I conducted follow-up interviews in Beijing regarding the impact of the Arab Spring on China's interests and behavior after 2010. Over the course of those fifteen months of field research, I officially interviewed Middle Eastern government officials with China-related responsibilities from Bahrain, Egypt, Iraq, Israel, Jordan, Oman, Palestine, Tunisia, Turkey, and the United Arab Emirates.

Question 1:
What drives Chinese policies, activities, and interests in the Middle East? Broadly speaking, what are China's economic and strategic interests in the region? How does Beijing balance these with its larger foreign and domestic interests?

In the post-Cold War era, China's interests in the Middle East are promoting China's own economic growth, fostering support for China in the international system, ensuring China's own domestic stability, and advocating for developing country causes.

China's most important interest in the Middle East is promoting its own economic development. Natural resource supply and export markets for Chinese goods and services are at the heart of this interest. China's imports from the Middle East have rapidly increased during the last two decades. China became a net oil importer in 1993 and today it is the world's second largest importer (5.5 mn. bb/d) after the United States.[1] As a result, China's imports from the Middle East (primarily composed of petroleum and gas) grew from $3.8 bn. in 1999 to $160 bn. in 2012.[2] As of 2011, the Middle East accounted for 55% of China's crude oil imports.[3] China's top crude oil suppliers in the region are Saudi Arabia (22%), Iran (12%), Oman (8%), Iraq (6%), Kuwait (4%), and the United Arab Emirates (3%).[4]

Although China's natural resource acquisition needs are a key component of its interest in promoting its own economic development, China's search for export markets in the Middle East is equally significant. China views the region as an immense economic opportunity for Chinese firms. China's product exports to the Middle East have dramatically increased over the last twenty years. They ballooned from $6.47 bn. in 1999 to $121 bn. in 2012.[5] China's top five export destinations in 2012 were the United Arab Emirates ($30 bn.), Saudi Arabia ($18 bn.), Turkey ($16 bn.), Iran ($11 bn.), and Egypt ($8 bn.).[6] China's primary exports were light industrial products (including consumer electronics and appliances), textiles, clothing, machinery, and automobiles.[7]

In addition to product exports, the Middle East is a huge service export market for China's construction, telecommunication, and finance industries. Contract services by construction firms are a particularly important segment of these services. In 2011, China's construction services in the Middle East were $21 bn.[8] China's 2011 top construction service markets in the Middle East were Saudi Arabia ($4.4 bn.), Algeria ($4.1 bn.), Iran ($2.2 bn.), United Arab Emirates ($1.9 bn.), and Iraq ($1.8 bn.)[9]

Foreign direct investment is not a major interest for China in the Middle East. Compared to its exports of goods and services, China's overseas direct investment (ODI) in the region is minimal. In 2010, it was merely $1.3 bn.[10]

[1] U.S. Energy Information Administration, *Country Analysis Briefs: China,* last updated September 2012, www.eia.doe.gov/countries/cab.cfm?fips=CH (accessed May 22, 2013).
[2] Data compiled from International Monetary Fund (IMF), *Direction of Trade Statistics Database,* www.imfstatistics.org (accessed May 22, 2013).
[3] U.S. Energy Information Administration, *Country Analysis Briefs: China,* last updated September 2012, www.eia.doe.gov/countries/cab.cfm?fips=CH (accessed May 24, 2013).
[4] Ibid.
[5] Data compiled from International Monetary Fund (IMF), *Direction of Trade Statistics Database,* www.imfstatistics.org (accessed May 22, 2013).
[6] Ibid.
[7] See Wang Lian, "Economic and Trade Relations Between China and Middle Eastern Countries," *International Studies*, No. 4 (2008), p. 26; and Jon B.Alterman and John W. Garver, *The Vital Triangle: China, the United States, and the Middle East.* (Washington, D.C.: CSIS Press, 2008), p. 57.
[8] Data compiled from *China Statistical Yearbooks 2000-2012.* China National Bureau of Statistics.
[9] Ibid.
[10] Data compiled from *Statistical Bulletin of China's Outward Foreign Direct Investment* (China Ministry of Commerce, 2009), p. 78-83, at http://chinainvests.files.wordpress.com/2010/12/2009-mofcom-investment-report1.pdf (accessed on March 17, 2011) and Statistical Bulletin of China's Outward Foreign Direct Investment (China Ministry of Commerce, 2011), p. 82-84, at

Related to China's interest in promoting its own economic growth are its concerns about economic security and regional stability in the Middle East. The region is viewed as a turbulent, U.S. dominated area which is a hotbed of great power competition, especially after the United States' invasion of Iraq in 2003 and the beginning of the Arab Spring in 2011. In order to ensure continued access to resources and markets in this region and to protect its own businesses and citizens operating in the region, China wants stability between countries and within countries.

After promoting its own economic growth, China's second most important interest in the Middle East is fostering international support in an emerging multipolar world order. Since the end of the Cold War, China has perceived an emerging multipolar order. Its proclamations regarding the inevitability of the trend toward multipolarity intensified after the 2008 Global Financial Crisis.[11] It envisions developing countries (including those in the Middle East) as playing an increasingly important role in this new order. As a result, one of its major interests in the Middle East is gaining political support from these countries through South-South Cooperation.

In addition to promoting its own economic growth and fostering support in the international system, China's third most important interest is ensuring its own domestic stability. Due to religious and ethnic strife in Xinjiang, China's Muslim dominated province, the Middle East is perceived as a potential source of domestic instability for China. In particular, Turkish support for insurgency activities (due to shared ethnic heritage with the Uigurs) is a key concern. This domestic stability interest in relation to the Middle East intensified after September 11, 2001 and became particularly acute after the Xinjiang riots in 2009.[12] To maintain domestic stability, China seeks support from Middle Eastern governments for its suppression of insurgency activities in Xinjiang. After the beginning of the Arab Spring, China's concern regarding domestic stability in relation to the Middle East has shifted from issues related to Xinjiang to a concern over preventing the spread of Arab Spring style upheaval from the Middle East to China.[13]

Finally, China also has a strong interest in advocating for developing country causes. In the post-Cold War era, China has consistently called for the establishment of a just and equitable new international

---

http://images.mofcom.gov.cn/hzs/accessory/201109/1316069658609.pdf.(accessed on May 24, 2013).

[11] For example, see *The Diversified Employment of China's Armed Forces* (2012). White Paper, Beijing, China: Information Office of the State Council of the People's Republic of China, April 16, 2013 (accessed on-line on May 30, 2013 at http://www.china.org.cn/government/whitepaper/node_7181425.htm); *China's National Defense in 2010.* White Paper, Beijing, China: Information Office of the State Council of the People's Republic of China, March 31, 2011, (accessed on-line on June 7, 2011 at www.china.org.cn/government/whitepaper/node_7114675.htm); *China's National Defense in 2008.* White Paper, Beijing, China: Information Office of the State Council of the People's Republic of China, January 20, 2009 , (accessed on-line on June 7, 2011 at http://www.china.org.cn/government/whitepaper/node_7060059.htm); *China's Foreign Affairs: 2009 Edition.* Beijing, China: Department of Policy Planning, Ministry of Foreign Affairs, People's Republic of China, World Affairs Press, 2009, p. 1-3; *China's Foreign Affairs: 2008 Edition.* Beijing, China: Department of Policy Planning, Ministry of Foreign Affairs, People's Republic of China, World Affairs Press, 2008, p. 1-2.

[12] In July 2009, there was large scale violence between ethnic Han Chinese and Uigurs in Xinjiang. According to Chinese authorities, 137 of those killed were Han, 46 were Uighur and 1 was from the Hui ethnic group. See Edward Wong, "China Raises Death Toll in Ethnic Clashes to 184," *New York Times*, July 10, 2009, available at: http://www.nytimes.com/2009/07/11/world/asia/11china.html.

[13] For example, see Bruce Dickson (2011). No "Jasmine" for China. *Current History, 110*(737), 211-216.

economic and political order which better represents the needs of developing countries. At the heart of this envisioned order is addressing economic and political inequalities between the developing world and the developed world, between the global South and the global North. During the Hu Jintao administration, China's self-identification as a developing country and calls for establishing this new order escalated.[14] The 2008 Global Financial Crisis also amplified China's demands for a new, more inclusive order.[15] Middle Eastern states are seen as key partners in South-South cooperation and pursuing this new order.

Question 2:
Characterize China's economic, diplomatic, cultural, and military engagement in the Middle East.

Since 2000, China relations with Middle Eastern countries have rapidly expanded to include a vast array of political, economic, cultural and military interactions. The following describes major aspects of that engagement: Cooperation Forums, the Middle East Issues Special Envoy,

---

[14] For example, see *China's National Defense in 2002.* White Paper, Beijing, China: Information Office of the State Council of the People's Republic of China, December 2002, (accessed on-line on June 7, 2011 at http://www.china.org.cn/e-white/20021209/index.htm); *China's Foreign Affairs: 2003 Edition.* Beijing, China: Department of Policy Planning, Ministry of Foreign Affairs, People's Republic of China, World Affairs Press, 2003, p. 1,6; "Comparison -- Text of Wen Jiabao's Speech at China-African Cooperation Forum," Xinhua Domestic Service, December 15, 2003, accessed via World News Connection on June 10, 2011; "Full Text of Hu Jintao Speech at North-South Leaders' Dialogue Meeting," Xinhua Domestic Service, June 1, 2003, accessed via World News Connection on June 10, 2011; *China's Foreign Affairs: 2004 Edition.* Beijing, China: Department of Policy Planning, Ministry of Foreign Affairs, People's Republic of China, World Affairs Press, 2004, p. 1, 7-8, 35-36; "Wen Jiabao Delivers Speech Marking Five Principles of Peaceful Coexistence Anniversary," Xinhua Domestic Service, June 28, 2004, accessed on-line via World News Connection on June 10, 2011; *China's National Defense in 2004.* White Paper, Beijing, China: Information Office of the State Council of the People's Republic of China, December 2004 , (accessed on-line on June 7, 2011 at http://www.china.org.cn/e-white/20041227/index.htm); *China's Peaceful Development Road.* White Paper, Beijing, China: Information Office of the State Council of the People's Republic of China, December 12, 2005, (accessed on-line on June 7, 2011 at http://www.china.org.cn/english/features/book/152684.htm); "Full Text of Hu Jintao's Speech at UN Summit 15 September," Xinhua Domestic Service, September 16, 2005, accessed on-line via World News Connection on June 10, 2011; "Full Text of Hu Jintao Speech at Asia-Africa Summit in Jakarta 22 Apr," Xinhua Domestic Service, May 5, 2005, accessed on-line via World News Connection on June 10, 2011; "Full Text of Hu Jintao's Speech at Asian-African Business Summit Reception," Xinhua, April 21, 2005, accessed via World News Connection on June 10, 2011; "Comparison – 'Full Text' of Hu Jintao's Speech at Opening of G-20 Meeting," Xinhua Domestic Service, April 16, 2005, accessed on-line via World News Connection on June 10, 2011; *China's Foreign Affairs: 2006 Edition.* Beijing, China: Department of Policy Planning, Ministry of Foreign Affairs, People's Republic of China, World Affairs Press, 2006, p. 3-4, 6, 38; "Text of Hu Jintao's Speech at Opening Ceremony of China-Africa Summit 4 Nov," *Xinhua Domestic Service*, November 6, 2006, accessed via World News Connection on June 10, 2011; *China's National Defense in 2006.* White Paper, Beijing, China: Information Office of the State Council of the People's Republic of China, December 2006 , (accessed on-line on June 7, 2011 at http://www.china.org.cn/english/features/book/194421.htm); "Full Text of Hu Jintao Speech at Dialogue Between G-8, Developing-Countries," Xinhua Domestic Service, June 9, 2007, accessed on-line via World News Connection on June 10, 2011; *China's Foreign Affairs: 2007 Edition.* Beijing, China: Department of Policy Planning, Ministry of Foreign Affairs, People's Republic of China, World Affairs Press, 2007, p. 4-5; "Full Text of Hu Jintao Speech at G8 Outreach Session 9 July in Toyko, Japan," Xinhua Domestic Service, July 10, 2008: accessed on-line via World News Connection on June 10, 2011; and *China's Peaceful Development.* White Paper, Beijing, China: Information Office of the State Council of the People's Republic of China, September 6, 2011, (accesssed online on October 14, 2011 at http://www.china.org.cn/government/whitepaper/node_7126562.htm).

[15] For example, see *China's Foreign Affairs: 2009 Edition.* Beijing, China: Department of Policy Planning, Ministry of Foreign Affairs, People's Republic of China, World Affairs Press, 2009, p. 4-5.

strategic partnerships, top leader visits, United Nations Security Council voting, the China-GCC Free Trade Agreement, government support for Chinese companies, special economic zones, Confucius Institutes, United Nations Peacekeeping Operations, antipiracy operations, conventional arms sales, and military exchanges.

Cooperation Forums

China has established two Cooperation Forums that include Middle Eastern countries, the Forum on China-Africa Cooperation (FOCAC) and the China-Arab States Cooperation Forum (CASCF).[16] These Cooperation Forums are China's primary multilateral coordination mechanisms with the Middle East.

FOCAC was established in 2000. The entire continent of Africa (including North Africa) is included in the organization. The current members of FOCAC are the People's Republic of China (PRC) and fifty African nations.[17] Four African countries (who still recognize the Taiwan) are not members of FOCAC: Burkina Faso, Gambia, Sao Tome Principe, and Swaziland. In North Africa, there are a number of countries that are members of both FOCAC and CASCF due to their affiliation with the Arab League. Those dual member countries are Algeria, Djibouti, Egypt, Libya, Mauritania, Morocco, Somalia, Sudan, and Tunisia.

CASCF was established in 2004. The League of Arab States represents its twenty-one members in this forum. Those states are Algeria, Bahrain, Djibouti, Egypt, Jordan, Iraq, Lebanon, Libya, Kuwait, Mauritania, Morocco, Oman, Palestine, Qatar, Saudi Arabia, Somalia, Sudan, Syria, Tunisia, United Arab Emirates, and Yemen. All of these states recognize the PRC (as opposed to Taiwan). As a result of coordination by the Arab League, in CASCF the Arab States actively negotiate for the inclusion of collective projects involving multiple Arab countries (e.g. railway projects, nuclear power projects, and Dead Sea initiatives).[18]

FOCAC meets every three years and most meetings are conducted at the ministerial level. From 2000 through 2012, five meetings were held: 2000, 2003, 2006, 2009, and 2012. The 2006 meeting was a summit which included most of the top leaders from African countries. The CASCF meets more frequently, every two years (2004, 2006, 2008, 2010, and 2012). To date, all CASCF meetings have been held at the ministerial level.

Both FOCAC and CASCF emphasize political cooperation between China and Middle Eastern states. The foundations of political cooperation in the Forums are China's Five Principles of Peaceful Coexistence (mutual respect for territory and sovereignty; mutual non-aggression; mutual non-interference in internal affairs; equality and mutual benefit; and peaceful

---

[16] Official website for FOCAC is www.focac.org. The CASCF website is www.cascf.org.

[17] African members of FOCAC include Algeria, Angola, Benin, Botswana, Burundi, Cameroon, Cape Verde, Central Africa, Chad, Comoros, Congo (Republic of), Congo (Democratic Republic of), Cote d'Ivoire, Djibouti, Egypt, Equatorial Guinea, Eritrea, Ethiopia, Gabon, Ghana, Guinea, Guinea-Bissau, Kenya, Lesotho, Liberia, Libya, Madagascar, Malawi, Mali, Mauritania, Mauritius, Morocco, Mozambique, Namibia, Niger, Nigeria, Rwanda, Sierra Leone, Seychelles, Senegal, Somalia, South Africa, South Sudan, Sudan, Tanzania, Togo, Tunisia, Uganda, Zambia, and Zimbabwe.

[18] Interview, Embassy of the Hashemite Kingdom of Jordan, May 24, 2010, Beijing, China; and Interview, Former League of Arab States official, October 26, 2010, Cairo, Egypt.

coexistence),[19] South-South Cooperation, the One China Principle, and support for Arab political causes (especially regarding the Arab-Israeli conflict). As already discussed, China's second most important interest in the Middle East is promoting international support for China in an emerging era of multipolarity. China utilizes these Forums to gain that support.

As discussed earlier in this testimony, China's most important interest in the Middle East is promoting its own domestic economic growth by acquiring resources, developing markets, and ensuring stability in the region. FOCAC and CASCF are the primary multilateral mechanisms through which China coordinates economic activities with the Middle East to support these interests. The main areas of economic cooperation in these Forums are trade, investment, infrastructure, and economic security.

Although China has established a Cooperation Forum with another region that does emphasize military cooperation (the Central Asian Shanghai Cooperation Forum), military cooperation is not a major component of CASCF or FOCAC. Military issues are referred to very broadly, usually just articulating regional support for China's multilateral military activities outside the Forums.

Though they will not be discussed in detail in this testimony, in addition to the areas of cooperation discussed above, both FOCAC and CASCF contain clauses for cooperation in the areas of environmental protection, cultural exchange, media, tourism, sports, legislative interaction and building party-to party ties.

Middle East Issues Special Envoy

China's Middle East Issues Special Envoy was the first special envoy ever appointed by China. The Envoy is focused on the Middle East peace process and other issues of concern in the region. China established the Envoy in 2002. The main reason that China established the Special Envoy was due to urging by Arab states for China to become involved in the issue.[20] Many Arab states perceive China to be a more balanced player in the Middle East Peace Process than other great powers (especially the United States) due to China's historical support for the Palestinians.

To date, the Special Envoys appointed have all been seasoned diplomats with deep experience in the Middle East: Wang Shijie (2002-2006), Sun Bigan (2006-2009), and Wu Siki (2009-present).

---

[19] The 5 Principles of Peaceful Coexistence were originally developed by China in the early 1950's. See http://www.fmprc.gov.cn/eng/ziliao/3602/3604/t18053.htm.

[20] Many interview respondents cited Arab expectations as the main reason for formation of the Envoy. Some examples include Interview, Beijing University Scholar, April 14, 2010, Beijing, China; Interviews, CIIS, March 30, 2010, Beijing, China; Interview, Embassy of the Sultanate of Oman, March 31, 2010, Beijing, China; Interview, Former Arab League official, October 26, 2010, Beijing, China; and Interview, Former African Union Official, November 9, 2010, Cairo, Egypt. See also, "Xinhua: Egypt Welcomes China's Active Role in Mideast Peace Process," *Beijing Xinhua in English*, November 7, 2002, accessed via World News Connection on October 16, 2006; "Syrian Vice President Discusses Mideast Situation With Visiting PRC Envoy 10 Nov," *Xinhua Hong Kong Service*, November 10, 2002, accessed via World News Connection on October 16, 2006 ; and "Jordan's King Welcomes China's Role In Mideast Peace Process," *Beijing Xinhua in English,* November 11, 2002, accessed via World News Connection on October 16, 2006.

China appears to have multifaceted strategic interests in the Middle East Peace process supported by the Special Envoy. First, similar to China's behavior in the CASCF, it appears to genuinely support the cause of the Palestinians and other Arabs involved in the Arab-Israeli conflict in seeking a solution to the conflict. Second, as discussed earlier in this testimony, regional stability in the Middle East is very important to China. It wants peace in the Middle East in order to ensure a stable international environment for its own economic growth and prosperity. China perceives the Arab-Israeli conflict as the core of problems in the Middle East, so solving this dilemma would help to guarantee peace. Third, China appears to consider its involvement to be the proper conduct for a great power who is a permanent member of the UN Security Council. Finally, China appears to see itself as uniquely positioned to function as a liaison and peacemaker between disputing powers because it maintains relatively good relations with all of the parties involved in the conflict.

Although the Arab states may want China to exert more influence in the Middle East Peace Process on their behalf, the specific role of the Special Envoy to the Middle East appears to be to gain a deeper understanding of the conflict and to serve as a liaison between various parties. At this point, its most important mission is to encourage the parties to negotiate at all. China's specific stance on the Middle East issue was most succinctly stated in its 2003 Five Point Proposal.[21] Basically, China supports the "road map" approach, peaceful negotiations, an end to violence, an independent Palestinian state, the establishment of an international supervisory mechanism, the land for peace principle as a basis for negotiations, negotiations with Palestine, Lebanon and Syria, and greater involvement of the international community in the peace process. In many press statements China has made clear that part of its "land for peace" concept is that the borders should be negotiated to pre-1967 lines, the Golan Heights should be returned to Syria, and Jerusalem should be the capital of Palestine. Even though China has maintained normal state-to-state relations with Israel since 1992, it appears to support the Arab side of the conflict more. Although China often points out that Israel's statehood is a fact and that its security must be protected, its criticism of Israel's aggression appears to be stronger than its condemnation of terrorist activities perpetrated by Hamas or Hezbollah. From 2002 to 2012, China's position on these issues has remained quite constant.

Strategic Partnerships

Starting in the mid-1990's, China introduced a new diplomatic mechanism called "strategic partnership." These strategic partnerships are established with individual countries and groupings of countries. **China's strategic partnerships are not military alliances (or quasi-military alliances). These relationships are labeled as strategic by the Chinese government because they include all aspects of bilateral relations (e.g. economic, political, cultural and military) and because both sides make a long-term commitment to bilateral relations.**[22]

China established a strategic partnership with Africa as a continent at the 2006 FOCAC

---

[21] See "PRC Middle East Special Envoy Elaborates 5-Point Proposal on Middle East Issues," *Beijing Xinhua Domestic Service in Chinese,* May 28, 2003, accessed via World News Connection on October 16, 2006.

[22] For a detailed discussion on China's strategic partnerships, see Evan S. Medeiros, *China' International Behavior: Activism, Opportunism, and Diversification (*Santa Monica, CA: RAND, 2009), 82-89.

Summit[23] **and with the League of Arab States via the CASCF at the 2010 Tianjin Ministerial Meeting.[24] To date, China has initiated strategic partnerships with the following individual countries in the Middle East: Egypt (1999), Saudi Arabia (1999), Algeria (2004), Turkey (2010), and the United Arab Emirates (2012).[25]**

Top Leader Visits

China's leadership has frequently visited Middle Eastern countries over the last two decades. Between 1990 and 2002, top leadership of the Jiang Zemin administration (President Jiang Zemin and Premiers Zhu Rongji and Li Peng) visited the following countries (number of visits in parentheses): Egypt (3), Morocco (3), Algeria (2), Turkey (2), Iran (1), Israel (1), Libya (1), Palestine (1), Saudi Arabia (1), and Tunisia (1).[26] Continuing an emphasis on the diplomatic importance of Middle Eastern countries, from 2003 to 2012 the Hu Jintao Administration (including President Hu Jintao and Premier Wen Jiabao) visited: Egypt (3), Saudi Arabia (3), Morocco (2), United Arab Emirates (2), Qatar (1), and Turkey (1).[27]

United Nations Security Council (UNSC) Voting

In general, China votes in alignment with the other permanent five (P5) members of the United Nations Security Council. That said, there are two issue areas in which China and U.S. votes tend to differ: territorial integrity and the Arab-Israeli conflict.

In the 1990's, China's UNSC vote differed from the United States in fifty cases. 22% of those votes involved Middle East issues. In the 2000's, there was a dramatic increase in the percentage of differing votes involving the Middle East. Out of thirty-three cases where votes differed between the China and the United States, 55% of differing votes were related to Middle East. Before 2011, China rarely utilized its veto power in the Security Council, but instead often employed abstention to voice disapproval without directly confronting the United States and other P5 members.[28] That pattern changed with the beginning of the Arab Spring. Out of seven differing votes from 2011 to 2012, three were vetoes over resolutions about Syria. Overall, in those two years, 72% of votes that differed between the U.S. and China involved the Middle East.

---

[23] See "Declaration of the Beijing Summit of the Forum on China-Africa Cooperation." November 5, 2006. www.focac.org (accessed November 28, 2011).

[24] See "Enhancing Mutual Understanding, Learning from Each Other, and Joint Contribution: Speech by President Jiemian Yang of Shanghai Institutes for International Studies (SIIS)," *Shanghai Institutes for International Studies,* http://www.siis.org.cn/en/zhuanti_view_en.aspx?id=10118 (accessed February 16, 2012).

[25] See Medeiros, *China' International Behavior: Activism, Opportunism, and Diversification* and various interviews and Chinese news reports.

[26] Jiang Zemin, Zhu Rongji, and Li Peng travel data compiled from various news reports collected via World News Connection on September 24, 2011 and data from Deborah Brautigam, *The Dragon's Gift: The Real Story of China in Africa (*Oxford: Oxford University Press, 2009), p. 84.

[27] Hu Jintao and Wen Jiabao travel data compiled from China Vitae Website, accessed on September 24, 2011 and May 25, 2013 at http://www.chinavitae.com/vip/index.php?mode=officials.

[28] Between joining the United Nations in 1971 and 2010, China only exercised its veto nine times in total. See Medeiros, *China's International Behavior*, 190, for a detailed list of vetoes 1971-2010. In 1972, its veto was used to support Palestine's PLO.

During the entire timeframe under consideration, the vast majority of China's abstentions were over issues of territorial integrity, particularly sanctions and jurisdiction of criminal courts. These votes directly correspond to China's promotion of the Five Principles of Peaceful Coexistence described in the above section on Cooperation Forums, especially the principles of mutual respect for territory and sovereignty and mutual non-interference in the internal affairs of other states. From 1990 to 2012, China's support for these norms was relatively constant. In fact, based on China's veto behavior in relation to Syria in 2011 and 2012, it could be argued that China's support for these norms actually increased over the last few years. That said, there are a few inconsistencies in China's behavior. In the 1990's, there were a number of cases where China abstained from votes concerning actions against Iraq. In the 2000's, there were not any Security Council votes on Iraq where China's vote differed. Also, in direct conflict with its general opposition to sanctions, it voted for sanctions targeting Iran's developing nuclear program. For example, China voted yes for the following UNSC Resolutions implementing sanctions on Iran: S/RES/1737(2006), S/RES/1747(2007), S/RES/1803(2008), and S/RES/1929(2010). One possible explanation for these discrepancies is that China did not want to oppose the United States on issues which involved vital national interests for the U.S. As discussed earlier in this testimony, China perceives the Middle East to be in the U.S. sphere of influence and does not want conflict with the United States in the region. As a result, it may have been more cooperative on issues (such as the 2003 Iraq War and actions against Iran's nuclear program) that were arguably vital national interests for the U.S.

China's yes votes that differ from the United States tend to involve Chinese support for the Palestinians in the Arab-Israeli conflict. These yes votes significantly increased in the 2000's. This directly corresponds to China's pledges via CASCF (and the China-Middle East Special Envoy) to support the Palestinians in the international arena.

China-GCC Free Trade Agreement

In July 2004, China and the GCC signed a Framework Agreement on Economic, Trade, Investment, and Technological Cooperation and announced the launch of free trade agreement negotiations.[29] GCC (Cooperation Council for the Arab States of the Gulf) country membership includes the United Arab Emirates, Bahrain, Saudi Arabia, Oman, Qatar and Kuwait.[30] The proposed FTA would include goods, services, and investment.[31] Between 2004 and 2012, six rounds of negotiations were held. Negotiations are ongoing and both sides appear to be optimistic that a final agreement will ultimately materialize.

Government Support for Chinese Companies

One of the most active and vigorously criticized facets of China's interactions with the Middle East is the engagement of Chinese companies in the region. As discussed earlier in this

---

[29] See "The Joint Press Communiqué between the People's Republic of China and The Cooperation Council for the Arab States of the Gulf (GCC)," *Ministry of Foreign Affairs of the People's Republic of China Website,* July 7, 2004, http://www.fmprc.gov.cn/eng/wjdt/2649/t142542.htm, ccessed January 12, 2010.

[30] For more information on the Gulf Cooperation Council (GCC), refer to its website at http://www.gcc-sg.org/eng/indexc64c.html?action=GCC

[31] See PRC Ministry of Commerce, *China FTA Network (China-GCC FTA Page),* http://fta.mofcom.gov.cn/topic/engcc.shtml (accessed January 12, 2012).

testimony, China's economic interests in this region (for resources and markets) dramatically increased from 1990 to 2012. In the Middle East, the vast majority of Chinese company activity is in three sectors: energy, construction and telecommunications. Chinese state owned enterprises (SOE's) are the most prominent Chinese corporate actors in the Middle East. Over the last two decades, the Chinese government has actively encouraged these enterprises to pursue opportunities globally and specifically in the Middle East. In addition to the fact that these enterprises are ultimately owned and controlled by the Chinese state, the Chinese state guides the behavior of these enterprises through a number of initiatives. These companies receive direct and indirect government subsidies; favorable financing in the form of generous credit lines and low interest loans from state-owned banks; preferential awarding of construction contracts tied to China's foreign aid and concessional loans;[32] and expedited mandatory approvals for large scale OFDI activities.[33] These companies have been encouraged to pursue overseas opportunities in target industries and regions through the creation of national champions and the Chinese government's "going out/ going global" programs. These companies have also been encouraged to aggressively pursue economic engagement through initiatives announced in the FOCAC and CASCF. Finally, the Chinese government provides strong political support for these companies.

Special Economic Zones

Between 1990 and 2012, China launched two Special Economic Zones (SEZ) in the Middle East: Egypt (1994) and Algeria (2006).[34] The Egyptian Suez Canal SEZ is strategically located near port facilities on the Suez Canal. Longer term, this location will facilitate product shipment to Europe as well as the Middle East and Africa for manufacturers in the zone. The SEZ encompasses 6.6 square kilometers of space, but only one square kilometer is currently utilized.[35] As of the end of 2010, $300 million USD had been invested in the SEZ.[36] The main Chinese company involved in the project is TEDA.[37] The SEZ is targeting the investment of small enterprises.[38] Specific industries include textiles, electronics, chemicals, automotive products, transformers, and pipes for transporting petroleum.[39]

The Algeria SEZ was suspended in 2006. The Chinese companies involved in establishing the SEZ were Jiangling Automobile and Zhongjing International. The primary industries targetted were automotive assembly and construction materials. [40]

---

[32] See Nargiza Salidjanova, *Going Out: An Overview of China's Foreign Direct Investment,* USCC Staff Research Report, U.S.-China Economic & Security Review Commission, 2011, p. 11.

[33] See Andrew Szamosszegi and Cole Kyle, *An Analysis of State-owned Enterprises and State Capitalism in China* (Washington, D.C.: U.S.-China Economic and Security Review Commission, 2011), p.89.

[34] For a detailed discussion of these SEZs see Deborah Brautigam and Xiaoyang Tang. "African Shenzhen: China's Special Economic Zones in Africa," *Journal of Modern African Studies* 49, no. I (2011): p. 27-54.

[35] Interview, Egyptian Ministry of Foreign Affairs, November 24, 2010, Cairo, Egypt.

[36] Ibid.

[37] Interview, Egyptian China Business Council, November 7, 2010, Cairo, Egypt.

[38] Ibid.

[39] Interview, Egyptian Ministry of Trade and Industry, November 22, 2010, Cairo, Egypt; and Interview, Egyptian China Business Council, November 7, 2010, Cairo, Egypt.

[40] *China Africa Economic and Trade Cooperation,* White Paper, Beijing, China: Information Office of the State Council of the People's Republic of China, December 23, 2010, accessed on-line on June 7, 2011 at http://www.china.org.cn/government/whitepaper/node_7107834.htm; and Deborah Brautigam Xiaoyang Tang.

Confucius Institutes

Since 2004, China has established Confucius Institutes in the following Middle Eastern countries (number of institutes in parentheses): Egypt (2), Turkey (2), United Arab Emirates (2), Iran (1), Israel (1), Jordan (1), Lebanon (1), and Morocco (1).[41] The purpose of these institutes is to promote Chinese language learning and cultural awareness in host countries.

United Nations Peacekeeping Operations

China is a relative newcomer to United Nations peacekeeping operations.[42] Its first contribution of UNPKO troops anywhere in the world did not occur until 1991.[43] China did not begin to contribute UNPKO troops to Middle East operations until after 2001. To date, China has participated in the following four UNPKO operations in the Middle East: UNTSO UN Truce Supervision Organization (1990-present, 108 observers, staff or police); UNIKOM UN Iraq-Kuwait Observer Mission (1991-2003, 164 observers, staff or police); UNIFIL UN Interim Force in Lebanon (2006-present, 3197 troops, 58 observers, staff or police) and UNSMIS UN Supervision Mission in Syria (April 2012-August 2012, 9 observers, staff or police). [44]

Antipiracy Operations

The free flow of goods through the Gulf of Aden has become an important national interest for China due to its connection to China's promotion of its own economic development. The Gulf of Aden leads to a number of African countries, Middle Eastern countries, the Suez Canal, and is the quickest sea route from China to Europe (and many countries in the Americas).

In 2008, China's trade shipments through the Gulf of Aden were increasingly threatened by piracy. Numerous Chinese vessels were hijacked.[45] In response to these threats to its economic interests, for the first time in modern history, China's navy (People's Liberation Navy or PLAN) deployed to engage in an operational mission outside East Asia and the Pacific.[46] The purpose of the mission was combating piracy off the Horn of Africa. The primary objectives of these

---

"African Shenzhen: China's special economic zones in Africa," p. 32.

[41] Confucius Institute Website administered by Han Ban, accessed online on May 28, 2013 at http://english.hanban.org/node_10971.htm.

[42] For a detailed analysis of China's global UNPKO involvement, see Bates Gill, Chin-hao Huang, and J. Stephen Morrison, *China's Expanding Role in Africa: Implications for the United States,* A Report of the CSIS Delegation to China on China- Africa- U.S. Relations, November 28- December 1, 2006 (Washington, D.C.: CSIS, 2007), accessed onlne on April 10, 2009 at http://www.csis.org/index.php?option=com_csis_pubs&task=view&id=3714.

[43] China's first UNPKO troops were deployed to Cambodia in 1991.

[44] See *The Diversified Employment of China's Armed Forces.*

[45] See Kuang Peng and Jiao Wu. "China's Piracy Fight to Boost US Ties." *China Daily*, December 12, 2008: (accessed online on January 11, 2012 at http://www.chinadaily.com.cn/china/2008-12/22/content_7327363.htm).

[46] See Alison A. Kaufman, *China's Participation in Anti-Piracy Operations off the Horn of Africa,* Conference Report, Center for Naval Analyses, July 2009, 1, accessed online on May 18, 2011 at http://www.cna.org/sites/default/files/Piracy%20conference%20report.pdf.

operations were to protect Chinese ships and personnel, guard ships delivering humanitarian supplies for international organizations, and to the degree possible shelter passing foreign vessels from pirate attacks. [47]

Overall, China's antipiracy operations in the Gulf of Aden have been cooperative with other nations and in alignment with relevant UN Security Council resolutions. Although China has cooperated with other nations and has participated in multinational initiatives, its involvement with antipiracy operations has been different from its other multilateral military behavior in the Middle East - UNPKO. UNPKO are commanded by an international organization, the United Nations, and Chinese troops are often commanded by military officials from other countries. Chinese antipiracy initiatives in the Gulf of Aden are conducted in cooperation with other countries, but all Chinese naval forces remain under Chinese control in these operations. China's reluctance to formally join multinational taskforces is likely due to the fact that the antipiracy taskforces in the region are led by Western governments or organizations which do not include China as a member. The primary taskforces are the United States' CTF-151, the NATO Operation Protector, and the EU Atalanta. [48]

One major reason China has chosen to participate in multinational antipiracy initiatives (as opposed to more unilateral action) is to demonstrate that China is a responsible great power and to improve China's international image. [49]

Conventional Arms Sales

Since the end of the Cold War, China's conventional arms sales to countries in the Middle East have been consistently limited. Between 1990 and 1999, China's top conventional arms customers in the Middle East were Iran ($1.4 bn.), Egypt ($164 mn.), Yemen ($150 mn.), Algeria ($130 mn.) and Tunisia ($38 mn.).[50] From 2000 to 2012, China's top customers in the Middle East were Iran ($874 mn.), Egypt ($423 mn.), Algeria ($116 mn.), Kuwait ($87 mn.), and Saudi Arabia ($66 mn.).[51] In 2012, China's conventional arms sales to the entire region totaled a mere $45 mn. ($44 mn. to Iran and $1 mn. to Egypt).[52]

Military Exchanges

Between 2001 and 2010, China performed high level military exchanges with every Middle Eastern country except Iraq. China's highest volume of military exchanges (number of

---

[47] See *China's National Defense in 2010*.
[48] See Erik Lin-Greenberg, "Dragon Boats: Assessing China's Anti-Piracy Operations in the Gulf of Aden," *Defense and Security Analysis* 26, no. 2 (June 2010): 215, accessed online via EBSCO on January 12, 2012, p. 220.
[49] See Kaufman, *China's Participation in Anti-Piracy Operations off the Horn of Africa;* Lin-Greenberg, "Dragon Boats: Assessing China's Anti-Piracy Operations in the Gulf of Aden"; Jonathan Hogslag, "Embracing China's Global Security Ambitions," *The Washington Quarterly*, (July 2009): 105-118, accessed online on January 11, 2012, via EBSCO); and Andrew S. Erickson and Justin D. Mikolay, "Welcome China to the Fight Against Pirates," *U.S. Naval Institute Proceedings,* March 2009, 34-41, accessed online on January 11, 2012, via EBSCO).
[50] Data compiled by author from SIPRI Arms Transfers Database at http://www.sipri.org/databases/armstransfers, accessed online on May 11, 2011 and May 26, 2013.
[51] Ibid.
[52] Ibid.

exchanges in parentheses) in the Middle East were with Egypt (29), Turkey (20), Syria (10), Jordan (9), and Tunisia (8).[53]

Question 3:
Does China seek to cultivate relationships with Middle Eastern states in order to advance and garner support for its positions and objectives in international organizations like the United Nations? Explain.

As discussed earlier in this testimony, one of China's major interests in this region is developing support for China in the international system during a time of emerging multipolarity. One important forum for China's behavior in the international arena is the United Nations. In the United Nations, China seeks support for the Five Principles of Peaceful Coexistence as the norms for interactions between states in the international system and attempts to shield itself from foreign interference and criticism of its domestic political system. Middle Eastern states are important partners in those efforts. Also, Middle Eastern states are important partners in China's quest for a greater voice in the international system for developing countries.

Question 4:
Which Chinese actors (official, semi-official, and unofficial) are most heavily involved in developing and implementing policies related to the Middle East?

China's foreign policy decision making for developing policies related to the Middle East is not transparent.[54] The most important official actors in implementing policy towards this region are the Ministry of Foreign Affairs, the Ministry of Commerce, and the International Department of the Chinese Communist Party (CCP). State-owned enterprises (SOEs) are also important players.

Influential think tanks and academic departments informing debates on China's policies towards the Middle East include the Chinese Academy of Social Sciences (CASS), Institute of West Asian and African Studies (IWAAS); China Institutes of Contemporary International Relations (CICIR); China Institute of International Studies (CIIS); Shanghai Institutes of International Studies (SIIS); Chinese Academy of Trade and Economic Cooperation; China Reform Forum; and Peking University's School of International Studies.

Question 5:
How do Middle East States (governments and people) view China? How do they view China's engagement in the region, especially vis-à-vis the United States? Do Middle East states seek increased Chinese involvement in the region as a counterbalance to U.S. influence? Explain.

---

[53] Data compiled from appendices of *China's National Defense in 2002, China's National Defense in 2004, China's National Defense in 2006, China's National Defense in 2008, and China's National Defense in 2010.* 2010 Appendices acquired online on March 26, 2012 at http://eng.chinamil.com.cn/special-reports/node_47506.htm
[54] For a discussion of China's general foreign policy making process, see David Shambaugh. *China Goes Global: The Partial Power.* (New York: Oxford University Press, 2013).

In general, the Middle Eastern government officials I have interviewed from Bahrain, Egypt, Iraq, Israel, Jordan, Oman, Palestine, Tunisia, Turkey, and the United Arab Emirates are quite positive about the impact of China in the Middle East. They view China as a formidable economic partner and a country that shares many of their worldviews as developing countries. China is also seen as a relatively balanced power in relation to the Arab-Israeli conflict which is positively received by Arab states and the Arab League. Government officials also tend to stress the long historical relationship between China and their countries and often reference appreciation for China's past stance in this region against colonization. Generally, Middle Eastern officials do not want relations with China to endanger their existing close relationships with the U.S., but they do want to continue to actively build relations with China.

It is important to note that China's vetoes in the UNSC regarding Syria (discussed above) did appear to negatively impact China's relations with some members of the Arab League, particularly Saudi Arabia and Qatar. My impression is that friction caused by this disagreement is temporary and that relations between these countries and China are already improving.

Although it is limited, public opinion polling from the region indicates that the broader public also views China favorably. For example, in recent years PEW's Global Attitudes Project reports the following country responses to the question "Do you have a favorable view of China?": Tunisia 69% (vs. 45% for the US); Lebanon 59% (vs. 48% for the US); Egypt 52% (vs. 19% for the US); Jordan 47% (vs. 12% for the US); Palestinian Territories 62% (vs. 18% for the US); Turkey 22% (vs. 15% for US); and Israel 49% (vs. 72% for the US).[55] Every Middle Eastern country polled (except for Israel) has a higher favorability score for China than for the US. Even the Turkish population, many of whom have deep concerns about China's treatment of Uighurs, has a higher favorability rating for China than the US. BBC Polling data reflects similar results for Egypt. 50% of Egyptian views of China were mainly positive in 2012 compared to 37% for the U.S.[56]

Question 6:
Historically, China has been widely perceived as reluctant to challenge U.S. interests and influence in the Middle East. Assess whether this is true today, and whether it is likely to be true in the future. As China and Middle East states likely become more deeply engaged in the coming years and decades, will China seek an expanded role in the region? Why or why not?

Yes, in general China still appears to be reluctant to challenge U.S. interests and influence in the Middle East. China's relative cooperation with the U.S. on various actions against Iran targeted at limiting Tehran's nuclear program is an example of China attempting to avoid confrontation in the Middle East over an issue that is vital to the U.S. That said, in recent years China is

---

[55]See PEW Global Attitudes Project. *Key Indicators Database.* http://www.pewglobal.org/database/ (accessed May 29, 2013). Data for Tunisia, Lebanon, Egypt, Jordan and Turkey are from 2012. Data for the Palestinian Territories and Israel are from 2011.
[56]See *Views of Europe Slide Sharply in Global Poll, While Views of China Improve.* BBC World Service Poll, 2012, (accessed online on May 29, 2013, at www.worldpublicopinion.org).

becoming more willing to challenge the US in the region. For example, although China abstained on the UNSC vote that ultimately resulted in NATO intervention in Libya in 2011 (in alignment with the wishes of the Arab League), China has broadly criticized the US and NATO for the military action that resulted. Also, despite heavy pressure from the United States, China has cast three UNSC vetoes on the Syrian issue in 2011 and 2012 in coordination with Russia.

Based on interviews I conducted in January 2013, my general impression is that as a result of China's increased confidence in the wake of the 2008 Global Financial Crisis, concerns over foreign interference in fragile Middle Eastern states since the beginning of the Arab Spring, and an escalated perception that China's relations with the United States may be deteriorating as a result of the U.S. Pivot to Asia, China may be becoming more willing to stand up to the United States in regions outside of Asia. To date, the only example of newly assertive behavior in the Middle East is China's behavior related to the Syria issue.

Question 7:
Are there ongoing Track 1.5 or Track 2 dialogues between the United States and China regarding the Middle East, or between the United States and other partners regarding China in the region? If so, discuss the participants, objectives, and effectiveness of these dialogues.

I am not aware of any Track 1.5 or Track 2 dialogues that specifically work on issues related to China in the Middle East.

Question 8:
The Commission is mandated to make policy recommendations to Congress based on its hearings and other research. What are your recommendations for congressional action related to the topic of your testimony?

China and the United States share common interests in the Middle East including a desire for energy security, regional stability, and economic and social development in the region.[57] As a result, I would suggest that joint initiatives in the following areas could be pursued to foster cooperation between the U.S. and China: energy source exploration; alternative energy research and development; further anti-piracy initiatives; joint economic policy guidance to emerging markets in the region; and water security projects. In light of the perception in the Middle East that China is a relatively balanced actor in relation to the Arab-Israeli conflict, the United States could also more actively involve China in Middle East Peace Process efforts. Formal dialogues discussing Chinese and American interests, activities, and opportunities for cooperation in the region would also be beneficial.

---

[57] For a more detailed discussion of shared interests between the United States and China in the Middle East and opportunities for cooperation, see David Shambaugh and Dawn Murphy. "U.S.-China Interactions in the Middle East, Africa, Europe, and Latin America" by David Shambaugh and Dawn Murphy in *Tangled Titans: The New Context of U.S.-China Relations*, edited by David Shambaugh. (Lanham, Md.: Rowan and Littlefield, 2013).

OPENING STATEMENT OF DR. YITZHAK SHICHOR
PROFESSOR EMERITUS
THE HEBREW UNIVERSITY OF JERUSALEM AND THE UNIVERSITY OF HAIFA

DR. SHICHOR: Good morning. Thank you very much for inviting me here. It's been a long *schlep*, believe me, but it was worthwhile, and I think it's very important.

Just a small point before I start so that we know who we are dealing with. I'm blacklisted in China. I'm not sure if you know that, but I am one of those 16 people, all of them American except myself who are blacklisted in China because of our association with research on Xinjiang. I haven't been to China since 2005. Even then, my visit was limited to the south of China, and just for a few days, and I'm still not allowed to go to China and certainly not to Xinjiang. I thought this is something you should know.

I'm not going to read directly from my paper. Instead, I wrote down 12 points and I'll try to cover them as far as I can, about 30 seconds each, and whatever is left we'll do in the discussion.

Number one, the Middle East, without getting into definitions, is not one of China's core interests. This is something we should know. It's on the margins. Despite its importance as an oil producer and supplier to China, it is not one of the most important regions in Chinese foreign policy. The Chinese don't understand the Middle East very much. They are amazed by all its complexities and contradictions.

Number two, many people believe that China's foreign policy is motivated by economic considerations, especially by the pursuit of energy and commodities. I think that ultimately Chinese foreign policy is still driven by political considerations, by the international constellation of power relations. Of course, economics is very important, but ultimately it's political issues that matter.

Point number three is about stability. This is some kind of a mantra that is being repeated, reiterated all the time by the media, by Western scholars and by Chinese scholars. The Chinese want stability. Well, everybody wants stability. This is nothing new. The Chinese believe that stability is beneficial to their economic relations, modernization and development.

But I just want you to know that in some cases *instability* is also beneficial for Chinese foreign policy, and if you look at Chinese presence in the Middle East and around the Middle East, the fact that China has a strong presence in countries like Sudan or some North African countries or Iraq, certainly Iran, is because of instability.

Just imagine that Sudan would be like Switzerland. So all foreign companies [that had evacuated these countries], would be coming back and the Chinese will have to face tough competition. So to a certain point, in certain countries, in certain situations, instability is quite beneficial to

China.

Number four, it's another mantra, which is called "non-intervention". According to conventional wisdom, China's policy is based on non-intervention. The Chinese do not want to become involved in regional conflicts, in settling outstanding issues, and so on. Again, this is something that has to be corrected. It's not that Chinese do not intervene. They *do* intervene, but they do it in a *Chinese* way; they do it in an indirect way; they do it in a subtle way, behind the scenes. This is the Chinese way of influencing other countries yet not directly, not by coming in full force, even by using the veto, as Dawn said, which the Chinese are very careful about. And there are certain stages, which I mention in my paper, of how the Chinese look at intervention.

Number five, Sino-U.S. relations. Some people believe, especially Chinese intellectuals, that the United States' role in the Middle East is really harmful to Chinese interests and to the stability of the region. I think that, unofficially and implicitly, the Chinese very much appreciate the role of the United States, maybe not so much in East Asia, which is considered China's backyard, but in the Middle East. I think the United States is doing great service to China by preventing further deterioration, by keeping stability, to use this term again.

Another term that is being used all the time is "dependence". Many watchers say that the key to understand China's policy towards a country like Iran or Sudan is the Chinese so-called "dependence" on crude oil or other commodities.

To begin with, the Chinese have managed to diversify the oil resources among many countries so as--and this is based on their experience with the Soviet Union in the 1950s and early 1960s--to avoid dependence on one supplier. Therefore, the Chinese have not only managed to avoid dependence on one country, but they have very smartly managed to create what I call "counter dependencies", or "reverse dependencies", making these countries--say Iran, Sudan and others--depend on China on political issues given China's position as a Permanent Member of the UN Security Council, given China's role in the International Atomic Energy Agency, and given China's investments in other sectors of these countries' economies besides oil. These are long-term relationships of what I call "mutual dependence".

The next point concerns military relations. Dawn has already mentioned that China is really a marginal player in the Middle Eastern military field. This is true. China used to be a major exporter of weapons in the 1980s, but not anymore. China is really marginal in terms of weapons exports and I bring some figures in my paper. Also, China does not get any more weapons. China used to get some military technology from Israel. Again, not anymore.

But the Middle East is still tremendously important in military terms. I think this is the key region in the world that serves as a laboratory for testing and experimenting with weapons, including Chinese weapons (in the 1980s), but mainly with Western weapons, with the state-of-the-art

American military technology, which provide a very significant input into China's defense modernization. This is something we have to keep in mind.

I'll just say a word about Sino-Israel relations in light of Prime Minister Netanyahu's recent visit to China. I think there was a very dramatic, significant change during this visit. The two sides decided to put aside thorny political issues and concentrate on economics and doing business. I think this is very important. It also shows a certain kind of asymmetry in China's attitude toward the Palestinians as against Israel despite the visit of Abu Mazen just the day before Netanyahu came. We can expand about it later on.

I just want to say another couple of words about the Chinese attitudes towards Islam and terrorism. Again, there is a kind of balance. On the one hand, of course, the Chinese are concerned about Islam, especially about radical Islam, certainly about terrorism, but in certain cases, it serves China's interests. We have to keep it in mind.

The same goes for the so-called "Arab Spring," which is not a spring anymore, as we all know. And I think the Chinese had become aware of the problems leading to the Arab Spring and managed to devise a policy-- they call it "social management"--to bridge the social gaps that have been created in China. I think the Chinese are very skeptical about the Arab Spring, and you can see in the Chinese media and journal articles, criticism about the Arab Spring that is leading to radical Islam instead of democracy.

My final point is that the Chinese profile in the Middle East, China's presence in the Middle East, is really unprecedented. Such high profile in the Middle East has never been in Chinese history, over 2,000 years.

The question is why? How do we explain this Chinese presence? On the one hand it has to do, of course, with Chinese policies, a change in Chinese priorities and Chinese perceptions, especially economic policies, and a willingness to "go out." On the other side of the coin, which is I think very important, especially sitting here in this room, is the fact that Western powers and the United States somehow evacuated some of these countries, sometimes voluntarily, afraid of becoming involved in domestic unrest and civil wars. This kind of withdrawal, backed by U.S. presidential executive orders in fact paved the ground for the Chinese presence in the Middle East.

Thank you very much.

PREPARED STATEMENT OF DR. YITZHAK SHICHOR
PROFESSOR EMERITUS
THE HEBREW UNIVERSITY OF JERUSALEM AND THE UNIVERSITY OF HAIFA

June 6, 2013

"China and the Middle East"

Yitzhak Shichor
Professor Emeritus, the Hebrew University of Jerusalem, the University of Haifa

"Testimony before the U.S.-China Economic and Security Review Commission"

Precisely a month ago, two prominent Middle Eastern leaders that represent to many (the Chinese included) the core regional problem, visited China. Mahmoud Abbas (known as Abu Mazen), President of the Palestinian National Authority, and Binyamin Netanyahu (known as Bibi), Prime Minister of Israel, were in China at the same time by invitation. To a great extent these two visits, to be discussed in more detail below, reflect Beijing's policy in the Middle East, trying to steer a mid-course between different and occasionally contradictory situations and dilemmas while promoting what they perceive as their main interests in the region. It should be underscored right at the beginning that international affairs are NOT a top priority for the Chinese leadership. In fact, a glance at the reports, speeches and other documents of the most recent CCP congress and NPC demonstrates that foreign issues are marginal and occupy ten percent or less of the text. Among these issues, the Middle East – despite China's heavy reliance on its oil – is by no means one of China's "core interests" although it is indirectly related to them.

There are a number of definitions of the "Middle East". The one adopted here follows the Chinese use of the term as reflected in the structure of the Chinese Foreign Ministry. The Middle East is handled by the Department of West Asia and North Africa that also covers Iran and Turkey. While these countries, some created artificially by Western colonialism, are all Muslim (save Israel), they represent different political systems; ethnic identities; economic development; international orientations; as well as religious inclinations within Islam. Beijing has to juggle among them using acrobatic diplomacy much more complex than ever before. This requires a more intimate understanding of the Middle East that has to rely increasingly on research institutes and intelligence (in the dual sense). Interpreting Middle Eastern affairs in black and white (as was done in Mao's time when all regional problems were related to "imperialism" or "social-imperialism") is over. Beijing has to become more sensitive to "fifty shades of grey"…

According to conventional wisdom, China's main incentive in its Middle East policy is the pursuit of crude oil to fill the growing gap between oil production and consumption. While this is undoubtedly a major consideration in China's foreign relations in general, and especially in the Middle East, Beijing's international activities are still determined primarily by its strategic outlook and global power politics. In this perspective, there is an intriguing continuity between Mao's China and post-Mao's China. Despite its impressive growth and emergence as a great power (some believe already a superpower), Beijing is still concerned about "encirclement" (less by Russia and more by the US) and displays lack of self-confidence and time-honored legacies of reluctance to become more active in world affairs – all the more so in the Middle East perceived as too complicated and full of contradictions that present China with tough dilemmas.

Heading the list is US-China relations. On the one hand, the US is a potential rival which appears to lose ground because of China's emergence. Given the long legacy of bilateral hostility (with the possible – and brief – exception of the 1980s), Beijing is vigilant and obviously suspicious about US presence in the Middle East. Some Chinese commentators consider US presence – almost in Maoist style – as the ultimate source of Middle Eastern instability. Yet there are indications that Beijing, at least implicitly, does believe that the US presence helps preventing a further deterioration in the Middle East. More concerned about US presence in the Asia-Pacific region, their backyard, the Chinese may have come to terms with the US presence in the Middle East, far away from their "core interests". To give one example, despite its consistent backing of Iran on its nuclear program, Beijing reduced its oil import from Iran to get an exemption from the US-imposed sanctions and, at the same time, increased oil import from Saudi Arabia, reportedly "recommended" by the US. The bottom line: ultimately, relations with Washington are far more important to Beijing than relations with Iran.

Given the Middle East diversity, it is commonly assumed that China's primary interest in the Middle East (and elsewhere) is maintaining stability. Any disruption of the prevailing order would be detrimental not only to China's economic interests but also to its political and strategic presence as it may entail increased intervention by other parties, notably the US. Nevertheless, occasional instability serves Chinese interests as it drives away most of its competitors (e.g. in Sudan, Iran, Syria), especially in the energy sector. Following the turmoil in Libya, for example, the role of Chinese oil companies has increased while that of Western ones (that represent countries that had been actively involved in the civil war) has diminished. Similarly, despite concerns about the US alleged attempts to monopolize Iraq's oil sector, China has emerged as the primary winner, at least among all foreign oil companies. Instability and unrest sometimes pay, also by offering Beijing an opportunity to play a political role using its membership in international organizations and extensive diplomatic network, as well as to sell arms and military equipment. Beijing's arms sales and the spillover of Chinese-made or designed weapons to terrorist organizations, such as Hezbollah and Hamas, further *increase* Middle Eastern instability.

Apparently, these options do not conform to Beijing's alleged "non-intervention" policy, frequently accepted at face value by Chinese as well as non-Chinese scholars, media and statesmen. According to this policy, the Chinese oppose external intervention (Beijing's included) in the internal affairs of other countries, especially in settling internal conflicts. China also rejects the imposition of sanctions, least of all the use of force. Nevertheless, Beijing applies these principles in a flexible, pragmatic and creative "Chinese" way. In many cases, Chinese passivity or inaction produces action. A notable example is the 1991 US-led offensive against Saddam Hussein that had been facilitated by China's abstention on UN Security Council Resolution 1678. On other occasions, China supported sanctions contrary to its stated policy and tried to convince the respective leaders (e.g. in Sudan and Iran) to comply with UN, EU or IAEA resolutions. Chinese troops also participate in UN peace-keeping forces and Beijing regularly sends a "special envoy" to conflict-infected countries, less as a trouble-shooter and more on fact-finding missions – of inconsequence operative value. When Beijing does intervene in the Middle East (and elsewhere) – and it does – it is usually done in subtle, indirect and behind the scene ways which may still be effective. China's non-intervention policy reminds of traditional *wuwei* principles of not exerting oneself and getting all things done.

Beijing's "non-intervention" policy is occasionally related to, and justified by, its alleged "dependence" on the countries from which China imports commodities, primarily (in this case) oil. According to this interpretation, Beijing is careful not to interfere in the internal affairs of those countries or to play an active role in their outstanding conflicts in order to guarantee the continued supply chain. As conventional wisdom goes, this is why Beijing supports Iran and Sudan. Yet this is a misconception. Precisely to avoid such dependence (based on the bitter memory of the Soviets' sudden withdrawal from China in 1960), the Chinese have managed to create "counter-dependence" or "reverse dependence" by using accelerated export and investments as well as their voice in international organizations in order to forge long-term relationships beyond their immediate need for commodities and energy. Sudan's import market is completely monopolized by China. Iran and Sudan are not less dependent now on China than China is on them not to mention the diversification of oil import sources and the constant search for substitutes along the traditional policy of "playing barbarians against barbarians" (e.g. Saudi Arabia vs. Iran).

Still, there is an expectation in the Middle East that China would become more proactive and decisive in its policy (though not necessarily in the Western sense of a "responsible stakeholder") as befits its growing economic power and perceived global standing. Many in the Middle East (in the words of a May 15, 2010, *Saudi Gazette* editorial) believe that "America's fall from grace opened the door to a resurgent China to make its presence felt on the international stage in a way it had never done before. [...] China, unlike the US, appears to have no messianic illusions about its role in the world, passing no ideological judgment on its partners. [...] It has intervened in a low-key manner in countries where the level of dysfunction has gotten out of control." This, however, by no means implies a wholesale Middle Eastern approval of China as a welcome power in the region.

Given its history and the legacy of its relations with the Middle East and its revolutionary activities, China is undoubtedly respected but at the same time suspected. According to a number of public opinion polls, while some (23 percent in 2011) already regard China as the only superpower, only few consider it a worthy place to live or study (Table 1). The share of those in the Middle East who have a favorable view of China tends to decline in several cases (Table 2), but more regard China as the leading economic power (Table 3). A relatively small percentage (15-17) thinks that China has already replaced the US as the leading superpower (the percentage in Western Europe is much higher) though more believe that eventually China will take over (Table 4). Still, most regard China's growing military power as a *bad thing* (but growing economic power as a *good thing*, Table 5) – despite the fact that the penetration of Chinese capital, goods and services caused a great deal of damage to Middle Eastern economies. Middle Eastern markets, especially in Iran, Sudan and the Persian Gulf, have been flooded with low-quality and "defective" Chinese goods that undermine local indigenous industries.

This is especially true in Turkey whose textile and toy markets are dominated by Chinese products while *all* leather goods manufacturing is under Chinese control. Turkish traders complain about "unjust competition" by Chinese official – and even more so unofficial – import. "Each ship full of Chinese products that docks at the Turkish ports is causing the closure of a Turkish factory." Criticism of Beijing is not limited to economics. The Arab League condemned China (and Russia) for their use of veto in the UN Security Council resolution that held the Syrian Government responsible for the atrocities and violence. A number of cartoons (attached below) demonstrate Arab misgivings about the behavior of China and Russia in the Syrian crisis. An article published in February 2012 in Turkey's *Hürriyet* titled "The Gang of Four: Syria, Iran, Russia, China" used harsh words:

> The still-communist China is the fourth member of the gang. Here, I don't even need to explain that "human rights" – including the most basic one, the right to life – means nothing for Beijing. This is simply a mercantilist dictatorship without any principles. "It doesn't matter whether a cat is black or white," the late Deng Xiaoping once said, "as long as it catches mice." Apparently, it doesn't matter how many innocents die while the cat gets fed.

Syria and Iran provide two examples not just of China's non-involvement policy but also of the sophisticated way by which Beijing leaves the "dirty work" to Moscow. Unlike the other permanent members of the UN Security Council, notably the US and Russia, China has used its veto power sparingly – and not just because it is a relatively latecomer to the UN. Even today, over forty years after its admission to the UN, this tool is NOT Beijing's first priority in settling outstanding regional conflicts. The Chinese prefer that the parties concerned should settle such conflicts without any intervention. If that option fails, then a regional or professional organization (such as the African Union in the case of Sudan, the Arab League in the case of Syria, or the IAEA in the case of Iran) should try to settle the conflicts on behalf of the parties and based on their prior agreement. Only if this option fails would the Chinese turn, reluctantly, to the UN. The worst option, to be avoided as far as possible, is unilateral intervention by external powers – sidestepping international and regional organizations as well as the parties concerned. China believes that economic relations may help overcome conflicts without undermining sovereignty.

Emphasizing economic growth is not just expediency. To some extent it is a philosophy – some would say an excuse – that the basic human right is the right to live in dignity and enjoy a higher standard of living. This is how Chinese, and other East Asians, rationalize their pursuit of economic growth while ignoring or downgrading human rights. They are not totally wrong. Economic ties can bind together nations that for centuries had been not only different but brutally hostile. The gradual creation of the European Union provides a pertinent example. This may also work in the Middle East. While the Chinese have their own interests in forging economic relations with the Middle East, these activities might benefit other countries. The problem is the asymmetry in size and resources. Except for oil-exporting countries, China has accumulated huge foreign trade surplus, most notably in the case of Turkey (around $20 billion. Turkey's overall trade deficit is the highest in the world next to the US). This imbalance in trade is a cause of concern to both China, but primarily Turkey, officially linked as "strategic partners". Chinese penetration of the local economy raises the alarm not only in Turkey but also in Iran, swept by cheap goods originated in China.

This represents a Chinese attempt to compensate for its huge import of crude oil. China has a trade deficit with 8 Middle Eastern countries, all of them energy suppliers, with the exception of the United Arab Emirates – by far the biggest market for Chinese export in the region. Despite its dependence on oil, the share of China's import from the Middle East is less than 8 percent, nearly the share of North America and nearly half the share of Europe. Import from the Middle East accounts for about 60 percent of China's regional trade, export for about 40 percent. Oil apart, Turkey is China's leading trade partner in the Middle East, Israel comes second. Yet Israel's export to China is about the same as Turkey's and twice that of Egypt – each with over ten times Israel's population. This is a clue to the outcome of Netanyahu's recent visit to China.

Indeed, economics play a major role in China's Middle East policy. Netanyahu's visit to China is a case in point. Whereas in the past all Israeli officials who visited Beijing raised the issue of Iran's nuclear program – but failed to convinced China to act, this time, while the Iran issue was mentioned, it was done perfunctorily and briefly. It seems that the two parties realized that this issue (or that of Syria or the Palestinians) are not directly related to bilateral relations and raising them would be pointless. Beijing, whose play in Iran has nothing to do with Israel, would not budge while Israel still insists on using force against Iran, if needed something the Chinese regard as an obsession. Thus, downgrading thorny political disagreements, the visit concentrated instead on bilateral relations, technological, scientific and primarily economic.

Initially, there have been rumors about a possible Israeli-Palestinian meeting between the two leaders, under Chinese auspices, unleashing a wave of media reports about Beijing's "decision" to start playing the peacemaker in the Middle East. These rumors proved to be baseless. In fact, unofficial Chinese sources suggested that Beijing may have not intended to invite the Palestinian president who perhaps forced himself on the Chinese. His visit – though of a higher level ("state visit") as befits a president – was shorter (just three days) and mainly rhetorical. While Beijing came up with a "Peace Plan", it was no more than a bunch of slogans. Despite media allegations, Beijing has yet no intention of increasing its involvement in the settlement of the Arab-Israeli conflict. In this respect – nothing much has changed. In fact, the Chinese seem to have retreated from any such interest. Beijing is aware that there is no symmetry between Israel and the Palestinians (or even the Arabs). The only thing they can get from the Arabs is oil while Israel can provide everything else. While Netanyahu's visit was of lower level ("official visit", since, as a prime minister he was invited by Premier Li Keqiang), his visit was longer (five days, exceptional for such visits) and more constructive.

Unlike earlier visits that had reached a dead end because the two parties could not agree on issues such as Iran and the Palestinians, this time it appears that Israel and China came to realized the futility of these policies and decided to put aside thorny political issues. In any case, these issues are not related to bilateral Sino-Israeli relations. It is this awareness and mutual disillusionment about each other limitations that set the tone for Netanyahu's visit. Beijing realized that Jerusalem could by no means defy Washington by selling arms and military technology to China. Jerusalem realized that Beijing has its own interests in Iran and would not influence Tehran to stop its nuclear program, certainly not in public. Under these circumstances the two parties decided to do business and increase bilateral economic activities. China, that already has a foothold in Israel's chemical industry, may invest even more. One expected project is a railroad from Eilat, a port city on the Red Sea in southern Israel – to the north. Planned to be built by Chinese companies, this railroad would provide China with a continental bridge that could bypass the Suez Canal in case it is blocked by unrest in Egypt. China is also a potential client for Israel's offshore natural gas. Chinese construction companies finished the building of tunnels underneath Mount Carmel ahead of time (in 2002 Israel was the fifth market in the world for Chinese labor export).

Israel appears to be less concerned about China's arms sales to the Middle East (although more about Russia's). Since the 1980s, when nearly *all* Chinese military export had been delivered to the Middle East, Beijing has become a marginal military seller to the region whose share in its arms sales from 2000 to 2012 was around 19 percent reaching no more than 2.5 percent in 2012 – and zero the year before. Indirectly, however, China's military presence in the region could be harmful. In July 2006, a Northrop Grumman-built Israeli corvette was attacked by a Chinese made (or designed) C-802 anti-ship missile handed to the Hezbullah by Iran. The vessel suffered damage but managed to survive. Additional Chinese weapons (rockets) and war materials – some intercepted – found their way to the Hamas and fired against Israel. Obviously embarrassed following the publicity as well as Jerusalem's protests, Beijing asked Israel to keep a low profile on this issue and probably reprimanded Tehran as the *end user* of its military shipments. Indeed, the last thing China wants is to become directly embroiled in the conflict. Since the 1980s China has avoided supplying arms to parties that immediately threaten Israel, ignoring the fact that Israel has been supplying advanced weapons to its adversary India.

Although Israel's military transfers to China had stopped completely by the beginning of the 21st century due to US pressure, the two parties have been searching for loopholes in the US objection so as to resume at least part of this relationship. Thus, the Chinese Chief of the PLA General Staff visited Israel in August 2011 – after he had been invited to the US – and in May 2012 the Israeli Chief of the General Staff went to China. Three PLA Navy ships visited Israel in August 2012 and China's People's Armed Police Force sends its troops to Israel for training. Most of these exchanges, however, have mainly symbolic value. Yet Beijing is still interested in Israel's military technology and innovations trying to get them occasionally through third countries. China maintains more extensive military relations in the Middle East with Iran and Turkey, especially in missile technology. But the Middle East is extremely important for China's military not because of arms import or export but for other reasons.

For years China has been watching the Middle Eastern military confrontations, including and primarily those involving Israel, long before the establishment of bilateral diplomatic relations. Chinese military journals discussed Israeli air battles and military technologies in detail as early as the 1970s, if not before, and their success in coping with Soviet arms that also confronted China. More than any other region in the world, the Middle East has become a huge lab for studying the performance of Chinese-made weapons sold earlier to the region and even more so of state-of-the-art military technologies, primarily of US and Western origin. Consequently, Middle Eastern military confrontations, especially those in the Persian Gulf (the Iran-Iraq War of 1980-87, the first Gulf War of 1991 and the second Gulf War of 2003) as well as the second Lebanon War of 2006, offered China invaluable lessons, ideas and incentives that have been incorporated in its defense modernization.

In addition, the greater Middle East has offered China unique opportunities – some would say excuses – to train its armed forces in long-range operations. These include naval and airlift evacuation of over 30,000 Chinese workers from Libya and Egypt; the deployment of naval forces to the Red Sea and the Indian Ocean in the joint international fight against piracy; the participation, at Ankara's invitation, of PLA's Air Force fighters in Turkey's Anatolian Eagle aerial military exercise held in September 2010 (after the US withdrawal protesting against Israel's exclusion); and a joint exercise of Chinese and Turkish Special Forces in counter-terrorism and assault tactics held in the mountainous parts of Turkey in November 2010. These were the first occasions ever of Chinese defense operations on a NATO member soil, definitely an important military educational experience, not to say a political coup of symbolic value and a snub at the US. In sum, the Middle East plays an outstanding and exceptional role in China's military perspective – another example that instability is occasionally beneficial to Beijing.

China has been more ambivalent about two other issues associated with the Middle East: terrorism and Islam. Although the two are separated, in the Chinese mind and in scores of Chinese books and articles, they are interconnected not just between themselves but also with the Middle East. Apparently, Muslims should not be a problem for Beijing. For one thing, at around 25 million their share in China's population is less than two percent. For another, while nearly all are *Sunni*, they are split into at least ten different ethnic groups that display little solidarity and a much historical animosity. Indeed, for many years the Chinese had not been terribly worried about their Muslims. *Haj* (pilgrimage) missions to Mecca had begun in the 1950s, long before the establishment of diplomatic relations with Saudi Arabia. Stopped by the mid-1960s due to the Cultural Revolution, they resumed in the late 1970s. As post-Mao China opened to the outside world, Beijing has become more concerned about its Muslims and their relations with Central Asia and the Middle East. In the 1990s Beijing warned Iran and Saudi Arabia not to interfere in China's internal affairs by distributing Islamic literature and financing the building of mosques. Indeed, for over 15 years these activities ceased – but they were resumed more recently, undoubtedly with Chinese approval. These Middle Eastern contributions are channeled primarily to Muslim communities of Han stock (*Hui*) mainly in Ningxia-Hui Autonomous Region, Gansu or Yunnan Provinces and to a lesser extent in Xinjiang.

About half of China's Muslims live in Xinjiang (whose population is half Muslim), most of them of Turkic stock. This is China's westernmost province with close ethnic, cultural, linguistic, historical and religious relations with Central Asia and the Middle East. China is particularly concerned about the lethal combination of Islam, nationalism and terrorism in this region. While Islam in Xinjiang is relatively moderate and even eclectic, it is open to external more extremist influences from Central Asia and the Middle East. Jihadi blogs and websites occasionally criticize Beijing treatment of its Muslims, primarily Uyghurs, and advocate the establishment of an Islamic *shari'a* emirate in northwestern China. The Chinese are depicted by Arabs who joined Al-Qaeda as enemies of Islam aiming to clean Xinjiang of its Muslim communities and obliterate its Muslim identity. Still, the official Middle East, unlike North America and Western Europe, is careful not to express support for the Uyghur national claims or condemnation for their persecution and suppression by China. A rare exception was the Turkish Prime Minister Erdoğan's angry response to the July 2009 riots in Urumqi that looked to him "like genocide". This was a brief episode. Shortly afterward Sino-Turkish relations returned to normal. Other regional leaders kept quiet. It is not only that they recognize and respect China's territorial integrity but also that many of them (Turkey included) face similar challenges of separatism and terrorism and by no means want to create a precedent – or to upset Beijing.

As mentioned above, it is possible that the Chinese have been changing their attitudes on Islam as a religion in order to win the goodwill of Muslims at home and abroad. Whereas the Chinese no longer need the political support of Muslim countries, goodwill is always good for business. This is an indication of a growing Chinese self-confidence and greater social control capabilities. But the Chinese still do not have the courage to offer Uyghurs and Tibetans greater and real autonomy that may undermine their separatist claims while upgrading Beijing's international image. Muslims are a dilemma for China, an asset but also a liability, especially with regard to terrorism.

There is no doubt that Beijing is deeply concerned about terrorism – a term that began to be used widely only since the mid-1990s and much more so after September 11. Before, terrorist acts had been dealt with as criminal acts. Yet, China's concern is reflected first and foremost in its domestic affairs, as evident in the 2008 Olympic Games. Otherwise, the Chinese contribution to the fight against terrorism worldwide is marginal (see State Department *Country Report on Terrorism 2012*, May 2013). Moreover, three of the four states defined as sponsors of terrorism are not only in the Middle East but also Beijing's close allies (Iran, Sudan and Syria). In addition, China does not recognized organizations such as Hezbollah and Hamas as terrorist and indirectly, and perhaps unwillingly, assist them. A lawsuit against the Bank of China (Los Angeles branch) revealed that since 2003 it provided the Hamas with financial services, including money transfers, breaching the US sanctions regime. For China, terrorism is a liability yet occasionally an asset.

Beijing's perceived links between terrorism, Islam and the Middle East shed light on its skeptical and doubtful attitude toward the so-called "Arab Spring". In fact, Beijing had become aware of domestic state-society tension, the problem of unfair wealth distribution and deepening social gaps long before demonstrations in the Arab world erupted. The call for democracy was not only meaningless for China, but the Chinese media also slighted the significance of the so-called "democratic revolution" saying that history shows that all such political upheavals ended in authoritarian Islamic governments, essentially anti-Western. China couldn't care less about the "Arab Spring", regarded as an internal affair in which no one should interfere anyway. Therefore, there has been no change in China's policy toward the Middle East, but there has definitely been a change in China's domestic policy of "social management" (introduced before the "Arab Spring") that catered for the public good, on the one hand, and on the other hand enforced stricter control of society, the Internet and the media, and gradually increased the budgets for internal security that over the last three years exceeded those of national defense.

To conclude, while the Middle East is still marginal to China's "core interests" and while Beijing is still reluctant to become more actively involved in the region's problems, there is no doubt that China's profile in the Middle East – economic, military and political – is unprecedented. To some extent this is an outcome of Beijing's own policies and growing activism worldwide. Yet to some extent this is an outcome the behavior of other powers, first and foremost the US. Washington's refusal to sell missiles to Riyadh had opened the door to the Sino-Saudi missile deal and to diplomatic relations. Similarly, the US refusal to sell weapons to Turkey helped to shape the Sino-Turkish strategic partnership and to the Chinese participation in military exercises together with a NATO member. Also, the withdrawal of US and Western oil companies from regions of unrest and conflict based on US Presidential Executive Orders, had paved the ground for the entry of Chinese oil companies (e.g. in Sudan, Iraq and Libya) – that was later criticized. The upcoming visit of China's President Xi Jinping to the US, that starts tomorrow, is a good opportunity to *mutually* recognize each other's global role and share responsibilities. There is simply no escape: the US and the PRC, interdependent unlike the earlier bipolar world must learn to live together – and let others live together.

Table 1: **Opinions about China in Arab Countries**
(in percent and rank)

Year	As One Superpower		As a Place to Live		As a Place to Study	
	Per Cent	Rank	Per Cent	Rank	Per Cent	Rank
2011	23	1	11	4		
2009	14	3	9	4	3	Last
2008	13	3	8	4	4	
2006	16	2	7	5	4	5
2005	13	2	2	7	1	
2004	13	2	2	7	1	Last

Source: *Annual Arab Public Opinion Survey* (various years), Univ. of Maryland.

Table 2: **Favorable View of China by Middle Eastern Countries**
(in percent)

Country	2005	2006	2007	2008	2009	2010	2011	2012
Egypt	-	63	65	59	52	52	57	52
Israel	-	-	45	-	56	-	49	-
Jordan	43	49	46	44	50	53	44	47
Kuwait	-	-	52	-	-	-	-	-
Lebanon	66	-	46	50	53	56	59	59
Morocco	-	-	26	-	-	-	-	-
Palestine	-	-	46	-	43	-	62	-
Tunisia	-	-	-	-	-	-	-	69
Turkey	40	33	25	24	16	20	18	22

Source: adapted from PEW Global Attitude Project.

Table 3: **Middle Eastern Perceptions of China as a Leading Economic Power** (in percent)

Country	2008	2009	2010	2011	2012
Egypt	27	25	37	-	39
Israel	-	26	-	35	-
Jordan	31	29	50	44	44
Lebanon	22	32	36	37	44
Palestine	-	32	-	28	-
Tunisia	-	-	-	-	29
Turkey	7	9	12	13	22

Source: adapted from PEW Global Attitude Project.

Table 4: **Middle Eastern Perceptions of China As a Leading Superpower** (in percent)

Country	Has already replaced the US	Will eventually replace the US	Total has or will replace the US	Will never replace the US
Turkey	15	21	36	41
Palestine	17	37	54	38
Jordan	17	30	47	45
Israel	15	32	47	44
Lebanon	15	24	39	54

Source: adapted from PEW Global Attitude Project.

Table 5: **Middle Eastern Attitudes toward China's Growing Military and Economic Power** (in percent)

Country	Growing military power		Growing economic power	
	Good thing	Bad thing	Good thing	Bad thing
Turkey	9	66	13	64
Jordan	28	52	65	28
Lebanon	24	57	57	29
Palestine	62	29	66	24
Israel	19	66	53	30

Source: adapted from PEW Global Attitude Project.

PANEL I QUESTION & ANSWER

HEARING CO-CHAIR FIEDLER: Thank you, Dr. Shichor. There's a lot we want to get into.

Dr. Wortzel.

COMMISSIONER WORTZEL: Thank you, both, for great testimony. It's good to see Yitzhak. Thank you for making that long ride.

I've got two questions, primarily based on your written testimony. Dr. Shichor in his written testimony notes that most Middle East financial support for Muslims goes to the Hui in Ningxia and less to Xinjiang's Uyghurs. Yet, Beijing is really still very concerned about the Uyghurs. So I wonder if either of you could describe any evidence that money is going to the Uyghur groups from Xinjiang?

And, second, Dr. Shichor, you note that Chinese policymakers have a sophisticated way of leaving the dirty work in the United Nations on the Middle East to Russia. Is that because China can pretty well count on the Russians to block Security Council actions or do you think there's some coordination going on about who does what?

DR. SHICHOR: Well, number one, I have difficulties in providing the information about this sentence in my testimony (concerning financial support for China's Muslims). I was in France last week and I met with people who are associated with China and who had just come back from there. This is based on what I heard from them. The Chinese have been very careful so far not to allow external financial or any other kind of support to Muslims in China.

In the early 1990s, there were indications of such attempts by Saudi Arabia and by Iran, and somewhere by the mid-1990s, the Chinese warned both Iran and Saudi Arabia not to interfere in China's internal affairs, and they stopped.

Now, it seems that in view, maybe of the Arab Spring or religious tensions inside China, that the Chinese are allowing some investments or financial support to Muslims in China, but primarily to Hui Muslims. These are *Chinese* Muslims or Muslims of Chinese ethnic origins, and they have always been considered loyal to the government.

Xinjiang, of course, is different. These are Turkic people affiliated with Central Asia, not Hui Chinese Muslim. The same people live on the other side of the border, including Uyghurs, Tajik, Kazakhs, Kyrgyz, Tajiks, and so on. The Chinese believe that these people, notably Uyghurs, still have the vision of restoring the Eastern Turkestan Republic that was established in 1944 for about five years until the Chinese reoccupied Xinjiang with Soviet support.

We can discuss these kinds of concerns maybe later if you're interested. I don't believe the Chinese are *really* concerned about it because if you look at the power balance in Xinjiang and the monopoly on force by the Chinese military, I'm not sure that they are really concerned, certainly not about the present, though they may be concerned about the future. So, this is number one.

Number two, I'm not sure if there is any kind of shared responsibilities or coordination or mutual consultation between Chinese and the Russians on the Middle East or anything else. But I think that for the Chinese, it is very convenient that the Russians do the dirty work for them, and they don't have to take the initiative by themselves.

I really don't know if it's going to change in the future. I'm not sure about it. I think that because the Middle East is so far away from Chinese immediate concerns, because they don't know much about the Middle East, they are still amazed by all these internal rivalries, religious, political, and ethnic, that it will take a long time until the Chinese become involved in the Middle East, if ever.

Thank you.

HEARING CO-CHAIR FIEDLER: Do you have a quick response?

DR. MURPHY: I would agree on the Hui. I think formal financing from the Saudis, other Gulf states, et cetera, is more prominent. In Xinjiang, they're much more concerned about informal financing coming in through channels, especially from Turkey, possibly from the Gulf states. But I don't have any numbers. I mean that's not something that could be quantified.

On the dirty work, I think, especially in relation to Syria, that Russia has stronger actual material and economic interests in the conflict so China is following Russia's lead. I don't know if Russia changed its position, if China also would. I think that remains to be seen.

I don't know if there is formal coordination, but there has been a lot of coordination over the last ten years or so in the Security Council between Russia and China.

DR. SHICHOR: May I have just a quick follow-up?

HEARING CO-CHAIR FIEDLER: Yes.

DR. SHICHOR: In my testimony, I attach a number of very interesting cartoons from the Arab press criticizing the behavior of China (and Russia) on the Syrian issue.

HEARING CO-CHAIR FIEDLER: I think we're going to probably have a lot more questions on Syria.

DR. SHICHOR: Sure, okay.

HEARING CO-CHAIR FIEDLER: Commissioner Shea.

VICE CHAIRMAN SHEA: Thank you, both, for your testimony, and for schlepping here, Dr. Shichor.

As I read your testimony, it appears that the role of China will grow over the next ten years--let's look at the ten-year horizon--will grow as their appetite for energy resources from the Middle East increases. And it seems as if the appetite for energy resources from the Middle East by the United States will decrease as we go to alternative forms, natural gas and other non-oil-based energy sources.

Also we're in the midst of beginning to pivot militarily to East

Asia. So project, if you will, ten years from now, what do you see the role of China in the Middle East? What do you see the role of the United States in the Middle East? But mostly China.

And if you're advising the Chinese leadership, what things should they be doing positively and what types of missteps should they avoid? They have made missteps in other areas of the world, but what types of red lines would you suggest that they not step over?

HEARING CO-CHAIR FIEDLER: Both of you.

DR. SHICHOR: I would say there are some things that I'm quite certain about and others that I'm not. One is about China's economic development. I think that despite the slowdown in China's economy it will still grow exponentially over the next ten, 20, maybe 30 years, according to some experts. So say ten years from now, China's economy will probably be more than twice what it is today.

And this is going to have a tremendous influence, effect, on the world and on China's relations with other countries, with Russia, with the United States, and so on. I think this is one of the basic conditions or basic explanations of China's behavior.

Now, it doesn't end with economics. Because the economy is bigger, there are more financial resources, resources for military development, for defense modernization, and so on, so China will probably be stronger than it is today.

Also, I always tell that I saw a television program a couple of years ago about England, and it was about people with IQ 170 and above, which is, I would say, very respectable to say the least.

[Laughter.]

DR. SHICHOR: Every society, they said, has about 1.5 percent (people with IQ 170 and above). A quick calculation shows that, if this kind of analysis is true, China has about 20 million, over 20 million, people with IQ 170 and above. Now, suppose I'm wrong, it's not 20 million, it's only ten million, perhaps only five million, still, given China's size, they have the manpower, the potential to do almost everything they want to do. It is going to take some time.

Now, how is this going to affect China's Middle Eastern situation or position? Let me first talk about energy. People talk about the revolution in energy, especially in the United States, with shale oil and shale gas, and some people have doubts about how far this is going to revolutionize the energy sector. Some people say, well, there's going to be a change, but not as dramatic as people believe, maybe only 15 percent. U.S. dependence on Middle Eastern oil has already been reduced over many years. I don't know if you know it, but China has also begun exploring shale oil and shale gas.

VICE CHAIRMAN SHEA: Right.

DR. SHICHOR: But the Chinese don't have the technology. Maybe they don't have resources but they're going to have them in the future. And so China may also--

VICE CHAIRMAN SHEA: Doctor, what kind of red lines —or

what types of actions could China conceivably take that would put its interests in the Middle East in jeopardy?

DR. SHICHOR: Well, again, I don't know in the long term, but right now, a conflict in the Gulf, a war with Iran, a confrontation that would block the Hormuz Strait, and the flow of oil should be a red line. About 40 to 50 percent of China's oil import comes through the Hormuz Strait. This is going to be a real problem for China. You asked in the end what the Chinese have to do, and what is the impact on U.S.-China relations. Xi Jinping is about to visit the United States, and I think there is something. It's not directly related to the Middle East. It's related to the international situation at large because the international situation now is completely different from what it used to be at the time the Soviet Union existed. We had then a bipolar world with two superpowers that were in conflict with each other, and I could not imagine, it's inconceivable that the Soviet Union would have bought American bonds, for example, or that the United States or Boeing would set up an airplane plant in Soviet Union at that time, but this is the situation now with China. So we still have a kind of bipolar world. It's not multipolar.

So what I mean is that the two countries have to come to terms about understanding that the world has changed, and they have to coordinate their activities in the Middle East and elsewhere.

HEARING CO-CHAIR FIEDLER: Dr. Murphy.

DR. MURPHY: Ten years from now I think China will be the major economic actor in the region, both for resources, markets, et cetera. On the military side, I think the only thing that will change is they may increase their presence to protect their economic interests. So you might see more antipiracy activities, needing the ability to evacuate citizens, that type of thing, but nothing else in the military realm. I don't think they have a lot of interest in being involved there.

On the political side, I think ten years from now, if things continue as they are, countries in the region may look to China as to be more of a balance against the U.S. and to lead them more as developing countries. You may see that dynamic emerging.

What China should avoid ten years from now or in the next ten years is competing with the U.S., making this an active realm of competition. I think there's a lot of areas for cooperation and that competition can be avoided. So Iran is one issue where making that a confrontational issue between the U.S. and China is not in Chinese interests.

HEARING CO-CHAIR FIEDLER: Thank you. The only thing I wanted to remind you is each Commissioner only gets five minutes so that's why we'd like shorter answers. Commissioner Wessel.

COMMISSIONER WESSEL: I don't know why you made the comment just before I spoke.

[Laughter.]

COMMISSIONER WESSEL: Thank you. And Larry, I've always bowed to your linguistic prowess. Your ability to translate Yiddish and

Chinese now is deeply appreciated. Thank you also for your schlep and, Dr. Murphy, for your participation.

I'd like to follow up on Commissioner Shea's question. And Dr. Murphy, I think you provided a good view of the ten-year projection. In addition to what people perceive as an energy renaissance here in the United States, I think we're also dealing with political fatigue here in terms of U.S. power projection in the Middle East. So there are many who are welcoming energy independence here not only for its economic benefits but for the power projection issues.

Dr. Shichor, you, I think, have moved quickly over the issue of Israeli support for Chinese technological advances, primarily I think in the UAV area, but in a number of others.

So we have a, if one looks at, quote-unquote, "core interests," and that was talked about vis-a-vis China I think the U.S. has had some core interests in the Middle East area that continue--Israel and our support there. But now we see some power balance change, it appears, as the fatigue sets in here, and China sees not only the energy needs increase for them, but the ability to expand its political support and international institutions.

Are we not going to see more U.S.-Chinese competition for political and larger support, putting aside the energy issues over the coming years, as it relates to Israel? Israel has reached out. It's got its hands slapped as it relates to some technological issues, but Israel is right to protect its core interests. Where does China fit into that vis-a-vis the U.S. in the coming decade as well?

And, Dr. Murphy, if you'd like to start?

DR. MURPHY: So before 2008, I probably wasn't as concerned about this power balancing in the Middle East, but I think three things have changed in the last few years that alter my views. One, after the global financial crisis, I think China has an increased confidence in its ability and desire to be active in the international realm.

In 2010 with the pivot to Asia, which is not only being perceived by China negatively both in Asia, but I would say globally, China is wanting more and more now to demonstrate to the U.S. that it is willing to stand up to the U.S. in the international arena.

And then finally with the beginning of the Arab Spring and the intervention in Libya, an increased concern over U.S. and foreign intervention in other countries.

Those three factors together I think are making China more willing to take a stand in the Middle East or other regions against the U.S. So, the potential for that power struggle I think is greater now as a result of these larger global issues than it was a few years ago.

COMMISSIONER WESSEL: And your reference to the three votes in the U.N. also would support that counterbalance, correct?

DR. MURPHY: Yes. My understanding, based on interviews and research, is that part of those three vetoes is demonstrating that China can and China will stand up. China is going to advocate for the Five Principles of peaceful coexistence and non-interference, and also to display its displeasure with Libya, with what happened in Libya, and finally to show that it is supporting Russia, a country that it sees as an important partner in an emerging multipolar world. There's many factors coming together, but I think Syria is the first piece of that.

On Israel, I'll let Professor Shichor speak in detail on that, but I do think China is a relatively balanced actor in the region, and that it does have a strong relationship with Israel and doesn't want to interfere too much with Israel's core interests.

COMMISSIONER WESSEL: Dr. Shichor.

DR. SHICHOR: First about China-Israel relations. As you said, all military technology transfers that began in the late 1970s, early 1980s (I was involved in them at the beginning) stopped. There are now, as far as I know, no military relations between China and Israel of any kind.

Israel is very, very careful--and there have been all kinds of mechanisms set up in Israel, in the Parliament (the Knesset), and in the new export supervision department in the Israeli Ministry of Defense--to avoid something like that happening again.

Nevertheless, the two sides are very much interested--I mentioned it my paper--in finding loopholes and watching what the United States is doing and take it as kind of a kosher [legitimate] activity for both of them [China and Israel].

I think the Chinese very much appreciate Israel's technological and scientific achievements, especially in the military field. Israel, of course, for economic and other reasons, would still like to sell arms to other countries, including China, I think, if it is possible. Of course, India has become a second, substitute, very important market, for Israeli military technology.

Now, about U.S.-China competition. Again, coming back to the question of what will happen ten years from now, if I try to run wild with my imagination, I would say that the Chinese would be happy with some kind of a division of the world into different spheres of influence, whereby East Asia will be a Chinese sphere.

It's always been a Chinese sphere--and this is why the Chinese are so concerned about the United States' pivot to Asia, which is mainly, by the way, rhetorical; it's not so much real. In return for a US withdrwal from Asia, Beijing would possibly accept a stronger U.S. position in the Middle East, because the U.S. presence in the Middle East is very important for China. Though on the margins of China's interests, it is still very important.

COMMISSIONER WESSEL: Thank you.

HEARING CO-CHAIR FIEDLER: Carolyn.

COMMISSIONER BARTHOLOMEW: Thank you very much to both of our witnesses for coming here, people who came from not that far away as well as, Dr. Shichor, for your travel.

Thank you, also, Dr. Shichor, in particular, for acknowledging that the Chinese government controls who has access to the country based on what your views are and your research. I think that's an issue that a number of us have been concerned about, that if you dare to speak up against what the Chinese government is doing, your ability to do your research is really limited.

I'd like to explore with both of you a little bit more how China manages its interests with the Islamic countries as it is trying to keep people out of the Islamic issues that it has going on within its own country.

So in the 1990s, if I remember correctly, there was a presumption that one of the reasons that China was selling the M-11 missiles to Pakistan was that it was kind of a deal, which is we'll give you some of this equipment and in return you stay out of what's going on inside of Xinjiang and other places in China.

And I just wondered if you could talk a little bit more about the levers that the Chinese government might be using with countries in the Middle East, with Islamic countries, in order to try to contain what's going on inside China with its Islamic population?

DR. MURPHY: I would say they explicitly deal with that, for example, in the cooperation forums that I discuss in detail in my testimony. The verbiage of those forums is very specific about China supporting Arab causes and Arab states supporting China in combating international terrorism. It's code words, but it's very clear that they're referring to Xinjiang.

I think part of the issue, though, is most of the interaction and the most important parts of the relationship are economic, broader political issues, not the Xinjiang issue. So the Arab states, in particular, understand that China wants that type of support, and they don't tend to allow that to eclipse the broader relationship.

But particularly in the cooperation forums, they are very clear about wanting that support in exchange for their own support of these countries.

COMMISSIONER BARTHOLOMEW: Dr. Shichor.

DR. SHICHOR: Islam is a very broad term. As far as China is concerned, there are about ten different Muslim groups in China, different ethnic groups. The Chinese are very much concerned about Uyghurs mostly and less about the other groups, which are either small or part of China's ethnic collective.

Every now and then the Chinese remind the Middle Eastern governments not to interfere in China's internal affairs. But the point is that Middle Eastern countries and Islamic countries with very few exceptions--I mentioned Prime Minister Erdogan's critical reaction to the July 2009 riots in Xinjiang, which was over very quickly--couldn't care less about Chinese Muslims or about the Uyghurs.

So Chinese have more or less a free hand. There have been a number of major incidents in Xinjiang over the years. I'm not speaking about Mao's time, but since the beginning of the 1990s; most of the Middle Eastern and Islamic countries kept quiet about it.

Every year now Chinese hajj missions go to Mecca. This began around 1957, stopped on the eve of the Cultural Revolution, and resumed in 1979. The last mission included about 20,000 people. They are under strict control, and everything is supervised.

DR. MURPHY: I just wanted to add that after the 2009 riots, I know that Turkey was elevated in China's foreign policy priorities in the region, particularly because they wanted to emphasize these other aspects of interactions.

COMMISSIONER BARTHOLOMEW: Just a clarification. So, the message to Turkey became a more positive one rather than if you continue to speak out, you'll be punished?

DR. MURPHY: Right--I mean there was a focus on economic interaction, but I don't know what was happening behind closed doors. I'm sure there was discussion about how that type of behavior could harm long-term relations, but I think it tends to be the emphasis that we have this great economic and political relationship, don't disturb that by this support in Xinjiang.

It becomes more complicated in Turkey, though, because a lot of the support is really grassroots level support. You see they've got very low approval ratings of China when you look at Turkish opinion polls. So I think public perception is quite negative, but government-to-government it is really positive right now.

COMMISSIONER BARTHOLOMEW: Okay, thank you.

HEARING CO-CHAIR FIEDLER: Commissioner Brookes.

COMMISSIONER BROOKES: Thank you.

I believe it was Dr. Murphy's testimony that talked about arms sales to the Middle East and said they'd basically held steady. But there have been some significant Chinese transfers, such as the C802 to the Iranians, which found its way, it appears, to Hezbollah in the 2006 war with Israel.

Are there any other advanced Chinese weapons that are being transferred because it's not quite clear from those numbers? I know that you weren't specifically asked.

And also, there has been some rumor floating around that the Chinese in the 1980s sold some Silkworm type ballistic missiles to the Saudis. These are nuclear-capable missiles. And there were rumors that the Chinese might be upgrading those missiles, especially in light of what's going on across the Gulf in Iran. Do you have any knowledge of that?

Thank you.

DR. MURPHY: On the Silkworm issue, other than what you've heard, and I've heard the same things, but I don't have additional information. On conventional weapons, partially to your point, last year, of the $45 million of weapons sold, 44 of that went to Iran, and one million went to Egypt. I cannot speak off the top of my head regarding weapon systems. I would be happy to look into that and send it to you outside of the hearing, but Professor Shichor actually may be able to speak more intelligently to that than I can.

Thank you.

COMMISSIONER BROOKES: Please.

DR. SHICHOR: According to the figures supplied by SIPRI and other organizations, when you say $45 million, in proportion to other sales in other regions and by other countries, is very small. In terms of arms sales, this is really small. So China has almost no place in the Middle East as an arms seller over the last few years.

The Chinese continue their relationships with other countries, especially with Iran. Pakistan is the major buyer of Chinese arms, but with Iran it's probably missile technology. The C802 missile [that hit an Israeli boat in 2006] had been supplied to Iran on the condition that Iran would be the end user. The Chinese found out that some of these weapons--either originally Chinese or Chinese designed and built in Iran--were transferred to the Hezbollah in Lebanon and perhaps to other Palestinian organizations as well.

There is no way China can test these weapons under real battlefield conditions, and the Middle East is the only place where it can be done. So there is a certain advantage to these transfers.

There have been a number of Sino-Israeli exchanges [concerning the spillover of Chinese weapons]. The Chinese ambassador was invited to the Israeli Foreign Ministry, and the Chinese asked to keep it quiet underscoring that they were not interested in their weapons becoming involved in the Arab-Israeli conflict.

Now, about Saudi Arabia's Chinese missiles. I don't have time to get into all the details of these deals. I was in Taiwan when the news broke out. I think it was March 1988 when China decided to supply Saudi Arabia with the DF-3, a missile which is an old 1960s type. As I said earlier, the Saudis turned to China only because the United States refused to supply them with missiles, and the same goes for Turkey. So the Chinese supplied an unknown number of missiles, somewhere between 12 and 24. But the point is that these missiles were never used. They were not effective for deterrence because we know Saddam Hussein invaded Kuwait and also Saudi Arabia in 1990. Iraqi Scud missiles hit American bases and Saudi bases in Saudi Arabia; and the missiles were not used for retaliation afterwards. So their value was just symbolic. I don't think there is any plan of upgrading these missiles to become nuclear capable.

COMMISSIONER BROOKES: Thank you.

HEARING CO-CHAIR FIEDLER: Commissioner Tobin.

COMMISSIONER TOBIN: Thank you.

I have a question for each of you. First, if I may, Dr. Murphy, you spent extensive time interviewing in China over different periods of time, and in reading your testimony, the reader finds a lot of good news. And you've stated here today that you find China to be a very balanced actor.

So, my question for you is, do you have any concerns as you think about the United States, this Commission, and our requirement to make

48

recommendations to Congress? If so, what would that be?

And Dr. Shichor, what specific step, what single specific action do you think would you recommend that we relay to Congress?

Thank you.

DR. MURPHY: My biggest concern is that on a normative level that China has advocated for norms that are quite different than the Western liberal international order. So the Five Principles of peaceful coexistence, non-interference, territorial integrity, which is important to all countries obviously, but this strong stance on these sovereignty issues versus the broader respect for human rights, democracy, et cetera.

I think that the Middle East could be one area where you see tension in that order because many states in the Middle East share China's view of the world on those issues more than they share the U.S. view at this point in time.

And on the economic side, I think that in China, the relationship between state and government is very close. That differs from the liberal economic order promoting free markets and laissez-faire economics. States in the Middle East are also quite comfortable with that approach.

So when I see these commonalities in normative stance, if we start to have a larger global tension between the U.S. and China, states in the Middle East, I think, may be more naturally inclined to lean towards China than towards the U.S. We need to be careful about that.

And I think the primary way to resolve that, at least in the short-term, is not to exaggerate that potential but to seek out opportunities for cooperation between the U.S. and China, because right now it's not a region of conflict, and we have shared interests. But I do think that in the very long-term scenario, if we ended up in a Cold War type environment, I don't know which direction these states are going to fall. I think we need to be conscious of those ideological affiliations between the global South and China, with the Middle East as part of that.

COMMISSIONER TOBIN: Thank you.

Dr. Shichor.

DR. SHICHOR: Again, I think we have to start looking at things from a more general perspective. And I would like to say a few words about the leadership in China and the United States. A very interesting phenomenon over the last 20 or 30 years is that there is no convergence between the power of the two leaders in China and in the United States. A new president has just been "elected" in China who'll stay in office for two five-year terms. He has just started his first term and he is relatively weak. He still doesn't have his own power base within the Party, and it's going to take time, somewhere between two or three or even five years until the next Party Congress when he'll change the composition of the CCP Standing Committee and Politburo in his favor.

Most of them are going to leave because of age, so he's going to be stronger in the next term. While in the United States now, we have a president elected for a second term, and he should be much stronger because he doesn't have to worry about being reelected. Consequently we have a situation whereby in China there is a relatively weak president, and in the United States there is a relatively strong president.

And when the Chinese president will become stronger in his second term, there will be a new American president in his first term, who is going to be a little weak. And the point is how to bridge this gap between the two leaders. I would say it starts with recognition.

Charles Taylor, a British political theorist now living in Canada, developed the term "recognition," not in the sense of diplomatic recognition but in the sense of solving problems in multicultural societies. This term can be applied also to the international system, meaning recognition of the legitimacy of the "other".

I think one thing that China needs is this kind of recognition from the United States, this kind of respect, and I think the United States has to come to terms with China's rise. The world has changed. There is a new power on the horizon--or already here. The two countries should somehow take the responsibility that they are going to be the main leaders in the world in the next few decades. And they have to coordinate their respective responsibilities.

COMMISSIONER TOBIN: Thank you.

HEARING CO-CHAIR FIEDLER: Thank you. We've got to get Commissioner Cleveland and one other Commissioner in before we're done.

COMMISSIONER CLEVELAND: Thank you.

In our additional reading that the staff kindly provided us, there is an article that refers to Wang Jisi, who is the Dean at the School of International Studies in Beijing, discussing a strategy called "marching West." And in that context, he talks about Zhou Yongkang, a top Politburo member, going to Kabul and offering training, funding, and equipping of the Afghan police.

As it seems to be an emerging concept not necessarily endorsed or embraced by the new leadership, I'm interested in your views of this concept of "marching West" and, in particular, where Afghanistan fits into that scenario.

DR. MURPHY: Wang Jisi was with us for the last several months at Princeton, so I've been able to discuss this concept with him directly. My understanding of his original intent in putting forward this concept is that right now there's quite a bit of tension with the U.S. in the Asia-Pacific, and in order to avoid conflict with the U.S., China should be broadening horizons and looking at other regions, in that it has traditionally had strong relations with the Middle East, Africa, et cetera, that direction.

So this was kind of a redirection of energy hopefully to have a positive cooperative result. How that's informing policy debates within China and the degree to which his work is informing debates versus just reflecting debates is another issue. I think there's a lot of discussion within China about whether it should be reorienting itself towards regions where it has opportunities, and the Middle East is one of those.

So I think it's an evolving discussion. I think his original intent was meant to be very positive, but also if you read between the lines, the Middle East provides China with a lot of resources and economic opportunity. It's kind of this global balancing so that China doesn't have all of its eggs in one basket.

Specifically, regarding Afghanistan, I think China wants stability there and wants to be a positive actor. I don't think that they have a lot of other interests there and the potential for insurgency activities to spread from Afghanistan over into China, which long ago with the Soviet invasion of Afghanistan, you did have some of that movement of actors across that border.

DR. SHICHOR: Well, I don't have much to add except that all these slogans such as "marching West," "developing the West," or the "Five-Antis", make things simple for people to understand. But it doesn't say much. When Abu Mazen visited China just before Netanyahu's arrival, the Chinese came up with a "peace plan". When you look at it, it's not a plan, it's not peace, it's nothing, just a collection of slogans. So I don't think we have to worry very much about it. Otherwise, I agree with what Dawn said.

COMMISSIONER CLEVELAND: You anticipated my next question, which is in your testimony. Dr. Shichor, you said that there had been a shift in this recent visit with Netanyahu and Beijing. Beijing plays a role in Iran, but has nothing to do with Israel, and it would not budge while Israel still insists on using force against Iran.

I'm wondering if you could elaborate on the shift in the bilateral relationship, sort of how that's come about, and how it might look a year or two down the road?

DR. SHICHOR: Thanks.

I was consulted before Netanyahu's visit to China, and I said: don't emphasize again the Chinese support of Iran because China has its own interests, nothing to do with Israel, and the Chinese do it not because they support Iran's military nuclear program. They don't like it at all, and they know probably a lot more about it than we do. And so I said just deemphasize these issues and try to concentrate on bilateral relations between the two countries.

For many years, the two sides entertained all kinds of myths about each other. The Chinese believed that Israel was the real force behind U.S. policy in the Middle East (and other places) and that Israel could deliver weapons and military technology, defying the United States. Israel looked at China as a backward country.

Now, the two parties came to realize that all of this is not true anymore, if it was at any time. Instead, they decided to forget about all these myths and "let's do business," I think to some extent this is a good policy. It's a long-term policy. The Chinese are very, very much interested in Israeli technology, not only military, but medical technology, electronics, and so on. And, of course, Israel is interested in the Chinese market and investments.

In terms of its size--Israel is a very small country. It has a population of about 7.5 million. Yet, Israeli trade with China is a little more than Egypt's trade with China, whose population is over ten times bigger than Israel's. And the same goes with Turkey. So I think it was good to put aside all political issues and stop the attempts by Israeli leaders and delegations to convince the Chinese to stop supporting Iran--a policy that has consistently failed anyway. I assume this is not going to be done anymore.

HEARING CO-CHAIR FIEDLER: Thank you.

Senator Talent.

HEARING CO-CHAIR TALENT: The Chinese supported, albeit with some reluctance, the U.N. resolution regarding Libya and have positively obstructed progress in Syria.

And this makes me curious because there are two incidents that are fairly close in time. The Europeans were really the leaders seeking both resolutions. What explains it? What's really going on? And when they say, well, we didn't know that the first resolution in Libya would lead to military action, I mean, come on. It authorized military action. They knew what the Europeans wanted to do. So what explains the change?

Is it a desire--does it indicate that they're really trying to move closer to Russia, that they're sort of throwing their sign? I mean I know that's part of it. So expound that if you would.

DR. MURPHY: Thank you.

So, first, I am also skeptical regarding their surprise, as I am also told over and over again in interviews with them and with members of the Arab League. So I think the fact that military intervention occurred strengthened their worries about foreign interference. But I think there is this increasing concern about the U.S. and the West altering the trajectory of these regimes.

But it perhaps could be because Syria is a different situation in that I think they are concerned that the Syrian situation could evolve into a much larger regional dispute that affects their interests in the region more, pulling in Iran, Saudi Arabia, the Gulf states, and Jordan. So I think they see it differently in that way.

I do think that they know that Russia is going to assert itself in the Security Council and so they have this opportunity to also voice opposition. I think it's part of this growing, as I discussed earlier, concern over the pivot to Asia and other regional dynamics in Asia-Pacific, that they're wanting to stand up to more.

But I think at the core of it, it probably is that Syria is just, in their mind, a much more serious situation that could evolve into a regional conflict.

HEARING CO-CHAIR TALENT: Well, but if nothing, it's evolving into a regional conflict. The point is by allowing the civil war to go on, there's a danger of greater instability in the region. Do they just not see it that way?

DR. MURPHY: I think their concern is that however one intervenes, that the result could be bad. So from what I was hearing in January with my interviews was concern about the composition of the opposition in Syria. It's not just the original anti-government opposition, but you have a lot of radical elements that ultimately could lead to a Syria with a much more Islamist regime in place, and China has some concerns about that.

That said, it's not transparent. I mean all of this is based on interviews. I think their stance is pretty much if we intervene, it could be a bad situation. If we don't intervene, it's a bad situation. So we should stay by this principle of non-intervention and be consistent.

And I do have to say that the Arab states that I interviewed were concerned about China's vote, but they at least understood that China has been consistent for a very long time regarding this principled stance. I don't think it's deteriorating relations between China and Arab states as much as it might seem to be.

HEARING CO-CHAIR TALENT: If you would like to comment on Syria?

DR. SHICHOR: Just very briefly. Is Syria so important for China? The answer is definitely not. Syria is not important in terms of oil supplies. Although China has interests in Syrian oil, it's not important in terms of trade. The Chinese couldn't care less about Bashar Assad.

So it must be something else. This is a very good question and I have to think about it a little more. If it's not Syria, it has to do with something else, and that "something else" is relations between China and Russia, on the one hand, and the relations between China and the United States, on the other hand. I think maybe it boils down to what I said earlier, the question of recognition and respect.

China expects to be consulted, to be part of the international decision-making process, and not let other countries do the work by themselves. In my paper, I said that there are four different stages in what Chinese call "non-intervention" in regional conflicts. First of all, the two parties have to settle the conflict directly between themselves without any intervention from outside. If this doesn't work, then a regional organization should intervene; in this case, the Arab League. And the Chinese managed to antagonize the Arab League as well. And if this doesn't work, then the United Nations Security Council should intervene. Only then comes that last and worst option, which the Chinese oppose, of unilateral response or action.

So, I think, maybe the Chinese are now looking for a ladder. Someone should provide them with a ladder to get down from the tree that they had climbed earlier.

HEARING CO-CHAIR FIEDLER: Thank you very much. We could certainly continue to go on, but we have another panel starting in ten minutes after we break. I want to thank you again for your long trip, Dr. Shichor, and Dawn, for coming and visiting us as well.

[Whereupon, a short recess was taken.]

PANEL II INTRODUCTION BY COMMISSION JAMES TALENT HEARING CO-CHAIR

HEARING CO-CHAIR TALENT: Our next panel will examine China's energy and economic interests in the Middle East. Our two expert witnesses for this panel are Dr. Erica Downs and Mr. Bryant Edwards.

Dr. Downs is a Fellow at the John L. Thornton China Center at the Brookings Institution. Her research interests include China's overseas investment and lending, government business relations in China, and energy governance and decision-making in China.

Before joining Brookings, she served as an energy analyst at the CIA. She holds a Ph.D. and an M.A. from Princeton University and a Bachelor of Science from Georgetown University. Dr. Downs has testified before the Commission in years past, and we're pleased to welcome her back.

Mr. Edwards is a partner in the Hong Kong Office of Latham & Watkins. Mr. Edwards relocated to Hong Kong after four years in Dubai where he led the opening of the firm's four Middle East offices and served as Chair of the firm's Middle East practice.

Before Dubai, Mr. Edwards spent eight years in the firm's London office where he was Chair of the Corporate Department. His practice includes representation of companies and investment banking firms in merger and acquisition transactions and in public and private offerings of securities.

We thank both the witnesses for being here, and we'll begin with Dr. Downs.

OPENING STATEMENT OF DR. ERICA DOWNS
FELLOW, JOHN L. THORNTON CHINA CENTER, BROOKINGS INSTITUTION

DR. DOWNS: Good morning. I would like to thank the members of the Commission for the opportunity to be here today. It's an honor to participate in this hearing.

My remarks today will focus on China's energy relations with the Middle East. I will discuss China's energy trade with, and investment in, the region and the implications of the resurgence of oil and natural gas production in the United States for China's role in the Middle East.

Regarding China's oil trade with the Middle East, China imports more oil from the Middle East than any other part of the world. In 2011, China imported 2.9 million barrels per day of Middle Eastern oil, which accounted for 60 percent of China's oil imports.

China's largest crude oil supplier is Saudi Arabia, which provided China with one-fifth of its crude oil imports last year. Saudi Arabia has been China's top crude oil supplier for the past decade. The kingdom has established itself as a very reliable supplier in both word and deed. Saudi officials have repeatedly assured the Chinese that they can count on Saudi Arabia to provide China with the oil it needs for continued economic growth. Saudi Aramco has backed up this commitment with its participation in a joint venture refinery in China to process Saudi crude.

China's oil imports from Iran--its fourth-largest supplier in 2012 and third-largest supplier for most of the previous decade--have recently declined, probably as a result of U.S. sanctions aimed at reducing Iran's revenue from crude oil exports.

The National Defense Authorization Act of 2012 (NDAA) prescribes penalties for foreign financial institutions which do business with the Central Bank of Iran, the main clearinghouse for oil payments. However, the NDAA also grants 180-day exemptions to countries that significantly reduce oil imports from Iran. China's imports of Iranian crude have fallen from 555,000 barrels per day in 2011 to 402,000 barrels per day during the first four months of this year. These reductions earned China exemptions in June and December 2012, and June 2013.

Regarding China's oil investments in the Middle East, the Chinese oil companies' largest upstream projects in the region are in Iraq and Iran. The firms have signed service contracts to develop oil fields in both countries. The projects in Iraq have progressed much more quickly than the projects in Iran.

China National Petroleum Corporation, or CNPC, moved quickly to develop a foothold in the post-war Iraqi oil industry and is one of the largest foreign companies, in terms of production, operating in Iraq. One of the crown jewels of CNPC's international upstream portfolio is Iraq's Rumaila oil field, which CNPC is developing in partnership with BP. Last year, Rumaila accounted for more than one-third of Iraq's oil output. It was also CNPC's top producing project overseas, accounting for almost one-half of CNPC's net overseas oil and natural gas production.

In contrast, the upstream activities of CNPC and its domestic peers in Iran have slowed in recent years. The Iranians suspended the contract of China National Offshore Oil Corporation, or CNOOC, for the development of the North Pars natural gas field in 2011 for lack of progress, and CNPC withdrew from developing Phase 11 of South Pars, the world's largest natural gas field, in 2012.

CNPC is behind schedule in developing the Azadegan oil field, and Sinopec's work on the Yadavaran oil field has reportedly suffered delays. The reasons for the shrinking presence of China's oil companies in Iran include sanctions that have made it difficult to secure necessary equipment and technologies, unhappiness with contract terms, uncertainty about whether Iran's nuclear program will spark a military conflict, and reported guidance from China's leadership to move slowly in Iran.

In sum, the Chinese oil companies' strategy for securing upstream projects in Iran has been one of "talk now and spend later." In the 2000s, the companies were happy to negotiate contracts for projects that almost certainly would have gone to major international oil companies in the absence of sanctions. However, they have not been in any rush to actually pump large sums of money into Iran.

I would also like to say a few words about how the resurgence of oil and natural gas production in the United States may reshape the roles of the United States and China in the Middle East. The International Energy Agency projects that the United States oil imports from the Middle East will fall from 1.9 million barrels per day in 2011 to just 100,000 barrels per day, or three percent of total imports, in 2035 as a result of increasing domestic oil production and decreasing demand.

In contrast, China's oil imports from the Middle East are projected to grow from 2.9 million barrels per day in 2011 to 6.7 million barrels per day, or 54 percent of total oil imports, in 2035.

These trends have prompted speculation about the future U.S. military posture in the Persian Gulf and, in turn, what it might mean for the security of regional oil flows to China. It is highly unlikely that the United States would completely disengage from the Middle East even if the United States is importing little or no oil from the region.

Washington will almost certainly retain a variety of interests in the region, including the free flow of oil, counterterrorism, and nuclear nonproliferation. However, if a diminishing appetite for Middle Eastern crudes and budgetary constraints were to prompt Washington to substantially reduce its military presence in the region, oil security concerns might compel Beijing to play a larger role in defusing the primary threat to the free flow of oil from the Persian Gulf--the closure of the Strait of Hormuz by Iran.

At a minimum, this might entail Beijing communicating to Tehran that it would regard the disruption of oil exports bound for China as a threat to one of China's vital interests, similar to the public warning that then-Premier Wen Jiabao issued in Qatar in January 2012.

A less likely but more active Chinese effort might involve reinforcing verbal admonitions with the stationing of a ship in the Persian Gulf, perhaps from one of the multinational regional antipiracy patrols in which the Chinese Navy participates.

Finally, it's worth noting that the boom in oil and natural gas production in North America may provide Washington with more leverage over the activities of Chinese oil companies in Iran. North America is now the epicenter of global mergers and acquisitions in oil and natural gas exploration and production.

In 2011, for example, 60 percent of all upstream mergers and acquisitions worldwide were in North America. China's oil companies are part of this story. Since 2009, almost half of the capital Chinese oil companies have spent on overseas mergers and acquisitions has been used to purchase assets in North America, including $8 billion spent in the United States.

The more Chinese companies are invested in the United States, the more they are likely to think twice about doing business in Iran. This is because involvement in the Iranian oil industry may undermine their efforts to expand in the United States in two ways:

First, any proposed acquisition that would result in foreign control of an American business should be reviewed by the Committee on Foreign Investment in the United States, or CFIUS, for national security risks, and it is likely that CFIUS would inquire about the nature of the acquirer's activities in Iran.

Second, Chinese oil companies are acutely aware of how public opinion can scuttle a deal, thanks to CNOOC's unsuccessful bid for Unocal in 2005. Strong opposition to a Chinese company's business in Iran might prevent that company from acquiring an asset in the United States by making the transaction costs unacceptably high. In sum, opportunities to invest in the United States might diminish the appetite of Chinese oil companies for undertaking projects in Iran.

Thank you.

PREPARED STATEMENT OF DR. ERICA DOWNS
FELLOW, JOHN L. THORNTON CHINA CENTER, BROOKINGS INSTITUTION

June 6, 2013

Erica Downs
Fellow
John L. Thornton China Center
The Brookings Institution

Testimony before the U.S.-China Economic & Security Review Commission

Hearing on *China and the Middle East*

Panel II: China's Energy and Other Economic Interests in the Middle East

I would like to thank the members of the Commission for the opportunity to testify. It is an honor to participate in this hearing.

My remarks today will focus on China's energy relations with the Middle East. I will discuss China's energy trade with and investment in the region and the implications of the resurgence of oil and natural gas production in the United States for China's role in the Middle East.

China's oil trade with the Middle East

China imports more oil from the Middle East than any other region of the world. In 2011, China imported 2.9 million barrels per day (b/d) of Middle Eastern oil, which accounted for 60 percent of China's oil imports. For comparison, the United States imported 2.5 million barrels per day of oil from the Middle East in 2011, accounting for 26 percent of US oil imports.[1]

China's largest crude oil supplier is Saudi Arabia, which provided China with one-fifth of its crude oil imports -- almost 1.1 million b/d – last year.[2] Saudi Arabia has been China's top crude oil supplier for the past decade. The Kingdom has established itself as a very reliable supplier in both word and deed. Saudi officials have repeatedly reassured the Chinese that they can count of Saudi Arabia to provide China with the oil it needs for continued economic growth.[3] Saudi Aramco has backed up this commitment with its participation in a joint venture refinery in China's Fujian Province, which processes Saudi crude.

---

[1] International Energy Agency, World Energy Outlook 2012 (Paris: OECD/IEA, 2012), pp. 85, 107; and data provided by the International Energy Agency by email on May 29, 2013.
[2] "Table of China December Data on Oil, Oil Product and LNG Imports," *Dow Jones Global Equities News*, January 21, 2013.
[3] See, for example, Ali Ibrahim Al-Naimi, Speech at the Conferment Ceremony of Honorary Doctorate, Peking University, Beijing, China, November 13, 2009, http://www.kaust.edu.sa/about/bot/speeches/PekingUniversitySpeech.html.

China's oil imports from Iran-- its fourth largest supplier in 2012 and third largest supplier for most of the previous decade-- have recently declined, probably as a result of US sanctions aimed at reducing Iran's revenue from crude oil exports. The National Defense Authorization Act of 2012 prescribes penalties for foreign financial institutions which do business with the Central Bank of Iran, the main clearinghouse for oil payments, but also grants 180-day exemptions to countries that "significantly reduce" oil imports from Iran. China's imports of Iranian crude have fallen from 555,000 b/d in 2011 to 439,000 b/d in 2012 to 402,000 b/d during the period January-April 2013, earning the country exemptions in June and December 2012.[4]

China's oil investments in the Middle East

The Chinese national oil companies' largest upstream projects in the Middle East are in Iraq and Iran. The firms have signed service contracts to develop several large oil fields in both countries. The projects in Iraq have progressed much more quickly than the projects in Iran.

China National Petroleum Corporation (CNPC), which moved quickly to develop a foothold in the postwar Iraqi oil industry, is the largest foreign company, in terms of production, operating in Iraq. One of the crown jewels of CNPC's international upstream portfolio is Iraq's Rumaila oil field, which CNPC is developing in partnership with BP and Iraq's Southern Oil Company. CNPC and BP plan to increase output at Rumaila, which was 1.35 million b/d last year, to 2.85 million b/d, which would make Rumaila the second largest oil field in the world in terms of production behind Saudi Arabia's Ghawar.[5] In 2012, CNPC's three projects in Iraq produced 704,000 b/d, accounting for one-third of the company's total overseas oil and natural gas output.[6]

In contrast, the upstream activities of CNPC and its domestic peers in Iran have slowed in recent years. The Iranians suspended the contract of China National Offshore Oil Corporation (CNOOC) for the development of the North Pars natural gas field in 2011 for lack of progress, and CNPC withdrew from developing phase 11 of South Pars, the world's largest natural gas field in 2012 (after the Iranians threatened to void CNPC's contract for lack of progress).[7] CNPC is behind schedule in developing the Azadegan oil field, and Sinopec 's work on the Yadavaran oil field

---

[4] Nidhi Verma and Meeyoung Cho, "India leads Asian cuts in Iran oil imports ahead of waiver review," *Reuters*, May 21, 2013, http://www.reuters.com/article/2013/05/22/iran-sanctions-waiver-idUSL3N0E30D720130522; "Market Eye: China Demand Growth Sputters to Seven-month Low," *International Oil Daily*, April 23, 2013; Judy Hua and Chen Aizhu, "Update 2 – China's Feb crude imports from Iran up 81 pct on yr," *Reuters*, March 21, 2013, http://www.reuters.com/article/2013/03/21/china-oil-iran-idUSL3N0CC0CS20130321; "Table of China December Data on Oil, Oil Product and LNG Imports," *Dow Jones Global Equities News*, January 21, 2013; and "Oil Data: Table of China December Oil, Oil Pdt, LNG Imports," *Dow Jones International News*, January 20, 2012.
[5] "CNPC, Petrofac Make Joint Bid for Rumaila Contracts," *International Oil Daily*, March 18; 2013; and "Iraq's Rumaila – A Field in Transition," *Petroleum Intelligence Weekly*, October 24, 2011.
[6] "CNPC, Petrofac Make Joint Bid for Rumaila Contracts," *International Oil Daily*, March 18; 2013; and "Unrest Hits CNPC's 2012 Output," *International Oil Daily*, January 18, 2013.
[7] "Iran Set to Replace CNPC with Local Firms at South Pars 11," *International Oil Daily*, April 23, 2013; and "CNPC to Withdraw from Iran's South Pars Project," *International Oil Daily*, September 28, 2012; "CNOOC Iran Gas Project Suspended," SinoCast, October 14, 2011; and "Iran suspends $16 billion Chinese gas deal," *Platts Oilgram News*, October 12, 2011.

reportedly has suffered delays.[8] The reasons for the shrinking presence of China's oil companies in Iran include sanctions that have made it difficult for China's oil companies to secure equipment and technologies needed to operate in Iran, unhappiness with contract terms, uncertainty about whether Iran's nuclear program will spark a military conflict, and reported guidance from China's leadership to move slowly in Iran.[9]

In sum, the Chinese oil companies' strategy for securing upstream projects in Iran has been one of "talk now and spend later." In the 2000s, the companies were happy to negotiate contracts for projects that would almost certainly have been awarded to major international oil companies in the absence of sanctions. However, they have not been in any rush to actually pump large sums of money into Iran.

The Implications of greater American energy self-sufficiency for China's role in the Middle East

I would also like to say a few words about how the resurgence of oil and natural gas production in the United States may reshape the roles of the United States and China in the Middle East. The International Energy Agency projects that the United States' oil imports from the Middle East will fall from 1.9 million barrels per day in 2011 to just 100,000 barrels per day --3 percent of total oil imports-- in 2035 as a result of increasing domestic oil production and decreasing demand. In contrast, China's oil imports from the Middle East are projected to grow from 2.9 million barrels per day in 2011 to 6.7 million barrels per day -- 54 percent of total oil imports-- in 2035.[10]

These trends have prompted speculation about the future US military posture in the Persian Gulf and, in turn, what it might mean for the security of regional oil flows to China. It is highly unlikely that the United States would completely disengage from the Middle East; Washington will almost certainly retain a variety of interests in the region, including the free flow of oil, counterterrorism and nuclear nonproliferation, even if the United States is importing little or no oil from the Middle East. However, if a diminishing appetite for Middle Eastern crudes and budgetary constraints were to prompt Washington to substantially reduce its military presence in the region, oil security concerns might compel Beijing to play a larger role in defusing the primary threat to the free flow of oil from the Persian Gulf – the closure of the Strait of Hormuz by Iran. At a minimum, this might entail Beijing communicating to Tehran that it would regard

---

[8] "CNPC, NIOC Eye Early Production at South Azadegan," *International Oil Daily*, April 1, 2013; "Sanctions Show Importance of China for Iran's Economy," June 24, 2012; and "Output of Iran's Yadavaran field reaches 16,000 b/d," *Platts Oilgram News*, May 2, 2012.

[9] For more on the government's guidance, see Chen Aizhu, "Exclusive: China slows Iran oil work as U.S. energy ties warm," *Reuters*, October 28, 2010, http://www.reuters.com/article/2010/10/28/us-china-iran-oil-idUSTRE69R1L120101028.

[10] International Energy Agency, *World Energy Outlook 2012* (Paris: OECD/IEA, 2012), pp. 78-80; and data provided by the International Energy Agency by email on May 29, 2013.

the disruption of oil exports bound for China as a threat to one of China's vital interests, similar to the public warning then-Premier Wen Jiabao issued in Qatar in January 2012.[11] A more active Chinese effort might involve reinforcing verbal admonitions with the stationing of a ship in the Persian Gulf, perhaps from one the multinational regional antipiracy patrols in which the Chinese navy participates.[12]

Finally, it is worth noting that the boom in oil and natural gas production in North America may provide Washington with more leverage over the activities of China's national oil companies in Iran. North America is now the epicenter of global mergers and acquisitions in oil and natural gas exploration and production. In 2011, for example, 60% of all upstream mergers and acquisitions worldwide were in North America.[13] China's national oil companies are part of this story. Since 2009, almost half of the capital Chinese oil companies have spent on overseas mergers and acquisitions has been used to purchase assets in North America. In the United States alone, Chinese oil companies have invested more than $8 billion since 2010. Chinese oil executives have indicated continued interest in acquiring additional assets in North America.[14] The more Chinese oil companies are invested in the United States, the more likely they are to think twice about doing business in Iran. This is because involvement in the Iranian oil industry may undermine the efforts of Chinese oil companies to expand their presence in the United States in two ways. First, any proposed acquisition that would result in foreign control of an American business -- such as CNOOC's recent acquisition of Nexen -- requires review by the Committee on Foreign Investment in the United States (CFIUS) for national security risks, and it is likely that CFIUS would inquire about the nature of the acquirer's activities in Iran. Second, Chinese oil companies are acutely aware of how public opinion can scuttle a deal thanks to CNOOC's unsuccessful bid for Unocal in 2005. Strong opposition to a Chinese oil company's business in Iran might prevent that company from acquiring an asset in the United States by making the transaction costs unacceptably high. In sum, opportunities to invest in the United States might diminish the appetite of China's national oil companies for undertaking projects in Iran.

Thank you. I look forward to your questions.

[11] "Records of Premier Wen Jiabao's Press Conference at Doha Just Before the End of His Official Visits to the Three Gulf States," January 18, 2012, http://www.fmprc.gov.cn/ce/cebel/eng/zxxx/t898607.htm.
[12] This paragraph is based in part on an email exchange between the author and Rear Admiral Michael McDevitt, US Navy (ret.) on May 28-30, 2013.
[13] "2011 Bumper Year for European Upstream M&A," El Finance, January 25, 2012.
[14] Rakteem Katakey, Aibing Guo and Sarah Chen, "China Joining US Shale Renaissance With $40 billion," Bloomberg News, March 6, 2013, http://mobile.bloomberg.com/news/2013-03-05/china-joining-u-s-shale-renaissance-with-40-billion.html; and Judy Hua and Fayen Wong, "China's Sinopec says still seeking assets in N. America," Reuters, March 4, 2013, http://www.reuters.com/article/2013/03/05/china-npc-sinopec-idUSB9E8LA02G20130305.

OPENING STATEMENT OF MR. BRYANT EDWARDS
PARTNER, LATHAM AND WATKINS LLP, HONG KONG

MR. EDWARDS: Thank you to the members of the Commission for the opportunity to testify today.

The Middle East is a critical trade, logistics, and financial hub for China's increasing trade and commerce both with Europe and Africa. Total Chinese trade with Europe was approximately $567 billion in 2011, making Europe China's most important trading partner, ahead of the U.S. with a total of $446 billion.

Chinese trade with Africa is booming. It's now over $120 billion per year. And interestingly, there are more than one million Chinese now living in Africa. That is up from 100,000 ten years ago.

Many Middle East countries have been eager to participate in this new stream of commerce emanating from China. Dubai, in particular, stands out. In the last decade, it has built the Jebel Ali Port into the largest container port in the Middle East, and the ninth largest in the world. Interestingly, Dubai's port now exceeds by 63 percent the shipping volume of the largest shipping port in the U.S., the Port of Los Angeles.

To give a sense of how much is physically being produced in China, if you look at the list of top 50 ports in the world, 14 of them are in China, and if you compare the outflow of goods from those 14 ports versus the four U.S. ports in that list, the Chinese exports shipping volume exceeds U.S. eight times. There are large volumes of physical goods being manufactured in China that must find their way to Europe, and that is one of the reasons why the Middle East is strategically important to China.

In addition, Dubai has built Emirates Airline into the fourth-largest airline in the world. Dubai is a small country, only two million people. Yet Emirates exceeds every airline in the world except United, Delta and American, in capacity. It has 20 flights a day to China, mostly A-380s, and those flights take Chinese visitors to 120 different cities. The same strategy is pursued by Qatar Airlines, which has a network of 100 international destinations, and Etihad, the Abu Dhabi based airline, with 86 international destinations. So three Gulf airports, a stone's throw from each other, serve as a hub for commerce between China, on the one hand, and Europe and Africa on the other. Also, Dubai has welcomed thousands of Chinese as permanent residents. Currently, Dubai has a population of 200,000 Chinese residents, almost ten percent of the population. That compares to an estimate of only 9,000 Americans living in Dubai.

The Consulate of Dubai estimates that there are 3,500 Chinese-owned companies operating in the UAE, mainly in Dubai, Abu Dhabi, and Sharjah. So China-Middle East commerce is not limited to the state-owned Chinese companies; much of the commerce is generated by the many smaller businesses operated by the large Chinese population in the Middle East.

The Middle East is more than just a hub for onward Chinese investment; it is also a major trading partner with China. Trade volume between China and the Arab world reached $195 billion in 2011, a 35 percent increase over the prior year, and experts expect it to continue to grow.

As Dr. Downs said, it's no surprise that the Middle East's major exports to China are petroleum and natural gas. It's interesting to see what's coming the other direction. Probably the best way to do that is to visit the DragonMart in Dubai. DragonMart is the largest trading center for Chinese goods outside of China. It is a shopping mall that looks like a dragon and extends for 1.2 kilometers. It has 3,950 separate wholesale and retail stores, and it serves as a gateway for Chinese goods and services being moved into Africa and North Africa and the Middle East area.

One of the largest Chinese exports to the Middle East is telecom equipment and services. Huawei has 3,800 employees in ten Middle East countries. Huawei provides services to the key telecom providers in the Middle East, Etisalat in the UAE, and Mobily in Saudi Arabia.

In examining the non-energy investments of China, it is interesting that they predominately are in infrastructure, particularly railway and highway construction, less at the higher-technological end. One of the most important projects bid out in the last few years in the Middle East was Abu Dhabi's nuclear power project, which totaled $20 billion. It was expected to be awarded to either the French or the Americans, but it was awarded to the South Koreans. The Chinese don't compete in that space yet, but I think they're coming. Increasing technological capability in China will mean they will move upstream.

Let me mention one important new project. Israeli Prime Minister Netanyahu visited China May 8-10, and he reached an agreement in principle with the Chinese on a railway that will run from Israel's port on the Red Sea to the Mediterranean. It's a new land bridge--180 kilometers long-- that will allow the Chinese to import goods to Europe, completely bypassing the Suez Canal.

I think it's a very important strategic development, very smart on the part of the Chinese, and it shows the Chinese interest in investments that will continue to allow them to pursue their commercial exploits.

Thank you very much.

PREPARED STATEMENT OF MR. BRYANT EDWARDS
PARTNER, LATHAM AND WATKINS LLP, HONG KONG

June 6, 2013
China and the Middle East
Statement of Bryant Edwards
Partner, Latham & Watkins, Hong Kong
Testimony Before the U.S.-China Economic and Security Review Commission

Thank you to the members of the Commission for the opportunity to testify today. It is an honor to participate in this hearing.

Just a brief word about why I am here. I am a partner at Latham & Watkins, a global law firm headquartered in the US. After eight years in London, I moved to Dubai in 2008 to help set up our firm's four Middle East offices—in Dubai, Abu Dhabi, Doha and Riyadh. After four years living and working in the Middle East, I moved to Hong Kong last year.

For the last three years, we, with the support of the Dubai International Financial Centre, have organized and presented an annual conference called "The New Silk Road," that has brought together government officials, economists, investors and others to examine trade and commerce between China and the Middle East. In 2010 and 2011, the conference was presented in Dubai and in 2012 it was presented in Beijing, Shanghai and Hong Kong.

Middle East as a Trade and Logistics Hub for China

The Middle East is an important trade, logistics and financial hub for China's increasing trade and commerce with Europe and Africa. Total Chinese trade with Europe was approximately $567.2 billion in 2011, making Europe China's largest trading partner, ahead of the US total of $446.7 billion.[1] Chinese trade with Africa totals $120 billion per year now.[2] There are over one million Chinese living in Africa now, up from 100,000 in less than a decade.[3]

The Middle East sits squarely on what we call "The New Silk Road"—the new version of the ancient roads over which caravans transported goods back and forth between China and Europe.

Many of the Middle East countries have been eager to support this new stream of commerce emanating from China. Dubai in particular stands out. In the last decade, it has built its Jebel

---

[1] Statistical Communiqué of the People's Republic of China on the 2011 National Economic and Social Development, National Bureau of Statistics of China, February 22, 2012, Table 10.
[2] Jacob Zenn, "Chinese, Overseas and Insecure," *Asia Times*, June 21, 2011.
[3] Id.

Ali Port into the largest container port in the Middle East and the ninth largest in the world.[4] Interestingly, of the eight larger shipping ports, one is in Singapore, one in South Korea and six in China.

Dubai's port now exceeds by 63% the shipping volume of the largest port in the US—the Port of Los Angeles.[5] And—to give a sense of how much China produces and how important these new trade routes are to China—the aggregate shipping volume of the 14 Chinese ports on the list of top 50 ports is *eight times* the total volume of the four US ports on this list.[6]

In addition, Dubai has built Emirates Airline into the world's fourth largest airline by capacity— after only United, Delta and American—with capacity growing 20% in the last year.[7] Emirates has 20 flights—mostly on A-380s—to and from China each day, connecting Chinese passengers to the Emirates network of more than 120 cities. Although not as large, Qatar Airways, the state-owned flag carrier of Qatar, has followed Emirates Airline strategy of linking over 100 international destinations through Qatar, and Etihad Airways, the Abu Dhabi state-owned flag carrier, links 86 international destinations through its base in Abu Dhabi.

Dubai has also welcomed thousands of Chinese as permanent residents. Currently, Dubai has more than 200,000 Chinese residents, constituting about 10% of Dubai's population.[8] That compares to estimates of 9,000 American residents in Dubai.[9]

Although some of the Chinese may have emigrated as workers on projects run by the large state-owned construction companies, most are professionals working in the Chinese banks in Dubai or middle class owners and employees of small to medium businesses. The Consulate-General of the People's Republic of China in Dubai estimates there are some 3,500 Chinese-owned companies operating in the UAE, mainly in Dubai, Abu Dhabi and Sharjah.[10]

Trade and Commerce Between China and the Middle East

---

[4] Top 50 World Container Ports (based on volume in 2011), World Shipping Council, http://www.worldshipping.org/about-the-industry/global-trade/top-50-world-container-ports.

[5] According to the World Shipping Council, Dubai's port had volume in 2011 of 13.02 million TEUs ("Twenty Foot Equivalent Unit") compared to volume of 7.94 million TEUs at the Port of Los Angeles.

[6] The 14 Chinese ports among the top 50 ports in the world had total shipping volume in 2011 of 176.84 million TEUs compared to 22.44 million TEUs for the four US ports on such list. World Shipping Council statistics referred to in footnote 5 above.

[7] Top 50 Airlines Ranked by ASK/Week (March 2013), http://www.theaviationwriter.com/2013/03/50-biggest-airlines-in-world_24.html.

[8] Daniel Shane, "Chinese Firms Eye Dubai for Africa Growth," *Arabian Business*, July 25, 2012.

[9] Overseas Digest, Private American Citizens Residing Abroad, http://www.overseasdigest.com/amcit_nu2.htm.

[10] Gillian Duncan, "Emirates a Big Draw for Small and Medium Chinese Firms," *The National*, July 31, 2011, http://www.thenational.ae/business/industry-insights/economics/emirates-a-big-draw-for-small-and-medium-chinese-firms.

But the Middle East is more than a hub for the onward Chinese investment and itself is a major trading partner with China. The trade volume between China and the Arab world reached $195.9 billion in 2011, a 35 per cent increase from the previous year, according to China's Ministry of Commerce.[11] Experts expect that figure to top $300 billion in 2014.

It is no surprise that the Middle East's major exports to China are petroleum and natural gas.

What is more interesting is what comes back from China. One of the best ways to see this is to visit DragonMart in Dubai. DragonMart is the largest trading center for Chinese products outside of the mainland China.

DragonMart, which snakes for 1.2 kilometers, has 150,000 square meters which contain over 3,950 wholesale and retail shops. It is a gateway for Chinese products in the Middle East and North African markets, offering Chinese traders and manufacturers an efficient way of introducing and selling their goods into these sizeable markets. Chinese products sold include home appliances, stationery, office appliances, communication and acoustic equipment, lamps, household items, building materials, furniture, toys, machinery, garments, textiles, footwear and general merchandise.

DragonMart has been such a financial success that work has started on an even larger second DragonMart next door that will have 175,000 square meters of space.[12]

In addition to DragonMart, the Middle East is a gracious host to numerous trade fairs promoting Chinese goods and services. As one example, the annual China Homelife exhibition at the Dubai World Trade Centre features over 1,000 Chinese suppliers of textiles and garments.[13] As another example, the Chinese Commodities Fair, held every year in Sharjah, features Chinese agricultural products, techniques and equipment.[14]

As Chinese products become more complex and sophisticated, Chinese manufacturers are setting up sales and service operations throughout the Middle East to be able to provide maintenance and repair services. For example, Honghua Group, a leading global land drilling rig manufacturer, announced late last year the opening of its sales and maintenance service center in Dubai's Jebel Ali Free Trade Zone. The new service center will provide sales, maintenance, refurbishment, spare parts supply and storage, equipment rental and after-sales service in the Middle East, Africa and Europe. In addition, the new service center will be able to assemble 10

---

[11] Li Jing, "Sino-Arab Trade Forum Told of Trade Opportunities in Resurgent Middle East," *South China Morning Post*, Sept 14, 2012.

[12] See "The Expansion of DragonMart" at http://www.dragonmart.ae/.

[13] "Chinese Textile Players Targeting Partners From the Middle East," *Khaleej Times*, December 4, 2012.

[14] "China Agricultural Products to Capture Regional Market," *Middle East Company News,* December 5, 2012.

drilling rigs annually.[15]

One of the largest Chinese exports to the Middle East is telecoms equipment and services. Huawei has 3,800 employees in offices in 10 Middle East countries. Revenues from the Middle East totaled $2.0 billion in 2012, an increase of 18% from the previous year.[16] Huawei provides services and products to most of the region's leading telecoms carriers. This year, for instance, Huawei entered into an agreement with Etisalat, the leading UAE carrier, for global consultancy services, and partnered with Saudi-Arabia's second leading carrier, Mobily, to expand Mobily's 3G and 4G services throughout Saudi Arabia.[17]

Chinese Investment in Banking and Finance in the Middle East

With such a growing and vibrant Chinese business community comes the need for Chinese financial services, including the ability to convert and clear yuan into other currencies.

The four largest Chinese state-owned banks–ICBC, Bank of China, Agricultural Bank of China and, most recently, China Construction Bank[18]–now have presences in the Dubai International Financial Centre. Trade in the Chinese yuan by banks in Dubai has been increasing—ICBC said it conducted $2.1 billion of yuan transactions in the Middle East interbank money market in the first half of 2012, up 58 percent. A number of non-Chinese banks, including HSBC, Standard Chartered and Dubai-based Emirates NBD, now offer RMB accounts in the UAE.

As part of Premier Wen Jiabao's visit to the Middle East in January 2012, the Central Bank of China and the Central Bank of the UAE reached agreement on a currency swap. The deal. which exchanges 35 billion RMB ($5.54 billion) for 20 billion AED ($5.44 billion), was reached to promote bilateral trade and investment. However, this one time exchange was a stop-gap measure until full yuan convertibility can be established.

Currently, yuan clearing is conducted in Hong Kong and Taipei and will soon be conducted in Singapore. China recently named ICBC as the clearing bank for yuan business in Singapore.

Officials at the DIFC would like Dubai to become the next market outside China to provide yuan clearing. But any such arrangement for Dubai would depend on discussions and agreement between UAE and Chinese authorities.[19] Dubai's intention to become the Middle East center of offshore RMB trading received a boost in February 2013 when the chief executive of the Hong Kong Monetary Authority (HKMA), Norman Chan, said that Dubai could follow in Hong

---

[15] "China Drilling Firm Opens Dubai Center," *TradeArabia*, November 15, 2012.
[16] Huawei Middle East Fact Sheet, http://www.huawei.com/en/about-huawei/newsroom/resources/middle_east/.
[17] Id.
[18] "CCB Opens Dubai Operation," *SinoCast Banking Beat*, May 13, 2013.
[19] "DIFC Targets China, South Asia, For Growth," *Reuters*, February 15, 2013.

Kong's footsteps as trade flows between China and the region continue to grow.[20]

Chinese Investment in Non-Energy Infrastructure in the Middle East

To date, Chinese contractors have not won—or even bid for—the most technologically sophisticated and complex projects in the Middle East. In recent years, such projects have been won mostly by the South Korean and the Japanese contractors.

For example, one of the most sought after recent Middle East projects was the $20 billion contract to design and build the nuclear power plant that will be operated by the Emirates Nuclear Energy Corporation (ENEC) in Abu Dhabi. This will be the first nuclear power plant in the Arab world. After a 12-month bidding process, ENEC awarded the project in December 2009 to a South Korean consortium consisting of Korea Electric Power Corporation (Kepco), Hyundai Heavy Industries, Samsung Engineering and Construction and Doosan Heavy Industries and Construction. The decision surprised industry experts, who had expected that the project would be awarded to the American or French bidders.[21]

Other high profile Middle East projects have similarly been awarded to South Korean or Japanese contractors. For example, the contract to build the Burj Khalifa in Dubai—the world's tallest building—was awarded in 2004 to a consortium led by Samsung Engineering and Construction and Arabtec. In 2005, the contract to design and build the Dubai Metro—the first fully automated driverless metro network in the world—was awarded to a consortium made up of Japanese companies including Mitsubishi Heavy Industries, Mitsubishi Corporation, Obayashi Corporation and Kajima Corporation.

Notwithstanding their later arrival, Chinese contractors have developed a strong market share in infrastructure and transport—areas of expertise honed at home during the enormous Chinese infrastructure build-out over the last two decades. Chinese contractors are building approximately 45% (by value) of the infrastructure and transport projects run by the non-Middle East contactors included in region's top 25 contractors.[22] By contrast, US-based contractors have approximately 9% of such contracts.

Israel

Red Sea Land Bridge: When: Israeli Prime Minister Benjamin Netanyahu visited China on May 8-10, 2013, he reached agreement in principle with the Chinese on a railway line that could turn Israel into a land and sea bridge for Chinese exports to Europe. The plan is to build a 180

---

[20] "HKMA Sees Dubai as RMB Centre," *Trade Finance, Euromoney Insitutional Investor,* February 5, 2013.

[21] Kevin Baxter, "Seoul Showcases its Talents in Nuclear Deal," *MEED Supplement: South Korea and the Middle East,* 2010

[22] "Region's Project Market Booms," *MEED,* May 12, 2013, Chart: Contractors by Project Value.

kilometer high-speed railway from Israel's southern port in Eilat on the Red Sea to its Mediterranean port in Haifa. From there, cargo can travel onwards to Europe. The route will be far faster than ships sailing through the Suez Canal to reach the Mediterranean. After it is built, ships arriving with goods from China will be able to off-load their containers in Eilat and by-pass the Suez Canal completely. The railway is expected to increase trade from China, India and other Asian countries through Israel, while also reducing Tel Aviv's dependence on a waterway controlled by Egypt. Construction is expected to take about five years to complete and will cost about $4 billion. [23]

Saudi Arabia

Haramain High-Speed Railway: The 450 kilometer Haramain high-speed rail link will connect the two holy cities of Mecca and Medina via Jeddah and the new King Abdulaziz International Airport. The line, which is now moving into its second phase of construction, is scheduled for completion in 2014. The $1.8 billion contract was awarded in February 2009 to a consortium including China's Railway Engineering. [24]

North-South Railway: The 2,400 kilometer North-South Railway is being developed by Saudi Railway Co. The $5.3 billion flagship project is on track with the start of passenger services scheduled for July 2014. It will link the country's northern mineral belt with Riyadh and the industrial city of Jubail. The rail link is due eventually to connect to neighboring countries as part of the GCC rail link. In September 2009, a consortium including China Civil Engineering Construction Corp (CCECC) was awarded a $720 million contract for the construction of a section of the North-South Railway. [25]

Mecca Monorail: The $1.7 billion 180 kilometer monorail project linking Mecca, Mina, Muzdalifah and Arafat was awarded in March 2011 to China Railway Company. [26]

Ras Al Zour Desalination and Power Plant: The $5.0 billion Ras Al Zour Desalination and Power Plant was awarded to a consortium that included China's Sepco III Electric Power Construction Corporation. The project is under construction and is expected to be completed in 2014. [27]

New Port in Saudi Arabia. On Saudi Arabia's east coast, Ras al-Khair Minerals Industrial City is being positioned as an export gateway for bauxite from mines in the north of Saudi Arabia. Ras al-Khair is being built as a hub for 80 industrial projects, including a $4 billion aluminum

---

[23] "Israel's Railway Plan Set to Boost China's Trade in Middle East, Europe," *Channel NewsAsia*, May 15, 2013.
[24] Saudi Arabia Infrastructure Report, Business Monitor International, Q2 2013, p. 20
[25] Id at p. 21.
[26] Id at p. 25.
[27] Id at p. 25.

smelter. To support these plans, Saudi Arabia is building a three-berth port to handle cargo. The $600 million construction contract for the new port was awarded to China Harbour Engineering Company.[28]

Egypt

High Speed Railway. The Egyptian Ministry of Transport has suggested to Chinese officials and Chinese investors that they contribute to the establishment of a high-speed railway linking Cairo, Alexandria, Luxor, Hurghada and Aswan. During his recent visit to China with Egyptian President Mohamed Morsi, Minister of Transport El-Meteny made the case for the new railway to a group of executives from 200 of China's largest companies.[29]

Egypt-TEDA Investment. The Tianjin Economic and Technological Development Area, or TEDA, runs an economic zone in northern China and has established five other such zones in Africa. Egypt-TEDA Investment, a joint venture with the Egyptian government, runs an economic zone in the outskirts of Cairo, where Chinese and Egyptian firms can set up manufacturing and trading operations with the help of certain government concessions. TEDA intends to invest over $200 million in the Cairo zone, which is popular because of its proximity to the Suez Canal and because of the trade agreements under the Suez Economic and Trade Cooperation zone. With about 30 textile, petroleum and automobile companies up and running, TEDA executives say they will need up to quadruple the size of the project in the coming years.[30]

Qatar

New Doha Port: The New Doha Port project is being constructed at an estimated cost of $8 billion. The port will be constructed in three phases; the initial phase is due for completion in 2014 and the final stage in 2025. It will be located 5 kilometers offshore, with a bridge connecting it to the mainland. The port will have five cargo terminals and four container terminals. In January 2011, China Harbour Engineering Company (CHEC) started construction on foundations and a breakwater. The project, valued at around $880 million, entails building a container wharf, general cargo wharf, naval forces wharf and breakwater at the port. The project will take around four years to complete.[31]

Iraq

---

[28] MEED 16-22 March 2012.
[29] Doaa Naguib, "Egypt Asks China to Build High-Speed Railway," *Amwal Al Ghad*, August 29, 2012
[30] Farah Halime, "Chinese Firms Brave Uncertainty in Egypt to Gain a Foothold in Middle East," *New York Times*, August 29 2012.
[31] Qatar Infrastructure Report, Business Monitor International, Q2 2013, p 17.

Gas-Fired Power Plant at Al-Najibiya: The $205 million Gas-Fired Power Plant at Al-Najibiya in Basra will generate 500 megawatts. It was awarded in April 2011 to the China National Machinery and Equipment Import & Export and one local contractor. It is under construction and is expected to be completed in September 2011.[32]

Samawa Cement Factory: The $250 million Samawa cement factory was awarded to the China National Building Material Company in September 2010 and the project was completed in 2012.[33]

Libya

Railway Projects: Chinese state-controlled company China Railways Construction (CRCC) has taken a strong investment position in Libya's railway sector. In January 2009, it signed a $805 million contract with the Libyan railway authority to construct a 172 kilometer rail line and in 2008 work started on a $1.7 billion project to connect the town of Sirte with Tripoli, a $2.6 billion project to connect Khums to Sirte and a $1.3 billion project to connect Sabha to Misrata. These projects have been delayed by the Arab Spring violence in Libya and the overall status of these projects is not clear at this time.[34]

Iran

East-West Railway: The Chinese government has made an offer to build a new freight rail line in Iran aimed at allowing continuous rail transport of goods from China, through the Middle East, to Europe. Iran's minister responsible for transport is reported to have invited bids to construct the line.[35]

Kuwait

Boubyan Port: The contract for phase 1 of the construction of the $1.14 billion Boubyan Port project was awarded in 2010 to a consortium that included China Harbour Engineering Company.[36]

College of Engineering & Petroleum, Kuwait University. The $505 million contract to build the new College of Engineering & Petroleum, Kuwait University, was awarded in 2011 to China Metallurgical Construction Corporation and another local contractor. The project is expected to be completed in 2014.

---

[32] Iraq Infrastructure Report, Business Monitor International, Q2 2013, p. 28.
[33] Id at p. 29.
[34] Libya Infrastructure Report, Business Monitor International, p. 8.
[35] Iran Infrastructure Report, Business Monitor International, Q2 2013, p. 7.
[36] Kuwait Infrastructure Report, Business Monitor International, Q2 2013, p. 15

Chinese Investment in Medical Devices and Pharmaceuticals

Acquisition of Alma Lasers Ltd. On May 28, 2013, Shanghai Fosun Pharmaceutical (Group) Co Ltd, the listed Chinese pharmaceutical and medical equipment manufacturer, via its subsidiary Sisram Medical Ltd, acquired 95.6% of the shares of Alma Lasers Ltd, an Israel based developer, manufacturer and marketer of medical laser equipment, for $221.1 million from independent third parties. Concurrently, Ample Up Ltd, a wholly-owned subsidiary or Fosun Pharmaceutical, acquired 9.5 million shares in Chindex Medical Ltd, which holds a 100% stake in Sisram Medical Ltd. As a result, Ample's shareholding in Chindex Medical increased to 70%. In addition, Pramerica-Fosun Fund contributed $50 million into Sisram Medical and owns a 33.80% stake in the company.[37]

Acquisition of Makhteshim Agan. In October 2011, state-owned China National Chemical Corp (ChemChina) acquired 60% of the shares of Makhteshim Agan (MA) from its parent Koor Industries Ltd for $1.43 billion. Makhteshim Agan is a pharmaceuticals, agro-chemicals and food additives manufacturer.[38]

Conclusion

The Middle East is vast and complex. Large state-owned Chinese corporations and small to medium-sized privately-owned Chinese companies have entered into a broad array of projects and have made a broad array of investments and acquisitions across the Middle East. But these seem to be early days. In spite of the substantial investments China has made, Chinese contractors, with their focus on roads and railways, in important ways lag behind the more technologically-advanced clean fuels, petrochemicals and nuclear generation projects being run by the South Korean and Japanese contractors. But it is only a matter of time before the fast-growing and cutting-edge technology companies maturing now in China begin to look outward towards the opportunities in the Middle East and beyond.

Ben Simpfendorfer, the founder of New Silk Road Associates, and one of the China experts we have had speak at our New Silk Road conferences, maintains that Chinese strategy in the Middle East to date has been primarily economic rather than political.[39] That would seem to be borne out by the fact that China invests in both Israel and in Palestine, and in both Saudi Arabia and Iran. To the extent that Chinese has a political strategy in the Middle East, it appears to be

---

[37] Dealogic acquisitions database.
[38] Dealogic acquisitions database.
[39] Jennifer Malapitan-Anguinaldo, "China and Middle East's Interdependency Grows," *MEED*, August 12-18, 2011

focused first and foremost upon keeping the Middle East countries open as a logistical and financial hub to permit the continued flow of Chinese products to, and Chinese investment in, the Middle East, Europe and Africa.

PANEL II QUESTION & ANSWER

HEARING CO-CHAIR FIEDLER: Thank you.
Commissioner Wessel.
COMMISSIONER WESSEL: Thank you, both, for being here.
Dr. Downs, good to see you again.

I've gotten conflicting information over the past couple of years about what Chinese investments in natural resources, oil, et cetera, actually gets them, in terms of their acquisition strategy to own assets at the wellhead. Some analysts have said that it gives them first right of refusal, et cetera, but gives them no preferential pricing access, that they are still paying world spot market prices or long-term prices are being applied.

Can both of you provide some guidance to what does China actually get when it makes these investments? Does it give them an assured stream of the oil? Do they have right of first refusal? Are they getting preferential pricing? What are they getting? Is it different than how Western firms, multinational firms, make their investments in these assets? Can you give us some comparison?

Dr. Downs, would you like to start?
DR. DOWNS: Sure. Thank you.

I think that when Chinese national oil companies make investments overseas, they are looking to do a number of different things. I think, one, like other oil companies, they are looking to grow reserves and production and profits.

COMMISSIONER WESSEL: But are they growing their own reserves or are they just growing world reserves? Meaning, what's the ownership stake interest that they have?

DR. DOWNS: It depends on the nature of the contract. If it's a production sharing contract, then the Chinese oil company typically will be entitled to a share of production, and whether they actually get that in physical barrels or a stream of revenue from the barrels that would be theirs that are marketed by someone else depends on the contract.

The Middle East is actually an interesting situation because many of the large oil reserve holders in the Middle East, including Iraq and Iran, don't allow foreign companies to make equity investments. In countries like Saudi Arabia, if you look at their upstream, it's completely closed to foreign equity investments.

And so what you have in Iran and Iraq is you have foreign oil companies that have been signing up for service contracts, and basically what that means is they agree to invest money up-front to develop an oil or gas field, and once that field goes into production, they will be paid back from the stream of revenue generated by that production.

COMMISSIONER WESSEL: But no ownership? No first right of refusal on the asset coming out? It's just a straight business deal then, is that right?

DR. DOWNS: It is a straight business deal. I will mention in

the case of Iraq, if you look at the Rumaila field, which is the biggest
producing asset in Iraq, which is being developed by CNPC and BP, my
understanding is that both CNPS and BP agreed to take their repayments in
the form of oil. So the companies agreed when they won the bid for that
contract to a $2 per barrel remuneration fee, and so they are taking--instead
of being paid back in cash, they are taking that in oil.

So in a way, it does sort of secure for CNPC, they can count on
getting a certain number of barrels from Iraq every month as a form of
repayment for money they've already invested.

COMMISSIONER WESSEL: Mr. Edwards, do you have any
comments on this?

MR. EDWARDS: It does appear that the Chinese state-owned oil
companies have had an advantage in Iraq because of their willingness to
accept the terms dictated by the Iraqi government. They do not have the
same pressure that the U.S. or other international oil companies have to
actually make a profit, and they seem more interested in securing that flow
of oil over the next decades than in actually generating a profit as an oil
company.

COMMISSIONER WESSEL: When you say generating the oil,
where they have the right to receive it or that it's just generating and
ensuring that there are broader reserves or flow of oil to the world market?

MR. EDWARDS: My understanding is ownership of interest in
the oil fields that will provide them with a steady flow of oil and natural gas
over the years. It seems to be their paramount interest in Iraq and other
regions in the Middle East, and it's given them an advantage over the other.

COMMISSIONER WESSEL: So just to sum, my confusion
continues.

MR. EDWARDS: Okay.

COMMISSIONER WESSEL: And continues because it's different
for different countries and different assets, meaning that everyone is right in
terms of some they have a right to the preferential receipt, some they have a
service contract that simply ensures that their assets--that there's a broader
reserves coming to market, and it depends on what the field is, what the
country is; is that right? That's what I heard from you, that it depends.

MR. EDWARDS: Yes.

DR. DOWNS: Yes, I mean I think a lot depends on the contract.

COMMISSIONER WESSEL: Right. Okay, thank you.

HEARING CO-CHAIR FIEDLER: Commissioner Wortzel.

COMMISSIONER WORTZEL: Mr. Edwards, I was intrigued by
the paragraph you had on the Egypt-Tianjin Economic and Technology
Development Area Cooperation. I'm interested in the technology focus. You
note textile, petroleum, and automobile in your written testimony, and those
are traditional strengths in Tianjin.

MR. EDWARDS: Right.

COMMISSIONER WORTZEL: But is that technology
cooperation limited to those areas? Do you know of other areas that they're

working on?

MR. EDWARDS: My understanding is they have committed to textile, petroleum and automobile parts for that particular park, but they're clearly interested in expanding. They have five parks in different African locations. I think they're taking advantage of the situation, the chaotic situation that exists in Egypt right now, where very few other outsiders are willing to invest. They view political uncertainty as an investment opportunity.

I think that's a theme throughout the more troubled areas of the Middle East. They show a lot of nerve by their willingness to invest during this period.

COMMISSIONER WORTZEL: Thank you.

HEARING CO-CHAIR FIEDLER: Commissioner Slane.

COMMISSIONER SLANE: Thank you both for taking the time to come here.

Dr. Downs, I just wanted to ask you, you talked about this enormous increase in demand for oil from China. I have read some studies that indicate that their shale gas could be three times the size of the United States, and I also understand the complexity of getting it out and their lack of infrastructure, but do you see that profoundly changing their future demand for oil?

DR. DOWNS: There are studies, as you've indicated, that show that China has considerable shale resources, at least on paper. In terms of how that's going to impact their demand for oil, it's hard to say. I think it's going to have a much bigger--the potential impact is much bigger in the area of natural gas, and I think whether that, in turn, impacts China's future oil demand will depend on the extent to which natural gas can be substituted for oil.

COMMISSIONER SLANE: Okay.

HEARING CO-CHAIR FIEDLER: Commissioner Bartholomew.

COMMISSIONER BARTHOLOMEW: Thank you very much, and thank you to both of our witnesses.

Dr. Downs, it's always good to see you, and Mr. Edwards, it's very interesting testimony and putting together all in one place some of these projects. I want to follow up on a question on the Egypt-Tianjin investment.

Are Chinese laborers being brought in to do the work in these factories? Egypt, of course, has an enormously high unemployment rate, and I wondered if there were any opportunities for Egyptians to be working in this zone or whether the Chinese are bringing in their own workers?

MR. EDWARDS: My understanding is that the Chinese are bringing in project managers, but they are providing employment opportunities for Egyptians. China's non-energy investments are generating local jobs. For example, Huawei has 3,800 employees in the Middle East, but 60 or 70 percent of them are non-Chinese. So it's one reason, I believe, that Middle Eastern governments welcome those type of Chinese investments because not only do they bring in revenue, but they're providing jobs for the local population.

COMMISSIONER BARTHOLOMEW: Is that true of these construction projects, too, that you were talking about?

MR. EDWARDS: Oh, definitely.

COMMISSIONER BARTHOLOMEW: So they're not bringing in Chinese laborers to build these?

MR. EDWARDS: Well, there are certainly some Chinese workers, but in my experience, and a lot of this is just driving around and seeing these huge projects in Dubai that are being constructed by the Chinese state construction companies, most of the actual workers are Pakistanis, Indians, Filipinos. They are doing the actual hard labor in the sunshine in the middle of the desert.

COMMISSIONER BARTHOLOMEW: Yeah.

MR. EDWARDS: And they're being managed in some cases by Chinese engineers and supervisors. So this is clearly providing opportunity for others in the region.

COMMISSIONER BARTHOLOMEW: For others, but not necessarily the people of those countries if they're using Pakistani and Indian.

MR. EDWARDS: Well, it depends. In the Gulf, the Emirates and the Saudis have no interest actually in that type of employment. So that's almost exclusively done by people brought in, laborers brought in from other countries, and my impression is that the Chinese are supervising the projects, but they're not providing all the labor.

COMMISSIONER BARTHOLOMEW: That's interesting because that's a changing pattern then.

MR. EDWARDS: Yes.

COMMISSIONER BARTHOLOMEW: Throughout Africa and other places, the Chinese have had a tendency to bring in their own workers, then leave some behind, or move people on to the next place.

Dr. Downs, do you have any comment on that, too?

DR. DOWNS: Sure. Yeah, no, I think you're right to observe--I think you're right that there appears to be a changing pattern. Most of my work on Chinese outbound investment has been in natural resource space, and if you go back to the late 1990s and early 2000s, at least within some of the Chinese oil companies, I think there was a perception that if we do overseas projects, these are great opportunities for us to send workers overseas, that the foreign country, in effect, can be a training ground for our own workers, as well as an important source for jobs.

Of course, as you probably know, a lot of host countries don't necessarily see things that way, and they would like for foreign investment to provide opportunities for the local population. I think in the past 20 or so years, for example, especially over the last decade, that we've seen Chinese oil and other companies investing overseas, and I think they've learned, in some cases the hard way, that you can't always bring all of your workers with you, and a lot is going to depend on what are the rules on the books in the host country and how strongly are they enforced?

I think there are some parts of the world where it might be easy to bring in your own workers. I think there are others where it will be more difficult, and I think certainly if you look at some of the investments made by Chinese companies in places like Australia, Canada, and the United States, there is a real recognition that jobs are important for the citizens of these countries. I think in some of the recent deals there's been a real effort to let the host country know that, yes, we're making an investment, but we're not going to take any jobs away, and, if anything, we're going to create them. But, again, I suspect this varies by country.

COMMISSIONER BARTHOLOMEW: Thank you. Mr. Chairman, is there an opportunity for another question?

HEARING CO-CHAIR FIEDLER: Yes.

COMMISSIONER BARTHOLOMEW: Okay. I guess I want to get to, again, looking at these projects, the issue of competitive bidding.

MR. EDWARDS: Right.

COMMISSIONER BARTHOLOMEW: And certainly there's a lack of freedom of press in many of these countries, and I'm wondering, just to get this on the record, do any of the countries in the Middle East where the Chinese are building big projects, do they have any anti-corruption restrictions or any functioning anti-corruption agencies in their governments?

MR. EDWARDS: I think it varies from country to country, but my experience in the UAE and in Saudi Arabia is that those two countries take the bidding process very seriously. They want the very best contractor for the particular project. The nuclear power project I mentioned in Abu Dhabi, $20 billion, they spent a full year evaluating bids before they awarded it to the South Koreans.

And it's an evaluation based not only on who can provide it at the lowest cost, but who has the expertise to get the project done. So my sense was that there is a high degree of integrity, at least in those countries, in the bidding process, and I've never seen any indication of the type of corruption you might expect to see, but that's a limited view of a few countries I have worked in.

COMMISSIONER BARTHOLOMEW: Okay.

HEARING CO-CHAIR FIEDLER: Commissioner Shea.

VICE CHAIRMAN SHEA: Thank you, both.

This question is for Dr. Downs. In your testimony you state that the more Chinese oil companies are invested in the United States, the more likely they are to think twice about doing business in Iran, and on its face, that seems very plausible to me, but I'd like to test that assertion or assumption a little bit.

Is it, you put in your testimony that the Chinese energy, state-owned enterprise energy companies are--their investments in the upstream activities in Iran have slowed down a little bit over the past few years. But isn't it fair to say that--is China, does China remain Iran's largest customer for oil? Is that correct, Dr. Downs?

DR. DOWNS: That is correct.

VICE CHAIRMAN SHEA: Does China remain Iran's largest supplier of gasoline, refined oil products, petroleum products?

DR. DOWNS: That I don't know.

VICE CHAIRMAN SHEA: But one of the largest suppliers.

DR. DOWNS: I mean certainly in the past--on the gasoline issue, certainly in the past, Chinese companies have supplied gasoline to--

VICE CHAIRMAN SHEA: Sinopec.

DR. DOWNS: --Iran, and one of them, Zhuhai Zhenrong, was sanctioned by the United States--

VICE CHAIRMAN SHEA: Right.

DR. DOWNS: --as a result of that.

VICE CHAIRMAN SHEA: But it's fair to say there's a tremendous amount of interaction in the energy space between China and Iran. And recently we've seen Chinese state-owned energy companies investing in the United States. Sinopec bought an interest in Devon Energy. CNOOC has bought Nexen, and Nexen has interests in the United States. CNOOC has a stake in Chesapeake Energy. CIC has a stake in AES.

So there's a lot of stuff going on between China and Iran on energy. China's companies are stepping up their investments in the United States. I don't see how you can make the assumption that greater involvement with Iran could slow down--greater interaction with the United States would slow down their interaction with Iran. I mean, could you?

DR. DOWNS: Sure. No, I'm happy to do so. And in my response, I'm going to distinguish between trade and investment. I think everything you said about trade is correct in that despite the sort of large reduction that China has made in its crude oil purchases from Iran, it still is Iran's largest oil customer.

But I'd like to focus on the investment space, which is what I was talking about in my remarks. I do think it is true that Chinese oil companies probably would like to have their cake and eat it too, and that they would like to, in their ideal world, they would be able to sort of continue to make upstream investments in the United States and hold on to their projects in Iran.

There are big fields, and I think the Chinese oil companies would like to keep them in hopes that one day when it's less risky to invest in Iran, that perhaps they'll have the chance to really develop those fields.

However, getting back to the United States and the extent to which having Chinese oil companies invest in the United States might make them think twice about doing business in Iran, there are a couple of points I'd like to make.

One of them has to do with the type of investment they make in the United States. Most of the investments that Chinese oil companies have made in oil and natural gas in the United States, to date, have been ones where they are minority stakeholders, and because they're minor stakeholders, those investments have not had to be reviewed by the Committee on Foreign Investment in the United States.

However, when CNOOC bought the Canadian company Nexen, that investment did have to be reviewed by CFIUS because Nexen has a Gulf of Mexico subsidiary. Now, obviously, I have not been privy to CFIUS' deliberations, but as I mentioned in my testimony, given that CFIUS reviews for national security risks, it would not be surprising to me if one of the questions at the top of CFIUS' agenda for CNOOC is what are you doing in Iran? And if you're still doing stuff in Iran, what's your plan to get out?

And I don't think it's surprising that prior to making this investment that CNOOC had basically walked away from a big natural gas project that it had been pursuing in Iran, and I would be surprised if CNOOC attempted to make any upstream acquisitions in Iran now that they did get approval from CFIUS for the Nexen acquisition.

So I actually do see having Chinese oil companies make investments that would either require them to file for CFIUS review, potentially as a way to, as a tool that would discourage them from investing in Iran, and then the other potential source of leverage that I mentioned in my paper has to do with public opinion.

If we think back to the summer of 2005 and the uproar that CNOOC's proposed acquisition of Unocal caused, I think that were something similar to happen in the case of Iran, or people decided that they didn't like the idea of a company that was investing in Iran also coming to the United States, that might put more pressure on the Chinese company to choose where to do business.

I think so far they are trying to maintain investments in both countries, but my understanding is that the companies are aware that if they want to do more business in the United States--which I think is a very attractive market for them for a variety of reasons--I think you could probably make the case that it is a more attractive market for them than Iran--that they need to be very cautious about what they're doing in Iran.

VICE CHAIRMAN SHEA: Counselor, that was a very good defense.

[Laughter.]

VICE CHAIRMAN SHEA: Thank you.

HEARING CO-CHAIR FIEDLER: Commissioner Tobin.

COMMISSIONER TOBIN: Thank you, both.

Dr. Downs, we've gotten detail on what the Chinese are taking from the Middle East, and then, Mr. Edwards, we also see what they are bringing, and I too was struck, as was Commissioner Bartholomew, on the range of activity there for which I had no prior knowledge, the delivering of railroads, for example, and I want to concentrate on that.

In Saudi Arabia, Egypt, Libya, Iran, and I probably missed two, if you think of railway systems, the Chinese build them, they leave, but the construction is there, and if we we're all concerned about Huawei in technology, do you have any concerns about those tremendous transportation infrastructures that are being built there, any security concerns?

MR. EDWARDS: Well, that is a very interesting question. My take is one reason they're winning a lot of projects to build railways is that they've successfully built an amazing railway system in China. In the last year, they just opened a bullet train from Guangzhou to Beijing, the longest in the world. Very technologically advanced. They have that expertise, and it is one thing that they've been able to export successfully.

I think the other reason China seems to have an interest in building railroads is that it will benefit their ability to trade. They're clearly interested in putting a railway through Iran that would link China with Europe eventually. Strategically that's very important for them.

Another Chinese railway project is the North-South Railway in Saudi Arabia, which eventually will link up with other railways in the Gulf to provide--for the first time--an integrated railway network in the Gulf. This again will benefit China with the huge flow of goods that must somehow get from China to Africa and Europe. So I think that's the reason they're doing it.

There may be security concerns with the Chinese building railroads throughout the Middle East. To me, however, it seems like these are mostly commercial ventures for them.

COMMISSIONER TOBIN: It makes sense commercially, but through your writing, it also brought awareness in terms of infrastructure and movement in a large region.

MR. EDWARDS: Yes.

COMMISSIONER TOBIN: Thank you.

HEARING CO-CHAIR FIEDLER: Commissioner Cleveland.

COMMISSIONER CLEVELAND: Mr. Edwards, I'm really interested in your observations about financial services and the steps towards being able to convert and clear yuan into other currencies.

MR. EDWARDS: Right.

COMMISSIONER CLEVELAND: And Premier Wen's visit in January where they reached agreement on a currency swap. I think that's potentially very interesting because it's one of just a few steps that's been taken.

Could you talk a little more about that and what you think it means in terms of providing a foundation for all these other activities that you've talked about?

MR. EDWARDS: Yes, first of all, the fact that there are 200,000 Chinese, 3,500 individual Chinese-owned businesses in the UAE creates a need for banking services and particularly for the ability to convert local currency into the *renminbi* and vice versa.

The four largest Chinese banks have set up operations in the UAE and do provide that service on some limited basis, and some of the local banks, Emirates NBD, for example, is also providing that service.

It's part of a bigger story of the internationalization of the Chinese currency, and the Chinese seem to be taking it step by step, very deliberately, but it is moving in one direction, and there is more and more Chinese currency circulating outside of China. As you know, they have very tight controls over how much Chinese currency they allow outside the country, but that is increasing on a very steady basis.

Right now, official yuan convertibility only occurs in Hong Kong, Taipei, and recently Singapore.

COMMISSIONER CLEVELAND: Right.

MR. EDWARDS: Dubai very much would like to be a financial center where there is full yuan convertibility. That requires an agreement between the Central Bank of the UAE and the Chinese Central Bank. Dubai is pushing for it, and I believe that's going to happen at some point in the next couple of years.

COMMISSIONER CLEVELAND: And my other question is do you see any differentiation in the conduct of state-owned enterprises versus privately-owned companies in terms of how they conduct business in the region? Either of you?

DR. DOWNS: So Chinese private enterprises versus Chinese state-owned enterprises?

COMMISSIONER CLEVELAND: Yes, to the extent that private is private, but, yes, the large state-owned enterprises versus medium and smaller?

DR. DOWNS: Most of the companies whose activities I look at in the Middle East and other regions of the world are largely state-owned, so I'm probably not the best person to address Chinese state-owned versus Chinese private companies. I can talk about Chinese state-owned versus foreign competitors, but I'll let Mr. Edwards take a stab at it.

MR. EDWARDS: Well, I think the Chinese private companies operate more as profit-making enterprises, and so they're actually interested in generating a profit. They don't have other strategic goals that the state-owned enterprises may have, and so you see them operating much the way you see Western private companies operating. There is an increasing number of private companies in China in the oil and gas exploration area and in the technology area.

We co-sponsored a conference in Shanghai a couple of weeks ago where we had the CEOs and CFOs of many of the top technology companies in China, and it feels like you're in Silicon Valley. For most of these companies, their executives running them spent time in the U.S. gaining skills, and now they're developing exciting technology companies of all stripes in China, and they're looking outbound now for the first time after they succeeded building the infrastructure in China.

That's why I think you'll see more sophisticated outbound investment by private Chinese companies.

DR. DOWNS: I'd also like to build on a point that Mr. Edwards made that I think is important, and that's just to recognize, as you did in your question, that when you look at Chinese companies that are investing overseas in the Middle East or in other parts of the world, that there is a broad range of actors. I think the most visible are the state-owned enterprises that are under the administration of the central government, and those are the companies about which I think most outside observers have questions about commercial versus national imperatives.

The heads of many of these companies are appointed by the Communist Party, and a lot of times they have ambitions to rise higher in the Party state so they really have a balancing act going on. On the one hand, they want to do a good job running their companies. They are under increasing pressure from the Chinese government to be profitable, to avoid disasters overseas and to make more successful and sustainable investments. In some cases they have international subsidiaries that are making these investments, so there is some pressure from minority shareholders as well. Yet, on the other hand, they do have to be responsive, or demonstrate that they're being responsive, to the interests of the Party state.

But when you start to look at the other groups of Chinese companies that are investing overseas, it's a bit of a different story. If you look at some of the provincially state-owned companies or the private companies, they don't have that same balancing act, or at least to the same degree that they need to take into consideration when they're doing stuff abroad.

COMMISSIONER CLEVELAND: Thank you.

HEARING CO-CHAIR FIEDLER: Thank you.

I have a couple questions. First, a point of information. How much does Japan, what percentage of Japan's total oil imports come from the Middle East; do you know?

DR. DOWNS: I don't know that off the top of my head.

HEARING CO-CHAIR FIEDLER: I mean they've always imported 90 percent of their oil, and in the discussion that we've been having about U.S. interests in the Middle East diminishing because of our growing energy independence, nobody has been pointing out the notion that many of our allies--whether they be Japan, India, South Korea--all are majorly dependent on Middle Eastern oil so that U.S. interests are continually effective. Am I correct in sort of making that observation?

DR. DOWNS: You are absolutely correct. If you look at projections that have been made by the International Energy Agency and others, looking where Middle Eastern oil is going to go in the future, the bulk of it is expected to go to Asia, and not just to China, but also other countries like India, Japan, and South Korea.

HEARING CO-CHAIR FIEDLER: And none of them are major naval powers who can protect their sea lanes as well as the United States can?

DR. DOWNS: I'm not a naval expert, but my understanding is that none of those countries have navies that are willing or able to step in and play the role that the United States does.

HEARING CO-CHAIR FIEDLER: I have a comment question on fracking in China. Fracking requires, to my understanding, a significant amount of water, and one of the biggest problems the Chinese have is the availability of drinking water, much less water to waste on fracking. And that would seem to me, even forgetting the fact that they haven't mastered the technology yet, that they probably in a sort of cost effective policy basis don't want to use their water for fracking with 1.3 billion people.

DR. DOWNS: I think you are correct that water is one of the many challenges that China faces in developing its shale gas resources. There are a variety of both above-ground and below-ground challenges, and water is one of them.

HEARING CO-CHAIR FIEDLER: I have another factual question on Iran and its oil and the diminution of Chinese purchasing of Iranian oil. Roughly, the figures were going from 500,000 barrels to 400,000 barrels. Do we have an idea on what the daily capacity of oil smuggling is with Iran?

DR. DOWNS: I personally don't know.

HEARING CO-CHAIR FIEDLER: I mean the history of oil sanctions has resulted in dramatic increases in the black market, as in the famous case of Marc Rich, the American oil trader, who was probably the world's biggest smuggler or seller of smuggled oil. So I'm wondering whether the Chinese are picking up their 100,000 barrels a day on the black market?

DR. DOWNS: I think you can probably find anecdotal evidence, anecdotal information, that supports that. On the broader issues of sanctions, you know, my sense is that with so many buyers and sellers of oil in the world, that sanctions are difficult to implement, and that they're difficult to ensure that a country can't sell or can't buy.

So my sense is that, I guess what I'm trying to say is that it wouldn't surprise me if there are other barrels of Iranian crude that are making their way to China but aren't showing up in Chinese customs data, but I don't have any information to support that.

HEARING CO-CHAIR FIEDLER: Do you have any information about the size of the Chinese strategic reserve at the moment?

DR. DOWNS: I don't know off the top of my head, but I can certainly look that up for you.

HEARING CO-CHAIR FIEDLER: It occurs to me that with China's dramatically increasing need for oil, that it dramatically increases their need for a strategic reserve of increasing amount, and that the closure of the Strait of Hormuz is an important strategic factor that raises the question of: how long can they tolerate a closing of the Strait of Hormuz?

So the strategic reserve number becomes very important to understand when considering their interests because I would say to you that the argument that you were having with--not argument--the discussion you were having with Commissioner Shea, that their interest in the United States might affect their behavior in Iran, my suspicion is the closure of the Strait of Hormuz is much more important to them than an equity investment in Devon Energy or any other such thing in the United States. But we apparently don't have enough information to sort of measure that.

DR. DOWNS: I can get information to you. I don't recall off the top of my head so I don't just want to throw random figures out there, but there is information out there in the public domain about the size of their reserve. About a year ago I did some calculations about what we knew regarding the size of China's strategic petroleum reserve (SPR) at the end of 2012 and the number of barrels and that implied was days of net import coverage. So the information is out there to make those calculations.

HEARING CO-CHAIR FIEDLER: Thank you very much. Commissioner Bartholomew

COMMISSIONER BARTHOLOMEW: I want to go back to follow up, Mr. Edwards and Dr. Downs, on where I left off in my other questions. But this is now about quality control in terms of the projects that are being done. Mr. Edwards, you noted the high speed rail. Of course, there were some pretty horrific accidents that happened in China because of shoddy construction.

MR. EDWARDS: Right.

COMMISSIONER BARTHOLOMEW: From what I've heard, the Bird's Nest is rusting out already so both the quality of the material that's been used and the quality of the construction inside China has raised some questions.

So I guess, first, on these projects that they're going to be doing, are they using Chinese-produced material like Chinese steel?

MR. EDWARDS: I think it's a mixture. I think it's project by project, and I think they use materials that are most cost effective and most available.

COMMISSIONER BARTHOLOMEW: Do you think that they're going to have to be building to a higher standard than the standard that they have been using in China?

MR. EDWARDS: My experience frankly in China is that the infrastructure is pretty high quality. The airports, the highways, the railways are all quite impressive. They've clearly had some problems, and I think you might expect that for any country that has built in the last 15 years the incredible amount of infrastructure that it has.

I also think they are learning. They're developing better technology and they're developing better materials and better processes. And the latest reports are that the high-speed rail, the brand new one that they built from Guangzhou to Beijing is very impressive and a technological feat.

I think that the quality of Chinese construction is coming up the curve. The Chinese to date received mandates for the most technologically challenging projects in the Middle East like the Abu Dhabi nuclear project or the Burj Dubai or the Dubai Metro. Those projects have gone to either the Japanese or the South Koreans who have a better reputation for quality. But my sense is that the Chinese are improving and improving rapidly.

COMMISSIONER BARTHOLOMEW: Again, I guess a question there is, is that there's technological innovation; there's learning.

MR. EDWARDS: Right.

COMMISSIONER BARTHOLOMEW: But if you look at a number of sectors, food safety, for example, and some other things, there's also been a tendency to cut corners. So what I'm wondering is if people inside China see the quality of the product being done by Chinese companies outside of China significantly better than what they are getting inside of China, what that dynamic might mean? And I'm asking you to speculate there.

MR. EDWARDS: Yeah, well, a fascinating question, and I think for the Chinese to play on the bigger stage outside of China, they have to bring their standards up to international standards so that they're competitive outside of China, and I think they're learning fast. It's hard for me to speculate what political effect that may have at home.

COMMISSIONER BARTHOLOMEW: Dr. Downs, any thoughts on that?

DR. DOWNS: I guess I'd just underscore the point that the Chinese construction companies that are building stuff abroad really do have a wealth of experience to draw on simply because they've built so much infrastructure in China, -- roads, railways, ports, and airports--that they do have a lot of experience to bring to bear on their projects overseas.

COMMISSIONER BARTHOLOMEW: I have just one final observation, which is that the quality of the infrastructure is ultimately the test of time. We'll have to see how well things hold up. Thank you.

HEARING CO-CHAIR FIEDLER: Commissioner Wessel.

COMMISSIONER WESSEL: Just a couple of quick follow-ups to Carolyn's point just a moment ago. The Verrazano Bridge, as you may know, the Chinese just won the bid for providing the entire upper deck despite the fact that there is a steel company that makes the product within a hundred miles of the bridge.

You talked about cost effectiveness, Mr. Edwards. I think that's a question of beauty is in the eye of the beholder. There are probably some subsidies involved there that might make it cost effective, and what happened with the Bay Bridge and the fact that the fabrication of that was given to a company that had never done it before, and they had to send the bridge structures back for rewelding and other things. I'm just not sure they have the capabilities.

And another point made, I think Dr. Downs--or it may--I apologize, Mr. Edwards--on terms of sourcing, I think we've seen in Canada, for example, that miners have been sent over from China to work in the mines in British Columbia, so there still is an effort--

DR. DOWNS: Right.

COMMISSIONER WESSEL: --to supply Chinese workers for projects. Whether they can get away with it or not is a question.

Dr. Downs, following up on Commissioner Shea's comments about or questions about CFIUS, I think the largest and most recent Chinese investment in U.S. energy infrastructure is Sinopec's $2.1 billion investment in Wyoming.

And just going to the Iran question that was raised, because that is not an acquisition but a greenfield investment, it's not covered by CFIUS. Should we have the same kind of concerns? I mean CFIUS is only involved if there's an acquisition. If it's a greenfield investment, there's no screening mechanism. What are your thoughts on that?

DR. DOWNS: Well, I think that the growth of Chinese investment in the United States is obviously prompting a lot of discussion about whether or not the United States needs to change their process for screening foreign investments, much the way the wave of Japanese investment in the U.S. in decades past did.

There are certainly lots of questions being asked about whether the United States needs to adopt a screening process, for example, more like that of the Australians or the Canadians? As you probably know, after or at the same time actually that the Canadian government announced that they were approving CNOOC's acquisition of Nexen, they also came out with a new list of undertakings regarding investment by state-owned enterprises in Canada.

So I think that these are questions that are out there, and I think the big question for the United States is does it make sense to continue screening investments narrowly for national security risks, or should that mandate be expanded to include other things like economic security and safety?

There's a big debate going on, and I'm not sure exactly where I come down on it. I think the process that we have so far has been working really well, but I guess--

COMMISSIONER WESSEL: But let's divide the question if we can.

DR. DOWNS: Okay.

COMMISSIONER WESSEL: I understand the net economic benefit test that Canada and Australia and some others have.

DR. DOWNS: Yes.

COMMISSIONER WESSEL: But if one goes just to the national security issue--

DR. DOWNS: Yes.

COMMISSIONER WESSEL: --which Commissioner Shea raised, and Iran sanctions, the question is should a greenfield investment be subject to the same CFIUS standard? Forget about an economic benefit. If you believe it's a true national security question, should it apply no matter what the nature of the investment, acquisition, controlling, et cetera?

DR. DOWNS: That's an interesting question. As you were speaking, one thought that occurred to me is that there have been some investments in the United States, including one by a Chinese company in wind farm projects in Oregon last year that was blocked, and one of the reasons that it was blocked was for proximity to a U.S. national security installation, which is one of the reasons we've blocked other investments by

Chinese and other companies in the past, and certainly other countries like Australia do this as well.

And so as you were talking, I was thinking what if a company wanted to make a greenfield investment in close proximity to a U.S. national security installation? To me, it seems like that potentially might raise the same national security risk--

COMMISSIONER WESSEL: Right.

DR. DOWNS: --as a foreign company acquiring a U.S. business with assets in proximity to that. So I think it's a very good question. I don't have an answer to it, but I think you've made an important point.

COMMISSIONER WESSEL: I understand. Thank you.

HEARING CO-CHAIR FIEDLER: Senator Talent.

HEARING CO-CHAIR TALENT: We know the Chinese are interested in markets in the Middle East. They're interested obviously in secure sources of oil. They're more comfortable dealing with stable governments, and to the extent they can do it without going too far out on a limb, they wouldn't mind raising their international profile and competing with the United States in the region.

So, in your view--and you can answer this very briefly if you want, even yes or no--does that make it almost certain that they're going to continue putting major efforts in developing their relationships with the Saudis and the Gulf states?

MR. EDWARDS: I think it's clear that they will. One point I would like to make is that the Chinese are benefiting from this movement of people into the Gulf region, and the development of a large permanent Chinese population with an independent business base. It concerns me that there are not enough Americans in the region. My own view, having lived there, is that one of the most important ways to advance our national interests is to have many Americans in the region doing business and contributing to society and having contacts and influence.

I think it's important that the U.S. do things to encourage Americans to take jobs in these regions. Unfortunately, Americans have a real disadvantage over any other people because of the U.S. tax code, which taxes income of American citizens on a global basis wherever they are.

What that means is that for companies to pay effectively the same wage in a low tax environment have to gross up American employees for their US taxes where they don't have to for Brits or New Zealanders or Australians. I was talking to a senior executive, an American, at a US bank in Hong Kong, and he said that if you bring in an American equally qualified with a Brit or an Australian, a U.S. company will always have to hire the non-American because of the additional tax expense for an American.

I think it is an important point. I think it's important that more and more Americans take advantage of these great opportunities in the Middle East and in China.

HEARING CO-CHAIR FIEDLER: Thank you very much. We will adjourn for lunch. I appreciate your testimony, and we'll see the rest of you at 12:30.

           DR. DOWNS: Thank you.

           HEARING CO-CHAIR FIEDLER: Thank you.

           [Whereupon, at 11:43 a.m., the hearing recessed, to reconvene at 12:31 p.m., this same day.]

PANEL III INTRODUCTION BY COMMISSIONER JEFFREY FIEDLER
HEARING CO-CHAIR

HEARING CO-CHAIR FIEDLER: We have the witnesses and we have a sufficient number of Commissioners to start. Welcome back.

The final panel of the day will focus on China's political and security challenges in the Middle East. Dr. Jon B. Alterman, Dr. Joel Wuthnow, and Dr. Andrew Erickson will be testifying.

Dr. Alterman is Director of Middle East Program at the Center for Strategic and International Studies. Prior to joining CSIS, in 2002, he served as a member of the Policy Planning Staff at the State Department and as Special Assistant to the Assistant Secretary of State for Near Eastern Affairs.

He also worked as a legislative aid to Senator Daniel Moynihan. He received his A.B. from Princeton University's Woodrow Wilson School of Public and International Affairs.

Dr. Wuthnow is an Asian analyst in the China Security Affairs Group at CNA in Alexandria, Virginia. His research interests include Chinese foreign and security policy, U.S.-China relations, and Chinese domestic politics.

He recently published a book entitled *Chinese Diplomacy and the United Nations Security Council*, and he contributes frequently to East Asia academic journals.

He received his A.B. from Princeton, a Master's in Philosophy from Oxford, and a Ph.D. from Columbia.

Dr. Erickson is an Associate Professor at the U.S. Naval War College and a founding member of the College's China Maritime Studies Institute. He is also a research associate at Harvard's Fairbank Center for Chinese Studies and a prolific writer on Chinese security issues.

Dr. Erickson received his Ph.D. and M.A. from Princeton University. Lots of Princeton guys here today.

Please, I think we'll start with Dr. Alterman, and I would say to you seven minutes, and when my colleagues show up from lunch, we'll do five minute rounds of questioning, and I'd like to keep your answers brief so we can get in as many questions as possible.

HEARING CO-CHAIR TALENT: You'll have a lot of opportunities to make any points you can't make in the opening statement in response to the questions.

HEARING CO-CHAIR FIEDLER: So, Dr. Alterman.

OPENING STATEMENT OF DR. JON B. ALTERMAN
DIRECTOR, MIDDLE EAST PROGRAM
CENTER FOR STRATEGIC AND INTERNATIONAL STUDIES

DR. ALTERMAN: Thank you, Mr. Chairman. Members of the Commission, it's a great honor and a pleasure to be here today.

China has an energy problem. Over the two decades since it became a net oil importer, it's grown increasingly reliant on energy supplies from the Middle East, a part of the world that's both prone to instability and in which China has very little influence.

Making matters worse, Chinese strategic thinking remains focused on a conflict with the United States, or the possibility of a conflict with the United States, which has far more influence in the Middle East than China does. China, therefore, is doubly vulnerable. Its economic growth, and the domestic political stability that growth helps provide, is dependent on energy that China cannot secure alone, and it relies on the goodwill of a country that China often sees to be its principal potential foe, and that country has to help provide security.

For China, there is no simple way out of this paradox. It's pursued fuels other than oil and gas, such as coal and nuclear power, but its needs are growing so rapidly--including to fuel its rapidly-growing automobile fleet--that its increasing reliance on oil and gas seems to be a certainty for the coming decades.

China also has sought to diversify its sources of oil, looking especially to invest in Africa so as to avoid reliance on the Middle East. But the Middle East is where the oil is, and whether it's tapping into growing Iraqi production or increasing supplies from Saudi Arabia, China finds that much of the increment of available oil in the world is held in the Middle East regardless of China's longstanding desire to diversify away from it.

Making the matter even more complex, the United States is increasing its military presence in China's immediate neighborhood, and many in the Middle East believe that this U.S. move is at the Middle East's expense. The U.S. ability to affect China's maritime ties with the Middle East will surely increase, while Middle Eastern states may themselves seek to increase China's maritime role in their neighborhood.

At the same time, the United States will be far more energy independent than it has been for decades, creating a stark contrast with China whose dependence on Middle Eastern energy is likely to grow.

That's a hard set of problems, and to complement the hard set of problems, China has a hard set of relationships. They have a difficult relationship with Iran. They see advantages in Iran drawing U.S. attention, drawing U.S. forces, and they appreciate both having a source of oil that the United States is unlikely to block and to also have oil that they can buy at discounted prices compared to the world market. Yet, as the world's largest oil importer, China suffers every time Iranian action causes oil prices to spike, and they feel pressure from their largest seller, Saudi Arabia, which believes it faces it an existential threat from Iran.

China has been also flummoxed by political developments in the Arab world which have created a need for nimble diplomacy. In Egypt and Libya, China faced enduring criticism for staying with a dying regime too long. In Syria, China sought to be more skillful standing by the government while quietly reaching out to the opposition. But China has a problem. Its instinct is to be a status quo power in a region where the status quo is shifting, and China is facing unprecedented diplomatic challenges.

China can't withdraw from the Middle East or avoid devising a strategy toward this region. It needs to navigate its way through what seems certain to be a sustained confrontation between Iran and the rest of the world, and it needs to craft an approach to the roiling politics that are reshaping the Middle East today, some of which threaten to tip the region into even more turmoil.

Some in China want a new role, and they see opportunities in the Middle East for China to establish itself as a responsible global actor. Many current and aspiring Chinese allies in the Middle East also want China to have a new role, in some cases to supplement close relationships with the United States, and in some cases to balance against U.S. power.

There is little unity in China or elsewhere on what a new Chinese role should look like or what China's priorities should be. Still it's all but certain that China will have a larger role in the Middle East in the coming decades, even if it takes on such a role more slowly and cautiously than many in China and the Middle East would prefer.

In a perfect world, it seems to me that China would really prefer not to have a Middle East policy. Closer to home, in Asia, which it knows well, it has a long history, and it occupies a dominant position. Strength in Asia propels China to a global stage, and it seems delighted at the prospect of being treated as a near peer by the United States.

While China still feels vulnerable to American might now, China also feels that power is shifting in its direction. If China could limit itself to thinking principally about Asia and the United States, it would have plenty of challenges on its hands, but it would also see the prospect of considerable reward. But it can't limit itself. It finds itself drawn continually westward toward more treacherous ground.

For China, the Middle East is complicated, it's conflictual, it brings tremendous scrutiny, and the United States has a home-court advantage. China's reliance on the Middle East highlights China's continued vulnerability to U.S. power, especially when it comes to safeguarding global trade, and China's instinct is to tread lightly.

Some in China seek to equivocate, while some advocate embracing the challenge head on and adopting a can-do attitude to further Chinese interests. I think many of you are familiar with the writing of Wang Jisi, a leading Chinese academic and Dean of the School of International Studies at Beijing University, who talked about looking West for China's strategy, embracing a strategy of looking West, going toward the Middle

East, but that, of course, is a controversial position in Chinese scholarship and policy thinking.

China's hesitancy toward the Middle East is mirrored in the actions of most other powers, which see peril and uncertainty in the unfolding politics of the changing Middle East. China, however, cannot lean against the region's volatility; it must somehow endure it. In addition, China's growing influence in the region means that its actions, and its inaction, will shape the Middle East to an unprecedented degree.

China has not yet concluded what tools it has at its disposal nor how it wishes to use them, and it must make that decision soon.

Thank you.

**PREPARED STATEMENT OF DR. JON B. ALTERMAN
DIRECTOR, MIDDLE EAST PROGRAM
CENTER FOR STRATEGIC AND INTERNATIONAL STUDIES**

TESTIMONY FOR THE U.S.-CHINA ECONOMIC AND SECURITY REVIEW COMMISSION

CHINA IN THE MIDDLE EAST

JUNE 6, 2013

JOHN B. ALTERMAN, PH.D.,
*Zbigniew Brzezinski Chair in Global Security and Geostrategy and Director, Middle East
Program, Center for Strategic and International Studies.*

China has an energy problem. Over the two decades since it became a net oil importer, it has grown increasingly reliant on energy supplies from the Middle East, a part of the world which is both prone to instability and in which it has little influence. Making matters worse, Chinese strategic thinking remains focused on the possibility of a confrontation with the United States, which has far more influence in the Middle East than China does. China, therefore, is doubly vulnerable. Its economic growth—and the domestic political stability that growth helps provide—is dependent on energy that China cannot secure alone, and it relies on the good will of a country it often sees to be its principal potential foe to help provide that security.

For China, there is no simple way out of its paradox. It has pursued fuels other than oil and gas—such as coal and nuclear power—but its needs are growing so rapidly, including to fuel its growing fleet of automobiles, that increasing reliance on oil and gas seems to be a certainty in the coming decades. China has also sought to diversify its sources of oil, looking to invest especially in Africa, to avoid reliance on the Middle East. However, the Middle East is where the oil is, and whether it is tapping into growing Iraqi production or increasing supplies from Saudi Arabia, China finds much of the available increments of additional oil in the Middle East, regardless of their long-held desire to diversify away from it.

Making the matter more complex, the United States is increasing its military presence in China's immediate neighborhood, and many in the Middle East believe the shift will be at their expense. The U.S. ability to affect China's maritime ties with the Middle East will surely increase, while Middle Eastern states may seek a greater Chinese maritime role. At the same time, the United States will be far more energy-independent than it has been for decades, creating a stark contrast with a China whose dependence on Middle Eastern energy is likely to grow.

China can neither withdraw from the Middle East nor avoid devising a strategy toward the region. It needs to navigate its way through what seems certain to be a sustained confrontation between Iran and the rest of the world, and it needs to craft an approach to the roiling politics that are reshaping the Middle East today, some of which threaten to tip the region into even more turmoil.

Some in China want a new role, and they see opportunities in the Middle East for China to establish itself as a responsible global actor. Many current and aspiring Chinese allies in the Middle East also want China to have a new role, in some cases to supplement strong relationships with the United States, and in some cases to balance against U.S. power. There is little unity in China or elsewhere on what a new Chinese role should look like or what its priorities should be. Still, it is all but certain that China will have a larger role in the Middle East in the coming decades, even if it takes on such a role more slowly and cautiously than many in China and the Middle East would prefer.

China's approach to the Middle East

China's interest in the Middle East did not begin with oil, but oil transformed it. Trade with the region dates back to antiquity and continued through the centuries of the Silk Road. In modern times, each grappled with crumbling empires and the European colonialism that capitalized on their internal weaknesses. As wars broke out, and revolutions occurred in both places, each was too absorbed in its own turmoil to take much notice of the other.

China's revolutionary fervor made the country a cheerleader for change in the Middle East in the mid-twentieth century, but China's impact was mostly symbolic, and it provided only token assistance to revolutionary forces. China's hostility to Western hegemony in the Cold War made recognition of China an appealing way for revolutionary movements to signal their departure from the status quo: in 1956, Gamal Abdel Nasser's recognition of Communist China alienated the Eisenhower Administration and helped set in train the Suez Canal Crisis; after Algerians won their bloody war of independence against France, they turned de Gaulle's old villa into the Chinese embassy. Few U.S. allies recognized Communist China, and most U.S. foes did.

But China had an overwhelmingly internal focus in this period, wholly occupied first with recovering from World War II and consolidating the revolution and later with the Great Leap Forward and the Cultural Revolution. China did not really turn to the Middle East until the 1980s, when a more market-oriented government sought markets for low-cost weapons to support a domestic arms industry. It was not until China became a net importer of oil in 1993 that the Middle East took on a strategic cast for the Chinese leadership.

Chinese diplomacy since the 1970s has focused on strategic objectives related to easing China's way in the world. Trumpeting a policy of non-intervention in others' internal politics and seeking positive relations with a wide variety of states, China generally has been content to play a modest role in global affairs. Simply put, China has been content to be a "market taker," seeking to maximize the benefit it derives from conditions it finds around the world. In the past, China pursued a policy characterized as "accomplishing something to some extent." It participated in international dialogues, insisted on non-interference in domestic affairs, and consistently opposed the use of force.[1] Sometimes these relations have been seemingly contradictory, as when it has pursued close ties with antagonists such as Israel, Iran, and Saudi Arabia. China has taken the attitude that it cannot affect the strategic decisions of any of these states. Where an international consensus has existed, China would often join it, but it is hard to recall circumstances in which it took the lead in shaping one.

---

[1] Liu Zhongmin, "On Political Unrest in the Middle East and China's Diplomacy," *Journal of Middle Eastern and Islamic Studies (in Asia)*, vol. 6, no. 1 (2012), p. 8.

The country's interests are outgrowing that approach, however. As China's global footprint rises, China increasingly finds itself thrust into the position of "market maker." Its demands are too large not to affect the global environment, and its external vulnerabilities are too large to rely on others to defend them. While China has played an outsized role in Asian affairs for centuries, its words and actions suggest a growing consensus inside China that the country must act more and more like a global power. The result is a somewhat awkward diplomacy in which China visibly struggles to define and carry out a new strategy.

Seen another way, Chinese diplomacy is being forced out of passively managing risk. As the stakes grow, an increasing number of Chinese analysts complain that such a conservative approach not only fails to protect Chinese interests, but it also elicits growing disappointment from Chinese partners who believe that China's growing power and their growing trade relationships with China should yield greater diplomatic benefits.

The Middle East has several characteristics that make it especially delicate for China. First, the region is unavoidable in a way that other regions are not. China need not have a strong position in Europe, and its ties to both Africa and Latin America are discretionary. China's swiftly growing energy needs, however, draw China ever-deeper into Middle Eastern affairs.

Second, the U.S. posture in the Middle East, and the strategic relations it has with virtually all regional governments, makes China feel vulnerable. China is relatively poor and militarily weak, and the United States has an ability to sustain tens of thousands of forces in the region for years on end in a way that China cannot emulate for decades. The United States' diplomatic and military strength in the Middle East influences all of China's relations in the region. The Saudi ambassador to China observed recently, "In order to understand China's relations with the Gulf states, one must understand Sino-American relations."[2]

Third, the region's swirling politics create a problem. As a status-quo power, China's instinct to support sitting governments has put it on the wrong side of victorious revolutionary movements in Egypt, Libya, and Tunisia. Broader change could make China more isolated in the region as it seeks to establish itself. Further, Chinese analysts are wary of delving too deeply into the region's internal developments, out of fear that their analysis of failing Middle Eastern authoritarian regimes will be taken as veiled critique of China's own leadership.

China's early efforts to explore a larger Middle Eastern role were somewhat awkward. After 2001, however, China acted quietly but effectively in the shadow of U.S. conflict with the region. China managed not to get drawn into U.S.-led wars in Iraq and Afghanistan, and it reaped benefits from what critics of the United States saw as a "war against Islam." As the United States waged a high-profile "Global War on Terror," Chinese companies moved in and won energy and infrastructure contracts. In the first decade of the twenty-first century, the Chinese economy boomed, fueled in significant measure by imported Middle Eastern oil.

There is something else drawing China into the Middle East—the Middle Eastern powers

---

[2] Khalid R. Al-Rodhan, "China's Strategic Posture in the Gulf, 1980-2010," Ph.D. Dissertation, Girton College, Cambridge University, 2011, p. 114.

themselves. Many of them, and especially several oil producers in the Gulf, are eager for a greater Chinese role. In part, the interest in China stems from insecurity about U.S. intentions, especially with visible U.S. fatigue at the posture it has maintained in the Gulf for decades. Taken at face value, the language the United States and China have used to describe the region was pointedly different: the United States called for "energy independence" and "ending addiction" to Middle Eastern oil; Beijing advocated "energy interdependence," "energy security," and "strategic partnerships."[3] The United States' language makes Gulf leaders uneasy, while China's language makes them feel more secure.

The attraction of China is more than merely language, though. Some powers seem to feel that having a competitor to the United States in the region would improve their bargaining position. This is true not only of Iran, which seeks leverage against the United States, but even countries such as Saudi Arabia, which have long and strategic ties to the United States. China's historic disinterest in domestic affairs, its willingness to sell weapons without Congressional meddling, and its ability to move swiftly gives these countries what they want quicker. It also spurs the United States to remove roadblocks to acquiring desired U.S. goods.

Finally, many petroleum producers see China as the future, a rising power that will be consuming their oil for decades more. China's eagerness for economic growth makes them a necessarily less fickle power, and one with a reliance on the Middle East that the United States does not share in the same way. Some see the U.S. relationship as something that can only diminish, while the relationship with China is something that will likely grow.

In 2011, China accounted for half of the growth in oil consumption worldwide, and the Energy Information Administration estimates that China alone will account for 64 percent of the growth in global consumption in 2011-13.[4] China now imports more oil than the United States,[5] and BP estimates that China will consume more oil than the United States by 2029.[6] With an increasing amount of U.S. imports coming directly from Canada and Mexico, China is a huge buyer from the rest of the world's producers.

China's strategy toward Iran and its neighbors

China's most difficult relationship in the Middle East is with Iran. On the surface, this seems unlikely. After all, China and Iran have a robust trading relationship, and they share a skepticism of U.S. intentions. Their common history dates back more than a millennium, and each former empire sees itself as much a civilization as a country. With a common view that the international order intends to constrain their actions unfairly,[7] each seeks a new order that allows it to achieve

---

[3] Al-Rodhan, p. 250.

[4] U.S. Energy Information Administration, China Country Brief, http://www.eia.gov/countries/cab.cfm?fips=CH

[5] Robin M. Mills, "Who's Winning the Great Energy Rat Race?" *Foreign Policy*, March 8, 2013, http://www.foreignpolicy.com/articles/2013/03/08/whos_winning_the_great_energy_rat_race_china_oil_importer.

[6] BP Energy Outlook 2030, p. 33.

[7] One author points out that while both countries are "revisionist" powers with regard to the international system, they are at odds because Iran is a revolutionary revisionist power intent on bringing down the existing international order while China is a reformist revisionist power that seeks to enhance China's position in that order. Mohsen Shariantnia, "Iran-China Relations: An overview of critical factors," *Iranian Review of Foreign Affairs*, vol. 1, no. 4

its rightful place in the world. A deeper investigation, however, reveals a deep Chinese unease with Iran, and a growing Iranian reliance on China that is not reciprocated.

There are many reasons for China's caution toward Iran. First, Iran's estrangement from many countries—most pointedly the United States—brings great scrutiny to the Chinese-Iranian relationship and imposes costs on China that it would rather avoid. The Vice President of the China Institute of International Studies told an Arab researcher, "We never hear the U.S. complaining about China's relationship with Saudi Arabia. But we hear them complain about Iran."[8] An Iranian scholar points out the problem from a Chinese perspective aptly: Chinese trade with Iran is a seemingly impressive $22 billion, but is less than one-fortieth of China's trade with its three largest trading partners: the United States, the European Union and Japan.[9] It is with these countries that China has a strategic imperative to manage its relations. At the extreme, the Chinese goal is to persuade the United States and its allies that it is a responsible global power and not a strategic rival; at minimum, the imperative is not to engage in a direct confrontation with the United States.[10] Sino-American relations remain at the center of Chinese strategic thinking, and whatever U.S. intentions, the Chinese government appears skeptical that China can win a confrontation with the United States in the near term.[11]

China is especially vulnerable when it comes to Middle Eastern energy. The United States has a unique ability to control the sea-lanes between China and Middle Eastern oil producers (in terms both of protecting Chinese supplies and being able to threaten them in case of conflict), and land-based pipelines are far from able to meet China's needs. In addition, Chinese scholars frequently note that the United States is the predominant external power in the Middle East, and while its absolute position may decline somewhat in the face of a re-emphasis on Asia and a retrenchment following the political upheavals of 2011, its position relative to any other outside power is overwhelming and likely to remain so for some time. If, as one Chinese scholar notes, "A peaceful geopolitical environment of the Middle East and North Africa is a requirement for China's energy security,"[12] there is little appetite for a confrontation with the United States, because, as the scholar admits frankly, "China lacks the capability of dealing with international energy politics and risks."[13]

Second, while China is concerned with reliable access to oil, Iran is not the preferred partner. Saudi Arabia is a far greater producer of petroleum products than Iran, and in the last decade it has gone from supplying slightly more oil than Iran to China to supplying more than twice as

---

(Winter 2011), p. 64.

[8] Al-Rodhan, p. 115.

[9] Mohsen Shariantnia, "Iran-China Relations: An overview of critical factors," *Iranian Review of Foreign Affairs*, vol. 1, no. 4 (Winter 2011), p. 75.

[10] One scholar wrote in 2011 that Chinese-Iranian political relations have not increased apace with their trade relations "due to the constraining impact of the ever-expanding complex relations between Beijing and Washington on the one hand and the simultaneous perpetuation of tension between Tehran and Washington on the other." Shariantnia, p. 82.

[11] One author writes, "The U.S. position as 'the only superpower' will not change within a short period, neither will its dominance over Middle Eastern affairs." Liu Zhongmin, "On Political Unrest in the Middle East and China's Diplomacy," *Journal of Middle Eastern and Islamic Studies (in Asia)*, vol. 6, no. 1 (2012), p. 6.

[12] Wu Lei, "The Oil Politics and Geopolitical Risks with China 'Going Out' Strategy toward the Greater Middle East," *Journal of Middle Eastern and Islamic Studies (in Asia)*, vol. 6, no. 3 (September 2012), p. 63.

[13] Ibid., p. 79.

much. Interestingly, Iran's share of China's oil imports has held relatively steady for the last decade, ranging between 9 and 14 percent and more recently trending at the lower end of that range. But because Iranian exports have been declining overall, Iran's China trade has rocketed from 5 percent to 25 percent of its oil exports.[14] From the Chinese perspective, the strategic relationship is with Saudi Arabia, which now accounts for more than 20 percent of all Chinese oil imports.[15]

The Saudi leadership is quite focused on what it sees as an existential threat from Iran, which includes but is not limited to Iran's proliferation activities. Saudi behavior in global markets has been to reassure customers while increasing production to meet demand. Iranian behavior, by contrast, has been to threaten the stability of supply in order to deter attack, while meanwhile presiding over a decline in actual production. Seen from the perspective of a consumer, which China assuredly is, Saudi Arabia's behavior tends to support China's economic needs, while Iran's undermines them. Saudi Arabia is not blind to the security implications of such a shift. According to one scholar, "China is increasingly focusing its attention on the Kingdom as a reliable energy partner, while Saudi Arabia sees China as an enormous potential market and strategic partner."[16]

Seen broadly, China has become increasingly strategic to Iran without the reverse being true. Instead, Saudi Arabia China's strategic bet in the Middle East seems to be on ties with Saudi Arabia. Yet Saudi reservations about China's ties to Iran do not trump China's other interests in Iran.

An energy relationship with Iran has two principal benefits to China. The first is economic. When global sanctions depress the demand for Iranian oil, China can obtain that oil at a discount. China is large enough to feel it is unlikely to be sanctioned by the United States, and it feels little obligation to sacrifice its own interests for U.S. strategy. China takes a dim view of sanctions overall, so subverting them—especially when they are not imposed by the United Nations— seems the natural approach.

Iran's other benefit to China is as a strategic hedge against U.S. influence. That is to say, in the event of conflict between the United States and China, it behooves China to have energy relationships that the United States cannot turn on and off. Chinese strategists continue to worry out loud about the potential of Sino-American conflict over Taiwan, even as the Chinese-Taiwanese relationship grows increasingly close, and they fear that one of the first U.S. steps in such an event would be to cut China's access to oil. China has taken many steps to ensure its energy supplies, from pursuing pipelines across the Asian steppes to developing port facilities in Burma that would allow some Chinese oil shipments to bypass the Straits of Malacca, which the U.S. Navy could conceivably control. One author urges, "Central Asia is a source of energy

---

[14] United States-China Economic and Security Review Commission, "China-Iran: A Limited Partnership," (Arlington, VA: CENTRA Technology, 2012), p. 19.

[15] One author points out that neither President Hu Jintao nor Premier Wen Jiabao visited Iran or Syria since October 2007, but Hu, Wen and then-Vice President Xi Jinping all visited Saudi Arabia. Bo Zhiyue, "China's Middle East Policy: Strategic Concerns and Economic Interests," *MEI Insight*, no. 61 (19 April 2012), Middle East Institute, National University of Singapore, p. 2.

[16] Naser al-Tamimi, "China-Saudi Arabia Relations: Economic Partnership or Strategic Alliance?" Discussion paper, Durham University, HH Sheikh Naser Al-Sabah Programme, Durham, UK, p. 1.

supply that demands no protection from any ocean navy. As China is still unable in the near future to build up an ocean navy strong enough to protect its oil shipping lines, this nearby energy source coming by land is obviously of great strategic significance for China's energy security."[17] A senior Chinese scholar of the Middle East put the Chinese balancing act well: He told an Arab researcher, "'It would be the end of the world' if China had to choose between the United States, Saudi Arabia and Iran."[18]

The Chinese government appears concerned but not alarmed over the Iranian nuclear program. Chinese interlocutors consistently assess that more time remains, oppose military action, and encourage the Iranians to negotiate with their adversaries. One possibility is that China is merely seeking to maximize its own bargaining position with both sides by finding a posture that is minimally acceptable to each and then playing one off against the other. It is possible, too, that Chinese diplomats do judge that a resolution is possible on these terms.

What is clearer is that China derives benefits from the current state of affairs. Many Chinese strategists seem delighted at the prospect of the United States being tangled up in enduring tensions with Iran, which draws U.S. attention and resources[19] and allows others to portray the United States as a global hegemon.[20] Looking broadly at the region, one analyst wrote recently that the basic orientation of China's Middle East strategy should strive to maintain peace and stability in the Middle East. On the other hand, the Middle East upheaval to a certain extent, contributed to the dispersion of the U.S. effort and contained the strategic eastward shift of the U.S. Therefore, there is no need for China to get the United States out of trouble.[21]

Overall, however, the Chinese position appears to flow from an assessment that China cannot much affect Iranian decision-making, and that the United States could manage the fallout of Iranian proliferation if it came to that. A senior think tank scholar close to the Foreign Ministry observed, "When we set our objectives, we know our means...[and] we have very limited means to influence the Gulf."[22]

Some argue that the Chinese position is not quite as strategic as it is often made out to be. John Garver makes the intriguing point that the apparent contradictions in Chinese policy toward Iran are a consequence of bureaucratic politics within China. One foreign researcher quotes an anonymous Chinese scholar of the Middle East to say that the Foreign Ministry's U.S. focus prompts many Chinese experts to refer to it as "the Ministry of American Affairs,"[23] so strong is

[17] Guang Pan, "China's Energy Strategy and Primary Role of the Middle East in This Strategy," *Journal of Middle Eastern and Islamic Studies (in Asia)*, vol. 2 no. 2 (2008), p. 67.

[18] Al-Rodhan, p. 115.

[19] International Crisis Group, "The Iran Nuclear Issue: The View from Beijing" Asia Briefing No. 100, 17 February 2010, p. 4.

[20] On Chinese schadenfreude over Iraq, see Xiong Guangqing, "The Iraq War's Weakening of U.S. Soft Power," *Academic Expression*, pp. 14-17, quoted in Michael Chase, "China's Assessment of the War in Iraq: America's Academic Expression, pp. 14-17, quoted in Michael Chase, "China's Assessment of the War in Iraq: America's 'Deepest Quagmire'" and the Implications for Chinese National Security," *China Brief*, vol. 7 issue 17 (September 19, 2007).

[21] Yao Kuwangyi, "The Upheaval in the Middle East and China's Middle East Policy," *Journal of Middle Eastern and Islamic Studies (in Asia)*, vol. 6, no. 3, (September 2012), p. 21.

[22] Al-Rodhan, p. 113.

[23] Al-Rodhan, p. 243.

its push for comity with the United States. Some argue that the People's Liberation Army emphasizes U.S. hostility and a desire to undermine U.S. global influence, and the Chinese oil companies seek commercial advantage not only by buying current supplies at below-market prices, but also by using Iran's relative weakness on the international stage to secure a unique and advantageous place in Iran's energy sector.[24]

China's strategy toward Egypt and the post-revolutionary Arab states

China's policy toward Iran has evolved over several decades and always in the shadow of U.S. policy. By contrast, China's policy toward the evolving revolutions in the Middle East required a more sudden shift in Chinese strategy and deft diplomacy. Overwhelmingly, the Chinese attitude toward political changes in the Middle East has been to view them with alarm. Further, its diplomatic approach has found limited success.

China's attitude toward political change in the Middle East is especially difficult because it is an avowedly revolutionary power that has developed its interests with governments that represent the status quo. While China's rhetoric supports popular empowerment, its actions have sought to develop ties with governments and to shun political movements. When those governments fell, sometimes despite official Chinese support, China found itself trying to build a position of influence on shaky foundations.

China's first challenge in the Middle East has been to understand it in a more sophisticated way than it has had to heretofore. Chinese policy has traditionally relied on a strict policy of non-interference in the domestic affairs of others, leading to a Chinese sense of disorientation when new political forces gained power in the Middle East. Chinese policy toward unrest in Asia articulated the "three evil forces"—terrorism, separatism and religious extremism—but that construction has little guidance to offer a government trying to navigate the uncertain terrain of post-uprising Middle East. Where, for example, does the Muslim Brotherhood fit into this schema, and what of the sectarian opposition party in Bahrain, al-Wifaq? Is al-Nahda in Tunisia a potential partner or a likely foe? In fact, China is not in a position to judge any of them, in part because it does not know the parties themselves, but also because it has not paid close attention to the societies from which they have sprung. According to an Arab researcher, some Arabic-speakers in Beijing refer to the Middle East section of the Foreign Ministry as majmu.at al-na.u wal-.arf, or "the syntax and morphology group," because its officials' Arabic is so refined that they sound like grammar teachers. And yet, they obtained their expertise almost entirely at the University of International Languages in Beijing, leading to "major mistakes that reflected badly on China regionally and internationally. Many of [their] actions reflected China's lack of expertise and true understanding of regional complexities."[25]

Seen broadly, the Chinese approach has been to see the Arab uprisings principally in material terms. Uneven economic growth and high unemployment throughout the Arab world[26] combined

---

[24] Prepared Statement of John W. Garver, delivered to U.S.-China Economic and Security Review Commission, April 13, 2011.
[25] Al-Rodhan, pp. 110-11.
[26] See, for example, Wu Bingbing, "Change in the Middle East: The case of Egypt," *Journal of Middle Eastern and*

with a global economic slowdown to upset a delicate internal balance.[27] While a diminution of U.S. global power and the communications revolution played a role, Chinese scholars have generally seen events in the Arab world as being a consequence of factors that, in a domestic context, the Chinese government is actively managing. One scholar judged that it was Egypt's privatization policy starting in 1991 that tipped the country to revolt, since as a result, "most middle class members have been laid off, restructured, marginalized, and finally added to the already large underclass."[28] Another echoed the overall assessment, saying, "The root cause of the unrest in the Middle East is a crisis of development, namely, a crisis of the development model."[29] In fact, however, what changed in Egypt was not the immiseration of the middle classes, but rather the spectacular enrichment of the upper classes, a phenomenon that has affected China as well.

China has tried to reach out to the new Arab governments tentatively. President Morsi of Egypt made his first trip outside of the Middle East to China, where he won the National Bank of Egypt a $200 million line of credit from the China Development Bank, as well as agreements for future cooperation in a number of areas. But for all of the excitement over the rising relations between Egypt and China, deep disagreements remained. Reportedly, Chinese officials were unable to get appointments with Egyptian counterparts for months after Mubarak fell, because of China's support for Mubarak through the period of street protests that brought him down. Further, Morsi sought to sway his Chinese hosts to change their non-intervention policy in Syria, which Egypt sees as threatening to security in the entire region. Taken as a whole, China's regional diplomacy has been more cautious than it has been deft, and its close ties to fallen regimes have damaged China's reputation.

For some Chinese analysts, the difficulties with new Arab governments in Tunisia and Egypt are a sign that Chinese diplomacy can no longer afford to be as reactive as it has been in the past. One author notes that "China's contact with the Muslim Brotherhood in Egypt and the National Transitional Council of Libya was apparently lagging behind that of other Great Powers,"[30] and urged "more efforts…to diversify China's diplomatic actors and channels in the Middle East, [and] in particular, increase China's contact with political oppositions in Middle Eastern countries."[31]

Uprisings in Egypt and Tunisia happened so quickly that it was hard for China to respond. Conflict in Libya and Syria, by contrast, dragged on for months and months, allowing China to consider (and sometimes reconsider) its policies. In Libya, China supported sanctions imposed in UNSC Resolution 1970 and abstained from UNSC Resolution 1973, which had the effect of allowing NATO troops to support rebels fighting against Muammar el-Qaddafi. China was unable to reap much benefit from its actions, however, for several reasons. First, it almost

---

Islamic Studies (in Asia), vol. 6, no. 1 (2012), p. 24.

[27] An Huihou, "The Reasons and Consequences of Political and Social Unrest in Arab Countries," *Journal of Middle Eastern and Islamic Studies (in Asia)*, vol. 6, no. 2 (June 2012), p. 3.

[28] Dai Xiaoqi, "Political Changes and the Middle Class in Egypt," *Journal of Middle Eastern and Islamic Studies (in Asia)*, vol. 6, no. 2 (June 2012), p. 72.

[29] Liu Zhongmin, "On Political Unrest in the Middle East and China's Diplomacy," *Journal of Middle Eastern and Islamic Studies (in Asia)*, vol. 6, no. 1 (2012), p. 4.

[30] Ibid., p. 10.

[31] Ibid., p. 16.

immediately tried to hedge on its support for isolating Libya, perhaps to protect more than $8 billion in contracts it had in the country. The rebels who eventually came to power noted months of Chinese statements expressing "regret" over NATO airstrikes and emphasizing respect for Libya's sovereignty. They saw the Chinese effort at neutrality as de facto support for Qaddafi.

Second, documentary evidence emerged of Chinese offers of support to Qaddafi in July 2011, five months after the rebellion started and after the imposition of a UN weapons embargo made such assistance illegal.[32] China seems to have been looking to bet on both sides, supporting the status quo while opening a door to Qaddafi's foes.[33] It did not work out so well in practice. China's efforts to split the difference between support for and opposition to Qaddafi received a blow when a spokesman for the Libyan oil company AGOCO said in August 2011, "We don't have a problem with western countries like Italians, French and UK companies. But we may have some political issues with Russia, China and Brazil."[34] China's instinct to support the regional status quo once again ran aground on the rocks of a changing Middle East.

The Libya lesson that Chinese decisionmakers seem to have applied to Syria, however, is that they were insufficiently opposed to international action. China has vetoed three UN Security Council Resolutions on Syria, and its calls for dialogue are consistent, regardless of the framework for such dialogue or the situation on the ground. China's Syria posture is likely guided by the geostrategic logic of supporting Russia and Iran against Western-led opposition. That support means that Bashar al-Assad is not as isolated as Qaddafi was and that Chinese policy opposing intervention in Syria is not isolated, either.

But while China remains adamant in its opposition to international military action, it has reached out to the Syrian opposition much more effectively than it did in Libya. In fact, 24 hours after China cast a UNSC veto, a Syrian opposition delegation visited Beijing at the government's invitation for consultations.[35] In China's careful fashion, one can note simultaneously that the group only met a mid-level official and did not represent a diplomatic affront to the government of Syria, and also that China has reached out actively to the potential future rulers of the country.

Overall assessment

In a perfect world, China would seem to prefer not to have a Middle East policy. Closer to home, in Asia, it knows the landscape well, it has a long history, and it occupies a dominant position. Strength in Asia propels China to the global stage, and it seems delighted at the prospect of being regarded as a near-peer of the United States. While China still feels vulnerable to American

---

[32] Graeme Smith, "China offered Gadhafi huge stockpiles of arms: Libyan memos," *Toronto Globe and Mail*, September 2, 2011, http://www.theglobeandmail.com/news/world/china-offered-gadhafi-huge-stockpiles-of-arms-libyan-memos/article1363316/.

[33] China's foreign minister hosted both Qaddhafi's foreign minister and the head of the Transitional National Council in Beijing in June 2011. See, for example, "Libya: China welcomes opposition figure Mahmud Jibril," *BBC*, June 21, 2011, http://www.bbc.co.uk/news/world-africa-13853210.

[34] Svetlana Kovalyova and Emma Farge, "ENI leads Libya oil race, rebels warn Russia, China," *Reuters*, August 22, 2011, http://www.reuters.com/article/2011/08/22/ozatp-libya-oil-idAFJOE77L0DN20110822.

[35] Yun Sun, "Syria: What China Has Learned From its Libya Experience," *Asia-Pacific Bulletin*, no. 152 (February 27, 2012), http://www.eastwestcenter.org/sites/default/files/private/apb152_1.pdf, p. 2.

might now, China also feels that power is shifting in its direction. If China could limit itself to worrying principally about Asia and the United States, it would have plenty of challenges on its hands, but it would also see the prospect of considerable reward.

And yet, it is continually drawn westward, toward more treacherous ground. For China, the Middle East is complicated, it is conflictual, it brings tremendous scrutiny, and the United States seems to have something of a home-court advantage. Chinese reliance on the Middle East highlights China's continued vulnerability to U.S. power, especially when it comes to safeguarding global trade. China's instinct is to tread lightly. As one scholar noted, "Many Chinese felt the Gulf was a 'graveyard of great powers' and they wanted to avoid getting involved. Many also understood the limits of Beijing's power and were reluctant to be involved in a region over which they had little influence."[36] And yet, China's energy consumption patterns make the region hard to avoid.

Some in China seek to equivocate, while some advocate embracing the challenge head on and adopting a can-do attitude to further Chinese interests. One of the latter is Wang Jisi, a leading Chinese academic and the dean of the School of International Studies at Beijing University. He wrote an article in October 2012 that seemed to argue for a different Chinese strategy for what the United States calls the Middle East and what Asian diplomats often call West Asia. It calls for China to turn to the Middle East with a more proactive strategy that seeks cooperation with the Western powers over shared concerns. Departing from the traditional Chinese approach, he urged "creative intervention" to further Chinese interests. His article contains an explicit call for broad investment in understanding the societies and cultures of the region and an implicit recognition that China will be reliant on the region for decades to come, while Western powers will not go away.[37]

China's hesitancy toward the Middle East is mirrored in the actions of most other powers, which see peril and uncertainty in the unfolding politics of a changing region. China, however, cannot lean away from the region's volatility; it must somehow endure it. In addition, China's growing influence in the region means that its actions—and inaction—will shape the Middle East to an unprecedented degree. China has not yet concluded what tools it has at its disposal, nor how it wishes to use them. China must make that decision soon.

---

[36] Al-Rodhan, p. 241.
[37] Wang Jisi, "March West: China's Geopolitical Strategy of Rebalancing," Wang Jisi, *Global Times*, October 17, 2012, http://opinion.huanqiu.com/opinion_world/2012-10/3193760.html.

OPENING STATEMENT OF DR. JOEL WUTHNOW
RESEARCH ANALYST, CHINA STUDIES, CNA

DR. WUTHNOW: Co-chairs and Commissioners, it's a great pleasure to be here today and I thank you for the opportunity to address the topic of China and the Middle East.

I've been asked to speak specifically about the current state of China's relations with Iran with an emphasis on China's policies and perspectives on Iran's nuclear program, and I'd like to do so by making two general observations.

My first observation is that China's relationship with Iran remains a limited partnership. On one side of the ledger, China has a relatively strong economic relationship with Iran. This includes oil exports, which, while down around 20 percent from 2011 levels, remain fairly robust; continuing investment in oil exploration and excavation activities in Iran, though these have been delayed in recent years; sales to Iran of gasoline, in addition to a wide range of manufactured products; and Chinese assistance to Iranian infrastructure development. In addition, there have been public reports of continued arms sales to Iran, though these reports are difficult to verify.

The substantial economic relationship has had negative implications for Chinese cooperation on the Iranian nuclear issue with China reluctant to approve sweeping economic sanctions against Tehran. To make matters more complicated, some Chinese firms that are already on the U.S. blacklist continue to operate in Iran. This includes the Chinese shipping firm Zhuhai Zhenrong and others.

On the other side of the ledger, China's involvement in Iran is bounded by Beijing's desire to maintain positive relations with the United States and other countries. China has been carrying out a balancing act regarding Tehran and Washington since the late '70s, and this continues on today.

In this respect, the United States has some political leverage at its disposal. For instance, President Obama's direct interventions with President Hu Jintao helped lead to China's approval for a fourth round of U.N. sanctions against Iran in 2010. President Obama has an opportunity this weekend to encourage President Xi Jinping to play an active role in the Iranian nuclear issue as well.

However, U.S. leverage on Beijing regarding Iran should not be overstated. China's economic interests in Iran remain large, and domestic politics may make it even more difficult for Beijing to make perceived concessions to the United States and its partners.

My second observation is that China's Middle East experts are debating the risks that Iran's nuclear program poses to the international community. This is important since China's risk assessments may help determine the extent to which China will work to forestall Iran's nuclear progress.

There are three areas of debate in China about Iran's nuclear program. First is about Iran's intentions. Very few Chinese analysts fully subscribe to Iran's argument that its nuclear program is peaceful in nature. Nevertheless, there's a range of opinion in China about whether and when Iran may cross the nuclear threshold with some more alarmed than others.

Second is about the risks of nuclear proliferation in the region. Some Chinese analysts doubt that Iran's nuclear program will spark a regional arms race, but others are more concerned. For instance, one security expert at the influential Central Party School argues that Iran's nuclear program may cause a chain reaction of proliferation in the region, and that new conflicts may envelop the whole region. However, this assessment is rejected by other analysts.

Third concerns the risk that Israel or the United States may use military force. Regarding the United States, a majority of PRC analysts seem to doubt that the U.S. would be willing to enter into another war in the Middle East, though a few believe that the U.S. may use force as a last resort.

Opinions about Israel are mixed. For instance, one Middle East expert at the China Institute for Contemporary International Relations writes that Israel, facing a grave threat and leery about the chances of negotiation as well as sanctions, could be tempted to use unilateral force to resolve the issue. However, other Chinese analysts remain skeptical about Israel's willingness to use force.

For the United States, there may be an opportunity to inform China's internal risk assessments encouraging more accurate risk assessments that acknowledge the dangers posed by Iran's nuclear program. The goal would be to convince China that its own interests require a more proactive bilateral and multilateral approach to addressing the Iranian nuclear issue, just as China seems to have been adjusting its course on North Korea.

The Congress should emphasize the following three points to Chinese interlocutors and ensure that the administration is doing the same:

First, Iran may be nearing a nuclear weapons capability. This could damage China's own interests in a nuclear nonproliferation regime that protects China's own rights to possess nuclear weapons.

Second, Iran's behavior may precipitate a regional arms race, which would create instability in the region. This, too, would harm China's interests by potentially destabilizing an area of the world critical to China's energy security.

Third, and last, there is a serious risk that if left unchecked, Israel or the United States may be tempted to use military force. This would also harm China's interests by threatening Chinese continued access to Iranian and Middle Eastern oil.

In conclusion, it is accurate to describe the China-Iran relationship as a limited partnership. However, beyond this limited partnership are debates within China about the risks associated with Iran's nuclear program. The U.S., including the Congress, should take steps to emphasize the very real dangers that Iran poses, both to the international community and to China's own interests in the region.

Thank you very much, and I look forward to your questions.

PREPARED STATEMENT OF DR. JOEL WUTHNOW
RESEARCH ANALYST, CHINA STUDIES, CNA

China and the Iran Nuclear Issue: Beyond the Limited Partnership
Joel Wuthnow, Ph.D.
CNA China Studies
wuthnowj@cna.org

Testimony before the U.S.-China Security and Economic Review Commission
Hearing on "China and the Middle East"
June 6, 2013

Co-chairs and members of the commission: thank you for the opportunity to testify today about China's role and interests in the Middle East, focusing on China-Iran relations. This is a topic of interest to me as a research analyst in the China Studies division at CNA, a federally-funded research and development center in Alexandria, Virginia.

In recent years, China has held a limited partnership with Iran. For Beijing, this partnership has involved an attempt to balance economic opportunities in Iran with the imperative to maintain positive relations with the United States and others. However, a key variable – one that is often overlooked by observers – is Chinese risk assessments concerning Iran's nuclear program. For the United States, there may be opportunities to inform and broaden China's consideration of the risks that Iran's nuclear program pose to China's own interests in the Middle East.

China's Limited Partnership with Iran

As several analysts in the United States have argued, China's contemporary relations with Iran can be characterized as a "limited partnership."[1] This partnership has two central features: (1) a desire by the PRC to seize economic opportunities, especially in the oil and gas sectors; and (2) an opposing need not to upset relations with the United States. This section briefly discusses both features.

Economic Opportunities

Economic opportunities sought by the PRC in recent years include the following:

- *Oil exports*. Despite fluctuation over the past year, Iran remains a key supplier to China. In 2011, China averaged a purchase of 555,000 barrels/day (bpd), a figure that dropped in early 2012 to 345,000 due to contract disputes between Chinese and Iranian state oil

---

[1] See, for example: Marybeth Davis, et al., "China-Iran: A Limited Partnership," a report prepared by CENTRA Technologies, Inc., for the US-China Economic and Security Review Commission (October 2012); Scott Harold and Alireza Nader, "China and Iran: Economic, Political, and Military Relations," RAND *Occasional Paper*, 2012; and John W. Garver, *China & Iran: Ancient Partners in a Post-Imperial World* (Seattle: University of Washington Press, 2006).

firms. By the first quarter of 2013, the figure had rebounded to 410,000 bpd. Iran remains China's third-largest supplier of oil, behind Saudi Arabia and Angola.[2] In addition to economic motives, analysts point to a strategic rationale for China's continuing energy relationship with Iran. As Harold and Nader argue, Iran may be a "supplier unlikely to be intimidated into cutting oil exports to China in the event of a U.S.-Chinese military conflict."[3]

- *Upstream investment*. China has been a key investor in oil exploration and excavation activities in Iran, including major investments in the Yadavaran and Azadegan oil fields by Chinese national oil companies. China has also reportedly considered expanding its involvement in Iran's petrochemical sector, especially in methanol production. Nevertheless, analysts have noted limitations on Chinese investments in upstream activities. As Downs and Maloney point out, this is associated with "tough operating environments and diplomatic sensitivities."[4] These factors were apparent in China's long-delayed participation in developing the South Pars natural gas field, involvement that was ultimately terminated in April 2013.

- *Manufactured goods*. China's overall trade volume with Iran rose from $10.1 billion in 2005 to $29.4 billion in 2010. Aside from the energy sector, much of this growth occurred in Chinese sales of manufactured goods, such as electronics, toys, and clothing. Under pressure from the United States, Chinese firms Huawei and ZTE, which have been condemned for providing surveillance technology to the Iranian regime, have both said they would curtail business activities in Iran. In addition to these products, China has also been a key supplier of gasoline to Iran, whose oil refinery capabilities are limited.

- *Infrastructure development*. Over the past two decades, China has contributed to several key infrastructure projects in Iran, with notable contributions to Tehran's subway system, as well as dams, bridges, and other infrastructure.

- *Arms sales*. Comparatively little is known about the nature of China's arms sales to Iran. There have been reports that China has sold anti-ship cruise missiles to Iran through 2012,[5] as well as indications that a state-owned Chinese firm has attempted to sell anti-aircraft missiles to Iran in March 2013.[6] However, the veracity of these reports, as well as the possible economic or strategic motives behind any ongoing arms relationship between the two countries, is uncertain.

- *Nuclear technology*. Although China's formal involvement in Iran's nuclear program ceased in the 1990s, there have been periodic reports that Chinese firms have supplied dual use technologies. John Garver writes that China may have a motive to facilitate a

---

[2] Data courtesy of the U.S. Energy Information Administration, online at: http://www.eia.gov/countries/cab.cfm?fips=CH.
[3] Harold and Nader (2012), p. 18.
[4] Downs and Maloney (2011), p. 3.
[5] SIPRI arms transfer database. Available online at: http://www.sipri.org/databases/armstransfers
[6] Robert F. Worth and C.J. Chivers, "Seized Chinese Weapons Raise Concerns on Iran," *New York Times*, March 2, 2013.

nuclear Iran since this could be a "a valuable check on U.S. influence in the Persian Gulf and move the world in the direction of multi-polarity."[7] However, the extent of potential Chinese violations of international sanctions is unclear.

In the context of the nuclear issue, China's economic interests in Iran have posed challenges for international cooperation. This is apparent in two respects. First, China has been reluctant to approve UN sanctions that target Iran's economy, including limiting Iran's access to capital markets, placing embargoes on Iran's shipping and air cargo industries, and toughening measures on foreign insurance of oil imports and exports.[8] Second, as Downs and Maloney point out, China's incentives to sanction Iran beyond those imposed by the Security Council are limited, especially in terms of reducing investments in Iran's energy sector and reducing sales of gasoline to Iran.[9]

Beyond these two areas, it is also possible that Chinese firms are violating UN sanctions, such as in sales of proscribed weapons and dual-use technology. However, public reporting on these issues is limited, and the role of the Chinese state, as opposed to individual firms, in any reported violations is difficult to determine.

Part of the U.S. approach to the Iran nuclear issue has been targeting PRC firms that do business with Iran, either legally or in violation of international sanctions. In some cases, including pressure against Huawei and ZTE, this approach has been successful. In other cases, the effects have been limited. For instance, Chinese shipping firm Zhuhai Zhenrong is already on the U.S. "blacklist," yet continues to be heavily involved in transporting oil due to profit motives.

Relations with the United States

On the opposite side of the ledger, China's partnership with Iran has been limited by Beijing's need to maintain positive relations with the United States. John Garver concludes that China's ties with Iran are a "second-order" relationship, surpassed in importance by its primary relations with the United States. As evidence, Garver chronicles how China's broader goals of economic and political cooperation with the United States led Beijing to eliminate formal cooperation in nuclear and missile programs with Iran in the mid-1990s, even though concerns remained about illicit cooperation between the two in these areas.[10]

More recently, the influence of the United States was apparent in China's decisions to support UN Security Council sanctions against Iran in 2010.[11] This episode is worth recounting because it illustrates that sustained high-level diplomacy by the United States can contribute to changes in Beijing's decision-making with respect to Iran.

---

[7] John Garver, "Is China Playing a Dual Game in Iran?" *The Washington Quarterly* 34:1 (Winter 2011), pp. 76-7.

[8] For more details, see: Joel Wuthnow, *Chinese Diplomacy and the UN Security Council* (New York: Routledge, 2012), pp. 85-7.

[9] Downs and Maloney (2011).

[10] Ibid, pp. 216-236.

[11] This section draws heavily from Joel Wuthnow, *Chinese Diplomacy and the UN Security Council* (New York: Routledge, 2012), pp. 87-92.

After international negotiations on Iran's nuclear program stalled in 2009, the United States opted to pursue a fourth round of UN Security Council sanctions. This measure was intended to pressure Tehran to comply with International Atomic Energy Agency verification requirements. In late 2009, U.S. officials began a diplomatic push for Chinese support at the UN. The argument of officials such as Kurt Campbell, Jeffrey Bader, and Hillary Clinton, was that China should agree to sanctions due to Iran's continued violation of IAEA requirements, the threat to regional stability posed by Iran's ongoing nuclear program, and the desire by many within the region for stronger international pressure against Tehran.

Despite some delays, China began to shift from its earlier opposition to sanctions in early March 2010. At that time, observers argued that China believed it had "overreached" in several aspects of its broader relationship with the United States, including its responses to several controversies: namely, those involving U.S. arms sales to Taiwan, the visit of the Dalai Lama to Washington, and alleged cyber-attacks on Google. These issues were compounded by the sense in the United States and elsewhere that China's foreign policy was becoming overly "assertive."

In mid-March 2010, President Obama became personally involved in efforts to gain China's support for sanctions, intervening on three occasions. First, President Obama held a long exchange with incoming Chinese ambassador Zhang Yesui, following the latter's credentialing ceremony at the White House, repeating the United States request for Chinese support. Second, on April 1, the President held an hour-long phone conversation with Chinese President Hu Jintao, underscoring the "importance of working together to ensure that Iran lives up to its international obligations."[12] Third, Obama met with Hu on the sidelines of the Nuclear Security Summit in Washington, reportedly indicating that the United States would take steps to mitigate risks to China's oil supply in the event of a crisis in Iran. The day following Obama's final encounter with Hu, China's deputy foreign minister, Cui Tiankai, promised that China would be open to "new ideas" regarding sanctions, and a day after that substantive negotiations on the text of a fourth resolution had begun at the Security Council.[13]

This sequence of events, coupled with the timing of China's acquiescence to sanctions, suggests that – along with other factors, such as a "watering down" of the final UN resolution in ways that protected key Chinese economic interests – U.S. diplomacy helped promote a shift in Chinese opposition to sanctions. Hence, in some circumstances, pressure from the United States may be effective in encouraging China to support stronger measures against Iran.

Nevertheless, there are three limits to this argument. First, the circumstances that facilitated President Obama's diplomatic success in 2010 (including support for sanctions among several Arab states, in addition to Russia, Israel, and the EU) may be unlikely to repeat themselves in future episodes. Second, despite fluctuations, China retains strong economic interests in Iran and may be unwilling to support more invasive sanctions that threaten those interests. Third, for domestic political reasons, China's new leadership may be unwilling to acquiesce in the face of perceived demands from Washington.

---

[12] "Readout of President Obama's Call with President Hu of China," *US Fed News*, April 3, 2010.
[13] "Six Major Powers to Resume Bargaining on UN Iran Sanctions," *AFP*, April 14, 2010.

Beyond the Limited Partnership: China's Debate about Iran's Nuclear Program

In addition to economic opportunities and relations with the United States, there is a third factor that may influence China's decision-making regarding Iran's nuclear program. This is the perception of Chinese leaders on the risks posed by Iran's continued nuclear development. Greater alarm in Beijing regarding Iran's intentions, the potential for a destabilizing arms race in the Middle East, and the chances of a U.S. or Israeli air strike may each affect China's willingness to accept international sanctions or exert bilateral pressure on Tehran to comply with IAEA requirements.

This section discusses debates within China about how to assess the risks associated with Iran's nuclear program.[14] Surveying the views of PRC analysts who may be influencing leadership perceptions, it demonstrates that there is a range of views on each of the topics mentioned above. The conclusion is that there may be opportunities for the United States and others to continue to persuade Chinese interlocutors of the risks that Iran's behavior could pose to regional security, and thus to China's own interests in Iran and the region.

Risks to the Non-Proliferation Regime

Not all Chinese political and military analysts—including those who may be informing key PRC leaders on how to approach Iran—submit that Iran is taking steps to develop nuclear weapons. However, very few Chinese analysts contend that Iran's nuclear program is of a purely peaceful character.

In general, Chinese analysts contend that there is a strategic rationale for Iran's nuclear program, but refrain from making predictions about whether Iran will actually acquire a nuclear weapons capability. This theme is evident in three examples:

- Ding Gong, a researcher at the influential Central Party School in Beijing, notes that Iran occupies a "precarious geostrategic situation," characterized by "few allies and many potential enemies," and asserts that Iran's "desire to recover past glories" is motivating its nuclear program. Ding also writes that Iran lacks the plutonium or highly-enriched uranium to produce a warhead, though warns that Iran's abundant uranium mines would be a valuable source of raw inputs should a sufficient enrichment capacity exist. However, Ding does not predict whether Iran will ultimately seek a nuclear weapons capability.[15]

- Jin Liangxiang, a Middle East specialist at the Shanghai Institutes of International Studies, argues that, as a "rational country," Iran knows that it will "pay a big economic, political and military price for crossing the red line," but also notes that, with an elevation

---

[14] This section draws heavily from Joel Wuthnow, "Pessimism without Alarm: Chinese Perceptions of Iran's Nuclear Program since mid-2010," paper presented at the American Political Science Association, September 2011. It also includes more recent sources.
[15] Ding Gong, "Cong Yilang he wenti kan Yilang de diqu daguo yishi," (Viewing Iran's Regional Great Power Ideology Through The Iranian Nuclear Problem), *Alabo Shijie Yanjiu* (Arab World Studies), 4 (2010): 48-49.

in uranium enrichment levels to 20%, "the possibility of Iran being able to produce nuclear weapons is increasing."[16]

- Gao Xintao, a lecturer at the PLA's Nanjing Army Command College, makes a slightly more nuanced argument. His argument is that, by drawing near to, but not actually crossing, the nuclear threshold, Iran can accomplish two goals: enhancing its bargaining leverage vis-à-vis the P5+1 and others, and mitigating the risks of a preemptive military strike. A decision to move from a potential to an actual weapons capability would result from "short-term factors," though Gao does not specify what those conditions might be.[17] In a separate article, Gao explains how national pride, domestic politics, geostrategic pressures, and historical experiences all inform Tehran's motives, though concludes only that a nuclear weapons aim is "within the range of the strategic thinking of Iran's ruling elite."[18]

Despite the skepticism apparent among Chinese security experts regarding Iran's stated goals of peaceful nuclear development, only a few PRC analysts go so far as to conclude that Iran is developing a nuclear weapons capability. One prominent Middle East expert who I interviewed in Beijing in 2012, for instance, argued that Iran is developing an "Islamic bomb," which could allow Tehran to claim the mantle of the "#1 power in the Middle East." However, this appears to be a minority perspective.

Although several Chinese analysts have doubted the sincerity of Iran's claims that its nuclear program serves peaceful purposes, very few in China have publicly considered the implications this poses for the strength of the international non-proliferation regime. Specifically, a weakening of the regime may encourage other countries to reject the authority of the IAEA and relevant international conventions, which in turn protect China's own status as a member of the nuclear club. Thus, there may be room to continue to inform China's debate by elaborating on the possible consequences of Iranian violations for China's interests in a stable non-proliferation regime.

Proliferation Risks

---

[16] Jin Liangxiang, "Yi he wenti jiqi dui diqu he daguo guanxi de yingxiang," (The influence of the Iran Nuclear Program on Regional and Great Power Relations), *Guoji Zhanwang* (World Outlook) 2 (2011): 64.

[17] Gao Xintao, "YaFei fazhanzhong daguo he xuanze de tedian: zhanlüe cengmian de kaocha," (Aspects of Nuclear Choices by Developing Great Powers in Asia and Africa: A Strategic-level Investigation) in *Guoji Luntan* (International Forum) 13 (2011): 1-7. Similarly, a prominent Middle East expert told me in February 2012 that Iran was aiming for "strategic ambiguity" about its ultimate aims, primarily as a way to extract bargaining concessions without paying the costs associated with a nuclear test.

[18] Gao Xintao, "Guojia anquan, guoji shengwang, heneng liyong yu guonei zhengzhi: yilang qiangli tuijin he kaifa de dongyin," (National Security, International Reputation, Nuclear Energy Use and Domestic Politics: The Motives Behind Iran's Aggressive Nuclear Development), in *Sichuan Shifan Daxue Xuebao* (Journal of Sichuan Normal University) 38 (2011): 19-25. Among the historical factors Gao cites is Iran's experience as the subject of Iraqi chemical weapons use during the Iran-Iraq War which, Gao argues, could motivate Tehran to develop a nuclear deterrent.

Regarding the risk that an Iranian nuclear weapons capability may spark a destabilizing arms race in the Middle East, Chinese analysts have exhibited a range of views. Some are relatively dismissive of the problem, while others are more concerned.

Li Baolin, a researcher at Fudan University, is a representative optimist. Li's argument is that the problem is confined to Saudi Arabia and Egypt, since others, such as Qatar and the UAE, have "fairly good" relations with Iran. Even then, the risks are mitigated by the fact that the technological base of the Gulf States is "too weak to support a [viable] nuclear program."[19] Buttressing this view, a prominent scholar told me in Beijing in 2012 that Iraq was "too weak" to pursue a credible program, Turkey would opt not to because of NATO security guarantees, and Saudi Arabia probably would not due to close ties with the U.S.[20]

Other writers express greater concern about proliferation:

- Ding Gong, an expert at the Central Party School, argues that Iranian acquisition of nuclear weapons would cause a "chain reaction" in the Gulf and as a result, "new conflicts may envelop the whole region."[21] Despite its professions of peaceful intentions and efforts to develop positive ties, according to Ding, Iran is still treated with distrust. Egypt, in particular, would view an Iranian nuclear weapon as an "assault on the fragile balance of power," a sense likely to be shared by Saudi Arabia and other Gulf states. Still, Ding allows that regional actors are unlikely to nuclearize while international talks are ongoing; this option would only be utilized as a "Plan B" if talks fail.[22]

- Yin Gang, a noted Middle East expert at the Chinese Academy of Social Sciences, writes that a nuclear Iran would "lead to a new balance of power in the Middle East and a very hard-to-control nuclear competition."[23] Yin also told a journalist in June 2010 that he feared an Iranian bomb would precipitate "a big war in the Middle East."[24] In an interview, another scholar feared that Arab states might be tempted to work towards an "Arab bomb" as a means of "balancing nuclear threats [from both Iran and Israel] and ensuring security."[25]

A slightly different version of this negative assessment is offered by Niu Song, a professor at the Shanghai International Studies University. Niu shares the view that an Iranian bomb would create insecurity in the Arab world. Niu writes that, "Iran is the greatest security threat to the

[19] Li Baolin, "Alabo guojia yu yilang he wenti," (Arab States and the Iran Nuclear Issue), in *Guoji Ziliao Xinxi* (International Data Information), 1 (2011): 3.
[20] Interview with scholar, February 2012.
[21] Ding, "Cong yilang he wenti kan Yilang de diqu daguo yishi," 48-5.
[22] Ibid, 50. In addition, Ding argues that the "power vacuum" left in the Gulf as a result of a drawdown of U.S. forces in Iraq will precipitate even greater insecurity among regional actors. Similarly, one of my interlocutors argued that there are not likely to be any "proliferation consequences" if Iran stays within the "red lines," meaning maintaining contacts with the IAEA and refraining from testing a nuclear device. Interview with scholar, February 2012.
[23] Yin Gang, "Yilang he wenti de shizhi shi yilang de guojia diwei wenti," (The Essence of the Iran Nuclear Problem is the Problem of Iran's National Status), *Dangdai Shiejie* (Contemporary World), 5 (2010): 51.
[24] Peter Ford, "At Shanghai Expo, Ahmadinejad Polite Despite China's Support for Iran Sanctions," *Christian Science Monitor*, June 10, 2010. See also, Swaine, "Beijing's Tightrope Walk on Iran," n48.
[25] Interview with scholar, February 2012.

Arab states and Israel, and it is unlikely that this threat will soon disappear."[26] However, the consequence of this shared threat perception is not necessarily nuclear proliferation—no specific opinion is offered one way or the other—but rather a tightening of political and military cooperation between the U.S., Israel and the Gulf Cooperation Council (GCC), as well as a closer relationship between Iraq and the GCC.[27] What this might mean for regional stability is left unstated.

Although some Chinese analysts accept the premise that an Iranian nuclear weapon might spark a regional arms race, few have publicly discussed whether and how such an outcome may damage China's own interests. While this lack of discussion may be due to sensitivity concerns, it may also reflect insufficient attention in China to the risks of a regional arms race, and lack of adequate attention to how such an outcome would negatively impact China's own interests in regional stability. Thus, there may be an opportunity to inform opinion within the PRC about the implications of a regional arms race.

Risks of U.S. or Israeli Military Action

A third risk assessment concerns the chances that United States or Israel may take military action to prevent Iran from acquiring a nuclear weapons capability. In this respect, Chinese analysts have come to a range of conclusions.

Several Chinese analysts argue that the United States may use force to prevent Iran from acquiring nuclear weapons:

- Gao Zugui, a Middle East specialist at the China Institute for Contemporary International Relations (CICIR), writes that Iran's "stridency" raises the chance for "a more hardline military solution" by narrowing President Obama's political and diplomatic options.[28]

- Tian Wenlin, another scholar at CICIR, argues that the war in Libya has increased the "appetite and confidence" of the United States to continue armed intervention in the Middle East. Tian describes the current similar as analogous to the period of saber-rattling towards Iraq in early 2003.[29]

[26] Niu, "Yilang yinsu dui Yiselie-Haihehui guojia guanxi de yingxiang," 115.

[27] The current members of the GCC are Bahrain, Kuwait, Oman, Qatar, Saudi Arabia and the UAE. Iraq's ties to the organization as an "associate member" were discontinued after the first Gulf War.

[28] Gao Zugui, "Aobama zhengfu Zhongdong zhengce," (Comments on the Obama Administration's Middle East Policy) in *Heping yu Fazhan* (Peace and Development), 6 (2010): 17. Similarly, Wang Liping and Xia Shi, professors at Jiujiang University in Jiangxi province, contend that, "the U.S. is clearly unwilling to tolerate a nuclear Iran," and that "a military attack is certainly an option." This, they argue, would have deleterious results for China, which would see its access to energy resources threatened. Wang Liping and Xia Shi, "He anquan beijing xia de Yilang he wenti yu Zhongguo waijiao zhanlüe xuanze," (The Iran Nuclear Problem in the Context of Nuclear Security and China's Strategic Options) in *Guoji Zhengzhi* (International Politics), 6 (2010): 60.

[29] Liu Qiang, et al., "Yilang 'he weiji' de shizhi yu qianjing" (The Substance and Prospects of the Iran 'Nuclear Crisis'") in *Shijie Jingji yu Zhengzhi Luntan* (Forum of World Economics and Politics), 2 (2012), pp. 171-2.

- Xu Jin, a scholar at the Chinese Academy of Social Sciences, makes a similar point by observing that the U.S. is preparing for a strike by enhancing missile defense cooperation with GCC states and deploying Blu-110 and -117 "bunker buster" bombs to a naval base in the Indian Ocean, which could be used to execute an attack on Iran's hardened and underground nuclear facilities. However, Xu cautions that "none of this means that the U.S. will definitely start a war."[30]

However, Chinese experts dismiss the possibility that the United States will use force. For instance, Liu Qiang, a researcher at the PLA Institute of International Relations (which is affiliated with the General Staff Department's military intelligence bureau), provides four reasons why the United States will not militarily intervene: (1) the U.S. public will not support a ground war in Iran, (2) the United States fears Iranian retaliation, such as a decision by Tehran to attempt to close the Strait of Hormuz, (3) the political influence of Iranian-Americans will militate against the use of force, and (4) the United States will be unwilling to face the long-term costs of reconstruction, especially after experiences in Iraq and Afghanistan. Rather, Liu states, the United States wishes to "win without fighting" (不战而胜) in Iran.[31]

Similarly, Jin Liangxiang, a Middle East scholar at the Shanghai Institutes for International Studies, argues that, after the tolls inflicted by the Iraq and Afghanistan wars, combined with the effects of the global recession, the U.S. will not want to get "mired" in another regional conflict.[32]

As regards Israel, some Chinese analysts concede that Tel Aviv views Iran as an "existential threat," and may thus be willing to use force for survival purposes:

- Tang Zhichao, a Middle East researcher at the CICIR, writes that, "Israel, facing a grave threat and leery about the chances of negotiations as well as sanctions, could be tempted to use unilateral force to resolve the issue."[33]

- Hua Liming, a former PRC envoy to Iran, told a reporter that, "Israel is more pressing than the U.S. in preventing Iran from acquiring nuclear arms, and its military strike preparations are more realistic."[34] Hua also mentioned reports that Israeli officials have conducted secret negotiations with Riyadh about permission to use Saudi airspace in any attack."[35]

---

[30] Xu, "Yilang he wenti 'he' qu 'he' cong," 2. Xu was referring to reports in the spring of 2010 that the U.S. had deployed these munitions to its naval facility at Diego Garcia in preparation for potential airstrikes on Iran. For details, see: "Report: U.S. Positioning 'Bunker-Busters' for Possible Iran Strike," *Haaretz*, March 17, 2010.
[31] Ibid, p. 172.
[32] Jin, "Yi he wenti jiqi dui diqu he daguo guanxi de yingxiang," 71-2.
[33] Tang Zhichao, "Yilang he tanpan chongqi duihua jiejue xianxinji," (A New Vehicle to Restart the Iran Nuclear Negotiations) in *Zhongguo Shehui Kexue Bao* (Chinese Social Sciences Today), 14 (2010): 1.
[34] Chen Xiaru, "Former PRC Envoy Views Possible Iran Retaliation Against U.S.-Israel Strike," *Zhongguo Qingnian Bao* (China Youth Daily), August 3, 2010. Accessed through World News Connection.
[35] Hua was likely referring to a 2009 report, which indicated that Israeli officials believed they had been granted tacit approval from Riyadh for raids on Iranian nuclear facilities. See: Uzi Mahnaimi and Sarah Baxter, "Saudis Give Nod to Israeli Raid on Iran," *The Sunday Times* (London), July 5, 2009.

However, other Chinese observers point to the difficulties inherent in an Israeli strike. One argument is that, whatever Tel Aviv's intent, the U.S., seeking to avoid another hot conflict in the region, will be able to prevent Israel from acting. Xu Jin, a scholar at the Chinese Academy of Social Sciences, writes that, "Israel's behavior depends entirely on the acquiescence and authorization of the U.S.," which will likely say "no" as long as diplomatic options remain.[36] A second argument concerns feasibility. Gao Xintao, a researcher at the PLA Nanjing Army Command Academy, writes that Iran would likely retaliate with ballistic missiles and that, in any event, an attack would only delay, and not halt, Iran's progress.[37]

Although some Chinese analysts argue that the United States or Israel may use military force, the potential consequences for Chinese interests are usually unstated. An exception is a report by the Center for National Defense Policy Studies at the Academy of Military Sciences, which notes that an "Iran crisis" is among those with the potential to have an "immense influence on China's oil supplies and prices." Moreover, the report notes that the Strait of Hormuz and other sea lines of communication are "lifelines for China's energy resources," exacerbating the vulnerability of China's economy to a potential military clash in the Middle East.[38]

Nevertheless, there may be an opportunity to inform Chinese views regarding the risks that unchecked Iranian nuclear development may lead to military conflict. Specifically, it may be possible to present detailed evidence about the risks that such a conflict would bring to the global economy, and to China's economic interests energy security throughout the region. If the PRC is alarmed that Washington or Israel may act militarily, Beijing may take more proactive steps to increase pressure on Tehran to comply with IAEA requirements.

Implications for the United States

The preceding analysis demonstrates that there is an ongoing discussion within China about the risks associated with Iran's nuclear program. For the United States, there may be an opportunity to inform this debate in order to emphasize the risks that Iran's nuclear program poses to regional security – and to China's own interests.

Indeed, this approach may have advantages over other policy tools, such as sanctioning PRC firms that invest in Iran (which may be ineffective) and leveraging the broader U.S. relationship (which may come at a high political cost). Conversely, encouraging more accurate risk assessments in China, including emphasizing the potential implications for China's own interests, may be a useful way to elicit broader Chinese cooperation in dealing with Tehran.

Specific steps that the United States Congress should take include the following:

---

[36] Xu, "Yilang he wenti 'he' qu 'he' cong," 2.

[37] Gao Xintao, "Yilang dui hebukuosan jizhi de renzhi jiqi genyuan," (Israel's Understanding of Nuclear Non-Proliferation Mechanisms And Its Roots) in *Alabo Shijie Yanjiu* (Arab World Studies), 5 (2010): 31-3.

[38] Major General Chen Zhou (ed.), *Strategic Review 2011* (Beijing: Academy of Military Sciences, 2012), pp. 71-2.

1. **Investigate whether the administration has been identifying and utilizing opportunities to inform Chinese risk assessments regarding Iran**. As stated above, the Obama administration has emphasized the risks posed by Iran's nuclear program in prior diplomatic interactions with the PRC. However, the Congress should investigate whether the administration has continued to identify and seize the full range of opportunities to inform Chinese risks assessments in the following areas:

   a. Evidence that Iran's intentions are not peaceful and the argument that Iranian pursuit of nuclear weapons would endanger PRC interests in a credible non-proliferation regime;

   b. Evidence that Iranian development of nuclear weapons may incite an arms race in the Middle East, which may endanger China's interests in regional stability; and

   c. Evidence that the United States and Israel may be able and willing to use force to respond to Iranian nuclear development, which would may result in a serious threat to China's energy security.

2. **Emphasize the risks of Iran's nuclear program in Congressional delegations to China and other countries.** Congressional delegations should seize opportunities to present evidence to Chinese interlocutors that strengthen and broaden perspectives in the PRC that the Iranian nuclear program may have negative consequences for regional security, and for China's own interests. In addition, Congressional delegations to other countries (such as Israel) should encourage those states to make similar arguments to Chinese officials and influential experts.

OPENING STATEMENT OF DR. ANDREW ERICKSON
ASSOCIATE PROFESSOR AND FOUNDING MEMBER
CHINA MARITIME STUDIES, U.S. NAVAL WAR COLLEGE

DR. ERICKSON: Chairmen Fiedler and Talent, Commissioners, I greatly appreciate this opportunity to discuss the timely subject of Chinese naval operations in the Middle East.

My testimony reflects my personal views and not the policies or estimates of the U.S. Navy or any other organization of the U.S. government.

It draws on research I've conducted with my colleague Austin Strange. We're about to publish a detailed monograph entitled "No Substitute for Experience: Chinese Anti-Piracy Operations in the Gulf of Aden." I'll focus on the key points here, and my written statement contains further details and answers to your other questions.

To date, antipiracy deployments have constituted China's primary naval presence in the Middle East. Over the past four years, the People's Liberation Army Navy, or PLAN, has deployed nearly 10,000 personnel in 14 task forces to protect more than 5,000 Chinese and foreign commercial vessels.

Chinese citizens living abroad number over five million and counting. In 2011, in the PLAN's first noncombatant evacuation operation overseas, it dispatched a frigate to symbolically oversee the seaborne component of China's evacuation of all 35,000 Chinese nationals from Libya. Meanwhile, in the PLA Air Force's first operational deployment overseas, it evacuated Chinese citizens from central Libya via transports.

This is part of a larger pattern far from China, particularly in distant seas or what Chinese strategists call "Far Seas." Beijing is making increasing, but still relatively modest, efforts to address challenges from non-state actors there. The Far Seas contain far more internationally-shared interests and cooperation than what Chinese strategists term the "Near Seas"--the Yellow, East and South China Seas--home to all China's outstanding island and maritime claims.

Lacking both interests and capabilities to pursue a comprehensive U.S.-style approach, China appears to be building a limited expeditionary capability best suited for handling nontraditional security missions.

China's antipiracy mission: offers new irreplaceable naval training and experience; forces personnel to address unpredictable situations; catalyzes development of skill sets critical for long-distance operations; stimulates unprecedented real-time coordination among the PLAN and other agencies; increases the PLAN's confidence and bureaucratic influence; and offers tentative indications of Beijing's approach to maritime governance as a great power.

For instance, mounting operational costs may stimulate gradual development of overseas access points.

The impact on international security thus far, while modest, is largely positive, in my view.

China has reached a level of aggregate national power at which it would be ineffectual for the U.S. to simply oppose all Chinese actions with which it is not entirely satisfied. In many cases, no amount of lecturing will change Chinese behavior.

With respect to communications, Washington's focus should instead be on ensuring U.S. and allied taxpayers and voters are fully informed and, hence, willing to continue robust military spending so that the U.S. approaches interactions with China from a point of strength. The Commission continues to play an important role in this regard.

With respect to actions vis-à-vis China, the U.S. must prioritize its interests vis-à-vis Beijing and support them with resources rather than just rhetoric. Washington should support positive Chinese approaches to cooperation and oppose specific negative Chinese approaches through a coordinated whole-of-government approach.

U.S. policy should emphasize thwarting Chinese attempts to carve out a zone of exceptionalism in the Near Seas within which existing international law and other norms do not apply and where China would have a freer hand to use the threat, or actual employment, of force to coerce its neighbors into resolving disputes in Beijing's favor.

Accomplishing this requires an Asia-Pacific rebalancing that is comprehensive, credible and sustained. In other words, properly funded. Here ship numbers will speak much louder than sermons or sound bites, both to China and perhaps equally importantly to longstanding and newly emerging U.S. partners in the region.

Generally speaking, China's Far Seas activities should be viewed as potentially far more positive--and as far more vulnerable to disruption-- than those in the Near Seas. Rather than involving nationalistic claims, they target non-state actors who threaten not only Chinese lives, property, and prosperity, but also those of other nations.

Far Seas military operations occur far from China's homeland with its extensive secure communications, logistics, and defenses. They are thus relatively unprotected, particularly vis-à-vis any fixed overseas access points that China may develop.

These key dynamics suggest the following policy recommendations, in my view:

One, encourage reduced Chinese free-riding in the Far Seas. The essence of U.S. concern with respect to Chinese Far Seas operations should not be an overactive China overall, but rather a "selfish superpower" China that husbands its military energies for Near Seas coercion.

Two, welcome constructive contributions but don't fixate on form. In keeping with its imperative to prioritize interests, the U.S. should show flexibility vis-à-vis Chinese actions that are largely positive in their impact.

Three, expand Far Seas cooperation as feasible. A key question for U.S.-China relations will be to what extent the two Pacific powers can broaden Far Seas cooperation amid ongoing Near Seas differences. Given China's Near Seas focus, this question will be answered largely in Beijing.

Thank you very much for your time. I look forward to your questions and insights.

PREPARED STATEMENT OF DR. ANDREW ERICKSON
ASSOCIATE PROFESSOR AND FOUNDING MEMBER
CHINA MARITIME STUDIES, U.S. NAVAL WAR COLLEGE

A Statement before the U.S.-China Economic and Security Review Commission, Panel III: "China's Political and Security Challenges in the Middle East," "China and the Middle East" hearing, Washington, DC, 6 June 2013

Andrew S. Erickson, Associate Professor, Naval War College

My testimony reflects my personal views and not the policies or estimates of the U.S. Navy or any other organization of the U.S. government.

It draws on research I have conducted with my colleague Austin Strange. We are about to publish a detailed monograph entitled **"No Substitute for Experience: Chinese Anti-Piracy Operations in the Gulf of Aden."**[581]

To date, antipiracy deployments have constituted China's primary naval presence in the Middle East. Over the past four years, in fourteen task forces, the People's Liberation Army Navy (PLAN) has deployed nearly ten thousand personnel on more than two dozen warships with more than two dozen helicopters. Through more than five hundred escorts, these forces have protected more than five thousand commercial vessels—Chinese and foreign in nearly equal proportion, the latter flagged by more than fifty nations.

Over 5 million Chinese citizens live abroad, a number that is rising rapidly. Strongly connected to the PRC in many cases, they, like their compatriots back home, have rising expectations of governmental protection in crises. As the Qaddafi regime fell to rebels, on 24 February 2011 the PLAN ordered guided-missile frigate *Xuzhou* to separate from the seventh antipiracy task force in the Gulf of Aden (GoA) and symbolically oversee the seaborne component of the evacuation of all 35,000 Chinese nationals from Libya. On 1 March, *Xuzhou* escorted a chartered civilian vessel transporting Chinese evacuees in the PLAN's first noncombatant evacuation operation overseas. In its first operational deployment overseas, on 28 February 2011 the PLA Air Force (PLAAF) dispatched transports to evacuate Chinese citizens from central Libya. Over 40 sorties, it evacuated 1,655 people (including 240 Nepalese) to Sudan, and returned 287 Chinese onward to China. Following the 5 October 2011 murder of 13 Chinese sailors on Chinese cargo vessels *Hua Ping* and *Yu Xing 8* in the Mekong River, a People's Armed Police (PAP) border unit began joint riverine patrols with Thai, Lao and Burmese counterparts in December 2011. As Beijing's 2013 Defense White Paper emphasizes, safeguarding its nationals abroad is a growing priority for China; it devotes three paragraphs to "Protecting Overseas Interests."[2]

---

[1] Andrew S. Erickson and Austin M. Strange, *No Substitute for Experience: Chinese Anti-Piracy Operations in the Gulf of Aden*, Naval War College *China Maritime Study* 10 (forthcoming summer 2013), http://www.usnwc.edu/Research---Gaming/China-Maritime-Studies-Institute/Publications.aspx. Unless otherwise specified, all data in this testimony are documented here.

[2] 中国武装力量的多样化运用 [The Diversified Employment of China's Armed Forces] (Beijing: 中华人民共和国国务院新闻办公室 [Information Office of the State Council, People's Republic of China], 16 April 2013), http://news.xinhuanet.com/english/china/2013-04/16/c_132312681.htm.

This is part of a larger pattern far from China, particularly in distant seas, or what Chinese strategists call "Far Seas." Beijing is making increasing but still relatively modest efforts to address challenges from non-state actors. The Far Seas contain far more internationally-shared interests and cooperation than what Chinese strategists term the "Near Seas" (Yellow, East, and South China Seas), home to all China's outstanding island and maritime claims. Chinese leaders are also likely to be more open to cooperative approaches in the Far Seas because they share many common interests there and realize that building a force capable of credibly challenging the U.S. there would require decades and massive budget increases that might prove unsustainable if China's economic growth continues to slow. Rather, China appears to be building a limited expeditionary capability best suited for handling non-traditional security missions, including protection of Chinese citizens in rough frontier markets and waterways.[3]

Antipiracy operations in particular offer valuable opportunities to enhance the PLAN's power projection capabilities and utility as a tool of diplomatic influence. China's GoA mission:

- Offers new, irreplaceable naval training and experience
- Forces personnel to address unpredictable situations
- Catalyzes development of naval skill sets critical for long-distance operations
- Stimulates unprecedented real time coordination among the PLAN and other agencies
- Increases the PLAN's confidence and bureaucratic influence
- Offers tentative indications of Beijing's approach to maritime governance as a great power
- For instance, mounting operational costs may stimulate gradual development of overseas access points

Antipiracy operations enable China to both respond to internal and external pressures to act on the international stage and raise its overall naval capabilities significantly. GoA challenges have compelled Beijing to adjudicate among diverse, often contradictory, domestic and international forces. As the first major window into China's Far Seas operations and its approach thereto, GoA operations foreshadow how Beijing will take its place in the world as its interests expand and its actions impact others increasingly. By allowing China to be seen providing public goods and cooperating to defend the global system, antipiracy operations afford China international status and influence that it covets. *The impact on international security thus far, while modest, is largely positive.*

Chinese Regional Maritime Security Perspectives, Drivers, and Approaches

China's first regularized overseas naval deployments were motivated in large part by piracy's threat to Chinese commerce. China's aggregate trade with EU countries in 2010 was approximately $500 billion.[4] Burgeoning China-EU trade further increases China's dependence on safe passage through the Bab al-Mandeb, GoA, and Indian Ocean. Adding to these routes'

---

[3] Gabriel Collins, "China's Military Gets Expeditionary," *The Diplomat*, 15 April 2011, http://thediplomat.com/2011/04/15/china%E2%80%99s-military-gets-expeditionary/.

[4] As of November 2012, the EU was China's largest trading partner and China was the EU's second-largest bilateral partner behind the U.S. See http://ec.europa.eu/trade/creating-opportunities/bilateral-relations/countries/china/.

strategic importance, China now obtains more than 20% of its oil from Saudi Arabia alone.[5] Riyadh has a contentious relationship with Tehran. It also faces a continual risk of insurgency and attacks on oil infrastructure in its strategically vital Eastern Province, which is home to both the bulk of the Kingdom's oil reserves and its restive Shia population.

As for the Strait of Hormuz and Persian Gulf, China has thus far taken a less confrontational tack than the U.S., cooperating with Iran in areas ranging from energy purchases (even in the face of Western embargos[6]) to military hardware sales. But as Beijing relies increasingly on Persian Gulf energy supplies, it will face corresponding pressures to become more deeply involved in the region's complex security arena.[7]

Political and defense budget gridlock in Washington, as well as reduction in North American reliance on Gulf oil through rising unconventional oil production in the U.S. and Canada, suggest that U.S. military oil protection activities in the Middle East will ebb. China's nascent but sustained forward military presence—an anti-piracy flotilla in the Gulf of Aden—now sits only a few days' sail from the Gulf and could assume much greater strategic importance if the U.S. scales back its presence. As China's naval and expeditionary military capabilities and Gulf oil imports continue growing, Beijing is likely to use its navy to ensure a deeper influence in the Gulf in coming years.

Growing reliance on Persian Gulf oil demonstrates the growing connection between China's domestic economic growth and external economic, political, and social forces that Beijing is unable to manipulate directly. While China may not be able or interested in controlling many of these risks, sea lines of communication (SLOC) security affects Chinese interests overseas directly: its trade relies on more pirate-infested waterways than that of any other country.

Beijing's leaders face both internal and external pressure to exert international leadership. The Chinese Communist Party (CCP)'s legitimacy rests in part on perceptions of how it handles threats to economic and human security. China's economic, political, and military rise over the past thirty-five years has prompted growing levels of scrutiny by international observers with respect to China's contribution (or lack thereof) as an interested party in the global commons. The PLAN's antipiracy mission has provided a highly visible vehicle by which China can respond to this challenge in a way that allows Beijing to balance concerns over international law and internal policy making.

China's military has accordingly been directed to broaden its missions beyond defense of controlled and claimed territory and maritime zones. China's leaders have emphasized the need to address nontraditional security concerns as part of fulfilling the "new historic missions" first

---

[5] "中美能源合作变量" [Variables in Sino-U.S. Energy Cooperation], 新金融观察报 [New Financial Observer], 27 August 2012, http://finance.jrj.com.cn/2012/08/27133814273855.shtml.

[6] Gabriel Collins and Andrew S. Erickson, "Chinese Traders Poised to Profit from Iran Oil Embargo," China Real Time Report (中国实时报), Wall Street Journal, 26 January 2012, http://blogs.wsj.com/chinarealtime/2012/01/26/with-eu-embargo-on-iran-oil-chinese-traders-set-to-seize-opportunity/.

[7] Gabriel Collins, "Essential Oil—The Rise of Iraq's Exports to China," *Jane's Intelligence Review* 25. 4 (1 April 2013).

outlined by former president Hu Jintao in 2004.[8] The persistence and complexity of modern piracy created a learning opportunity for China's navy, which is particularly unproven in Far Seas. Representing the only major Chinese military effort to date that addresses all four missions, antipiracy operations are critical for demonstrating Chinese military ability to protect citizens and investments abroad.

Antipiracy operations are an ideal training opportunity in large part because they avoid ideological sensitivities: piracy is a private, apolitical, largely economic act, allowing Beijing to maintain that its expeditionary military operations adhere to its longstanding policy of "noninterference" in other nations' domestic affairs. Furthermore, using naval power to protect Chinese-flagged and China-bound maritime commerce—even if in nominal fashion—bolsters the CCP's popular legitimacy and gives the naval brass powerful ammunition to pursue increased funding, shipbuilding, and training in inter-service resource competition.

PLAN GoA experience should pay dividends for China's leadership as Chinese overseas interests proliferate. As China's economic ties sprawl further beyond its continental borders, the costs of security failure will grow, especially in a 'fishbowl' environment where domestic and foreign audiences observe China's behavior intently. Beijing's leaders can now use the PLAN's GoA experience as a foundational guide for addressing economic, political, and military factors simultaneously to solve complex challenges to the security of China's overseas interests.

Impact on Far and Near Seas Operations

Sustained distant sea operations demand effective performance across multiple dimensions. The PLAN's anti-piracy mission has enhanced its supply and replenishment capabilities, civil-military and inter-military coordination and communication, crew health maintenance, convoy protection abilities, and perhaps most importantly, its ability to improvise and respond to sudden and unpredictable situations. This is a tremendous learning experience for a navy with few opportunities to operate extra-regionally. Future PLAN Far Seas operations will undoubtedly build off of this foundation. *Escort operations are likely to persist for some time and hence will continue to offer the first major insights into China's Far Seas operations and its approach thereto.*

Four years on, the PLAN's GoA antipiracy mission has yielded multiple Chinese naval breakthroughs, all of which underscore **China's most significant lesson: *the PLAN had to learn many things by doing them.*** Select PLAN personnel have sharpened their skills, improved coordination mechanisms, and tested new technologies and platforms. China's navy has realized operational and procedural improvements, with impressive speed and resourcefulness.

The mission's greatest organizational value is its *forcing and facilitating of real-time interagency coordination* of a scope, duration, and effectiveness rarely seen in Chinese civil-military and security affairs. The PLAN has assumed unprecedented responsibility and initiative in coordinating operations with such civilian agencies as the Ministry of Transportation

---

[8] They require the PLA to: ensure military support for continued CCP rule; defend China's sovereignty, territorial integrity, and national security; protect China's expanding national interests; and ensure a peaceful global environment and promote mutual development.

(MoT), transcending traditional bureaucratic and civil-military stovepipes and bringing the service out from the PLA's organizational shadow. Geographic and operational exigencies may increasingly allow the PLAN to come into its own as China's most externally-focused military service and a growing tool for Chinese policymakers. Antipiracy and related operations can spur needed improvements, and even serve as a test-bed for their realization. Transformation in organizational coordination is aided by the application of new technology. For instance, the PLAN has been able to test Chinese satellites and new communications technology under operational conditions far from home.

Chinese ships and crew deployed to the GoA must *master the logistical concepts and skills associated with protracted, long-distance naval operations*, **including balancing underway and in-port replenishment and maintaining crew morale during protracted hardships.** The PLAN has traversed a steep learning curve with impressive speed and resourcefulness, enhancing procedural, training, and operational techniques as well as associated support. Maintenance procedures and even ship design may be improved accordingly. PLAN GoA achievements transcend antipiracy best practices: they support broader future capabilities. At the tactical level, many fundamental skills that the PLAN is learning are what the U.S. Navy terms mission-essential tasks; e.g., proficiency in nighttime shipboard takeoff and landing is required of a helicopter crew for maritime special-forces operations. China's navy is increasing out-of-area capabilities, but would require tremendous improvements in force structure, human capital, training, and experience to translate present resources into an ability to engage in high-intensity combat operations in the Far Seas.

The *mission's greatest operational value is forcing personnel to face unscripted, unpredictable situations*—**the most intense operational experience presently available to China's navy**, which might otherwise remain an unwieldy and risk-adverse service. If officers and personnel who participated in the GoA mission are rewarded for risk taking (in the PLAN context), initiative, and innovative problem solving, this could also catalyze a gradual culture change that makes the PLAN a more dynamic and flexible organization. In the long-term, such leveraging of operational experience could make the PLAN a much more effective fighting organization than, e.g., the PLAAF, which receives expensive new hardware, but lacks real forward operational experience.

Benefits are already being applied in other areas, such as training in the Near Seas. That ~20-25% of the PLAN's surface ships (and nearly all its most modern platforms) have served in the GoA has implications for potential Near Seas contingencies. Compared to its smaller neighbors, China continues to accumulate operational expertise that should raise its readiness for manifold future contingencies. China's navy spreads GoA mission benefits throughout its ranks through systematic training, and by cycling ships and personnel through GoA task forces. For example, PLAN officials such as former East Sea Fleet Deputy Commander Zhang Huachen assert that their service should integrate systems, ideas, and practices from its Near Seas and Far Seas operations.[9] PLAN ships en route to the GoA often first train in the Near Seas. For example,

---

[9] 彭超 [Peng Chao] and 钱宏 [Qian Hong], "加强我军海外非战争军事行动能力建设: 专访军队人大代表, 东海舰队原副司令员张华臣" [Strengthening the Construction of Chinese Military's Capability for Overseas Military Operations Other Than War—Exclusive Interview With Military Delegate to the National People's Congress and Former Deputy Commander of the East Sea Fleet Zhang Huachen], 人民海军 [People's Navy], 14

the 11th escort task force conducted three months of "pre-war" training after leaving its homeport in Qingdao.[10] It underwent over 260 hours of training while transiting the Yellow Sea, East China Sea, Miyako Strait, and Northwest Pacific.[11]

To be sure, *increasing Far Seas activity does impose costs*. Principle expenditures of China's antipiracy mission include **fuel, food, and health supplies, and the ammunition and equipment** used in training exercises and live fire, as well as **depreciation of PLAN vessels and equipment**. Additionally, Chinese naval planners are surely calculating the ***opportunity cost*** of deploying supply and landing ships to the GoA when these ships could be preparing for Near Seas operations, such as a potential Taiwan contingency or, even more likely, a militarized South China Sea dispute or escalation in the East China Sea. Some basic operational procedures applicable to the GoA mission may be transferrable to these scenarios, but amphibious vessels like the *Yuzhao*-class Type 071 landing platform dock (LPD) could derive more relevant benefits from specialized training in regional waters.

Naval Diplomacy and Emerging Regional Logistics Footprint

The PLAN is assuming a niche role in Chinese diplomacy, as warships work increasingly with other navies and call on foreign ports for resupply and exchanges. Chinese task forces initially only docked in foreign ports one or twice per deployment. But following the extension of deployments from 4 to 6 months, task forces often dock several times. PLAN escort forces have already completed port calls in nearly 30 countries on four continents to refuel and replenish, as well as to enhance bilateral military ties through joint drills and other onshore exchanges. As **Appendix 1** indicates, Chinese escort forces have called on most major Middle Eastern countries, but have logged the most extensive replenishment visits by far in Port Salalah, Oman, and Djibouti. Pakistan and Saudi Arabia have served as overhaul locations.

China is utilizing its protracted anti-piracy deployments for naval diplomacy with dozens of littoral states and providing financial and material assistance for port construction in many of those states. Chinese experts differ regarding whether and to what extent China should pursue overseas "bases." Most agree that China cannot rely on its current Far Seas logistical framework indefinitely, as ships and resources are increasingly strained. Despite notable logistical innovations and resulting efficiency gains since 2008, Chinese planners are keenly aware of the great expense of sustaining Far Seas antipiracy missions. Lacking permanent bases, PLAN escort forces must refuel at sea or during official port calls arranged well in advance. Auxiliary vessels cannot provide the same services as would permanent onshore basing facilities. Yet large traditional bases would be difficult to reconcile with Beijing's nonintervention policies. Bases might also be regarded as lightning rods for political opposition; similar concerns reportedly imposed extreme limitations on early antipiracy task force port calls.

China is therefore likely to gradually pursue what the U.S. Navy would term a "places, not

---

March 2012, 2.

[10] 米晋国 [Mi Jinguo] and 崔岳 [Cui Yue],"战鼓声声旌旗猎—声声旌军第十一批护航编队出征之际" [Battle Drums Sounding and Hunting Banners and Flags—Written at the Departure of the 11th Escort Task Force], 人民海军 [People's Navy], 28 February 2012, 3.

[11] Ibid.

bases" approach. Port Salalah is already a de facto 'place' for the PLAN. In March 2013, Djibouti, already home to U.S., French, and Japanese bases, reportedly invited China to establish a military facility. Port Aden, Yemen, ranks a distant third, likely because of its perceived vulnerability to instability and terrorism, as demonstrated by the USS *Cole* incident. **Appendix 2** offers details on present and potential PLAN access points.

Responsible Stakeholding and Prospects for Further Cooperation

Pirates' ability to disguise themselves as innocent civilians and to disperse their activities makes piracy a complex, expensive problem for naval forces to address, necessitating international cooperation. China, desiring its rise to be seen as peaceful and mutually beneficial, has dispatched the PLAN to join other forces in the GoA. Perhaps most importantly, this offers China an opportunity to participate meaningfully—if, thus far, modestly—in the construction of twenty-first-century global governance architecture.

China's participation in Shared Awareness and De-Confliction (SHADE) is constructive, if circumscribed. SHADE is the first organization to coordinate efforts among established regional naval organizations such as Combined Task Force 151 (CTF)-151, NATO and Operation Atalanta/European Union Naval Force Somalia (EU-NAVFOR-ATALANTA); and is co-run by these three groups. China and other independently deploying nations have participated consistently, despite lacking access to chairmanship. This suggests that China is willing to cooperate with the U.S. and other powers for mutual gain in increasingly innovative fashion.

Propelled by domestic and international expectations, GoA antipiracy operations increase expectations in both. While PLAN antipiracy operations to date have succeeded operationally, at the strategic level they also illuminate a growing gap between Chinese and Western perceptions of China as a "responsible stakeholder" in the international system. By contributing useful public goods they offer China increased global maritime influence; nevertheless, they remain insufficient in degree or scope to earn Beijing the status that it covets. China, while conceding that there remains ample room for improvement, portrays itself as an increasingly responsible actor in the global commons—yet some Western audiences worry increasingly about Beijing's lack of integration into, and perhaps subtle rejection of, the existing international structure.

The PLAN seems open in principle to the possibility of greater cooperation in the GoA and possibly beyond. While Beijing is eager to increase cooperation quantitatively off the Horn of Africa, official statements to date suggest that this would likely entail increasing basic coordination, low-level information sharing, navy-to-navy exchanges, and joint operations—all of which China's navy does already, and none of which would represent a qualitative breakthrough. There are no signs that China will decide to operate within a multinational organization in the near future: Beijing appears to believe that the costs of joining a collaborative effort outweigh potential benefits. Independent operation avoids any situation in which China would have to subordinate itself—even symbolically—to another state or organization, and provides the PLAN with considerable freedom to alter its missions without having to notify partners or undergo lengthy multilateral deliberations. Even were China willing to interoperate with U.S. or other Western forces directly, the requisite sharing of software, information, and other interoperability enablers might not be possible due to security concerns.

Conclusion and Policy Recommendations:

China has reached a level of aggregate national power at which it would be ineffectual for the U.S. to simply oppose *all* Chinese exercise of power with which it is not entirely satisfied. In many cases, *no* amount of lecturing will change Chinese behavior. With respect to communications, Washington's focus should instead be on ensuring that U.S. and allied taxpayers and voters are fully *informed*, and hence willing to continue to fund robust military spending so that the U.S. approaches interactions with China from a point of strength; the Commission continues to play an important role in this regard. With respect to actions vis-à-vis China, the U.S. should not waste time on unrealistic proposals. Instead, it should support positive Chinese approaches to cooperation and oppose with great care and selectivity specific Chinese negative approaches by marshaling concrete resources through a whole-of-government approach that combines information, economic, diplomatic, and military policies all oriented toward achieving a common strategic outcome in U.S. policy toward China.

To make this possible, Washington must prioritize its geostrategic interests vis-à-vis Beijing and support them with resources rather than rhetoric. U.S. policy should emphasize thwarting Chinese attempts to carve out a zone of exceptionalism in the Near Seas within which existing international law and other norms do not apply and where China would have a freer hand to use the threat, or actual use, of force to coerce its neighbors into resolving disputes in Beijing's favor. Accomplishing this objective requires an Asia-Pacific Rebalancing that is comprehensive, credible, and sustained (properly funded). Here ship numbers (particularly of nuclear-powered attack and guided missile submarines) will speak much louder than sermons or soundbites, both to China, and perhaps equally importantly, to longstanding and newly emerging U.S. partners in the region.

Generally speaking, China's Far Seas activities should be viewed as far more vulnerable to disruption, and potentially mutually-beneficial, than those in the Near Seas. Rather than involving nationalistic zero-sum claims, they target non-state actors who threaten not only Chinese lives, property, and prosperity but also potentially those of other nations as well. At a minimum, this allows for sovereign exercise of Chinese rights; in many cases, it permits productive pursuit of common interests. Far Seas military operations occur far from China's homeland, with its extensive secure communications, logistics, and defenses. They are thus relatively unprotected; particularly any fixed overseas access points that China may develop. Chinese firms extracting oil in unstable regions supply the global market, lowering prices for everyone. Even Chinese cooperation with nations of concern, such as Iran, is likely to be tempered by China's desire for positive economic conditions and pariah states' own self-defeating approaches.

These key dynamics suggest the following policy recommendations:

- ***Encourage reduction in Chinese 'free-riding' in the Far Seas.*** The essence of U.S. concern with respect to Chinese Far Seas operations should not be an 'overactive' China, but rather a 'selfish superpower' China that husbands its military energies for Near Seas coercion.
- ***Welcome constructive Chinese contributions, don't fixate on form.*** In keeping with its imperative to prioritize interests, the U.S. should *show flexibility* vis-à-vis Chinese actions

that are largely positive. Washington should anticipate Beijing's hesitancy to simply integrate into Western-established security mechanisms (e.g., CTF-151) and look for ways to deepen cooperation incrementally through other mechanisms, such as SHADE.

- ***Expand Far Seas cooperation as feasible.*** A key question for U.S.-China relations will be to what extent the two Pacific powers can *broaden cooperation* in the Far Seas amid ongoing differences in the Near Seas. Given China's Near Seas focus, this question will be answered largely in Beijing.

Thank you very much for your time. I welcome your questions and comments.

Appendix 1: Selected Port Calls by First 14 PLAN Antipiracy Task Forces in the Middle East and North Africa, February 2009-April 2013

ALGERIA **Algiers** • 2-5 April 2013, *Friendly Visit* **BAHRAIN** **Al Manamah** • 9-13 December 2010, *Friendly Visit* **DJIBOUTI** **Djibouti** • 24 January 2010, *Replenish/Overhaul* • 3 May 2010, *Replenish/Overhaul* • 13 September 2010, *Replenish/Overhaul* • 22 September 2010, *Replenish/Overhaul* • 24 December 2010, *Replenish/Overhaul* • 21 February 2011 *Replenish/Overhaul* • 5 October 2011, *Replenish/Overhaul* • 24-29 March 2012, *Replenish/Overhaul* • 14 May 2012, *Replenish/Overhaul* • 13-18 August 2012, *Replenish/Overhaul* • 1-6 December 2012	KUWAIT **Shuwaikh** 27 November-1 December 2011, *Friendly Visit* **MOROCCO** **Casablanca** • 9-13 April, *Friendly Visit* **OMAN** **Muscat** • 1-8 December 2011, Friendly Visit **Salalah** • 21 June-1 July 2009, *Replenish/Overhaul* • 14 August 2009, *Replenish/Overhaul* • 2 January 2010, *Replenish/Overhaul* • 1 April 2010, *Replenish/Overhaul* • 8 June 2010, *Replenish/Overhaul* • 10 August 2010, *Replenish/Overhaul* • 19 January 2011, *Replenish/Overhaul* • 28 January 2011, *Replenish/Overhaul* • 10 April 2011, *Replenish/Overhaul* • 23 June 2011,	QATAR **Doha** 2-7 August 2011, Friendly Visit **SAUDI ARABIA** **Jiddah** 27-31 November 2010, Friendly Visit 3 September 2011, Replenish/Overhaul 17 June 2012, Replenish/Overhaul 1-6 January 2013, Replenish/Overhaul **UNITED ARAB EMIRATES** **Abu Dhabi** 24-28 March 2010, Friendly Visit **YEMEN** **Aden** 21 February 2009, Replenish/Overhaul 25 April 2009, Replenish/Overhaul 23 July 2009, Replenish/Overhaul 28 September 2009, Replenish/Overhaul 5 February 2010, Replenish/Overhaul 16 May 2010, Replenish/Overhaul 26 July 2010, Replenish/Overhaul 1 October 2010, Replenish/Overhaul

Replenish/Overhaul **EGYPT** **Alexandria** • 26-30 July 2010, *Friendly Visit* **ISRAEL** **Haifa** • 14-17 August 2012, *Friendly Visit*	*Replenish/Overhaul* • 8-11 August 2011, *Replenish/Overhaul* • 7-10 November 2011, *Replenish/Overhaul* • 21-24 February 2012, *Replenish/Overhaul* • 1-3 July 2012, *Replenish/Overhaul* • 9 July 2012, *Replenish/Overhaul* • 28-29 March 2013, *Replenish/Overhaul*	

Appendix 2: Ports for Potential PLAN Overseas Access and PLAN Visits Thereto

Port	Country	Quality of Repair Facilities	# PLAN Anti-Piracy-Related Visits Since 28 December 2008	Nature of Visits
Salalah	**Oman**	Only small craft facilities currently available.	15+	Replenish/Overhaul
Aden	**Yemen**	National Dockyard Company offers range of limited facilities, services. Workshops, large lathes, electrical, casting, refrigeration, other repair shops; in-water repair services. Two floating docks.	8+	Replenish/Overhaul
Djibouti	**Djibouti**	Multiple foreign naval/military bases; China reportedly invited to establish its own military facility. Small repairs possible; container terminal phase 1 construction completed; can berth 2 large container vessels together.	11+	Replenish/Overhaul
Gwadar	**Pakistan**	500 acre shipyard. 2 600kdwt drydocks planned. VLCC + ULCC construction planned. Expansive second phase of the port was supposed to be completed in 2010 but has not yet begun construction. Further development to include 15-20 berths, ship cargo handling equipment, port machinery, and warehouses; not commercially viable at present. China contributed $198 million of initial $250 million port investment. China Overseas Ports Holding Company Limited assumed port management control on 23 May 2013, with China Communications Construction Company (CCCC) as project contractor. 19 million tonnes/yr. capacity oil refinery planned.	N/A	N/A
Karachi	**Pakistan**	PLAN's preferred Indian Ocean repair facility. Two drydocks available; 18,000/ 25,000 DWT; development of bulk cargo, deepwater container terminals, and other expansion underway, including 18-m container terminal.	4+	Friendly Visits/ Joint Drills
Hambantota	**Sri Lanka**	Ship serving capabilities planned; port to be constructed in 4 stages over 15 years. Phase 1 accommodated first	N/A	N/A

		vessel in 2010; general cargo berth of 610 m; handles vessels up to 100,000 DWT; phase 2 initiated		
Colombo	Sri Lanka	Multiple afloat repair berths. Drydocks available up to 120,000 DWT; Deepwater port opened in 2012; Colombo South Harbor Development project will increase depth to 18 m then 23 m; phased development of 4 new terminals with 3-4 berths each.	N/A	N/A
Trincomalee	Sri Lanka	Minor repairs possible. Slipways for naval, commercial vessels.	N/A	N/A
Chittagong	Bangladesh	Private repair yards available. Drydock available for vessels up to 16,500DWT. New collocated port to be completed in three phases by 2015; will increase capacity from current 1.1-million to 3-million TEU for container traffic, and 30.5-million to 100-million tons for bulk cargo.	2	Replenish/Overhaul/Joint Drills
Sittwe	Burma	Available; Kyaukpyu deep sea port on Maday Island by Than Zit river mouth; initiated in 2009, project will produce 91 berths, accommodate 300,000-ton oil tankers.	1	Friendly visits
Victoria	Seychelles	Limited repairs. Divers, underwater welding equipment available. Drydock shipways available for vessels <300 GT.	1+	Friendly visits
Singapore	Singapore	Excellent; 1 terminal, 9 sub-ports; military ports.	1	Replenish/Overhaul/Friendly visits
Bagamoyo	Tanzania	Not yet built. Announced in March/April 2013 that China plans to fund Bagamoyo port with capacity of 20 million TEU/year to be completed by 2017. China to commit 800 billion Tanzanian shillings ($500 million) in 2013 for starting port construction; remainder of Chinese financial aid package will follow in 2014-15; $10B total Chinese investment; will include the building of new 34-kilometre road joining Bagamoyo to Mlandizi, 65 km railway connecting Bagamoyo to Tanzania-Zambia Railway (TAZARA) and Central Railway.	N/A	N/A

Plus signs indicate the possibility that not all port calls have been included.

PANEL III QUESTION & ANSWER

HEARING CO-CHAIR FIEDLER: Thank you very much. Commissioner Wessel has the first question.

COMMISSIONER WESSEL: Thank you and amazing how true to time each one of you were, so thank you.

HEARING CO-CHAIR FIEDLER: Experienced.

COMMISSIONER WESSEL: Experience, yes.

Dr. Alterman, you made the comment that the U.S. still has the home-court advantage. Dr. Erickson, you referred to sort of the naval balance, Far Seas, et cetera. We're dealing with a stated policy by the United States government of a pivot towards Asia, which as I understand it could mean, for example, with regard to naval assets, moving from 55 to 60 percent in terms of Pacific projection.

But we're also dealing with a suppressed budgetary situation with fairly significant resource reductions coming, and already occurring, but also coming in the future. As China's economic wealth continues, as its growth rates continue and the support for all of its currency policies and acquisition of dollar denominated and other assets, it seems that they have the ability to expand their naval resources pretty quickly. They also understand they still have a training issue and the ability to be able to project that power efficiently, while at the same time we are going through this resource problem as well as political fatigue from having been projecting power throughout the Middle East.

Where does this leave us? How do both the Chinese--and each of you touched upon it a bit--Chinese, Middle Eastern nations, but also as you look at naval assets, do we have what we need to be able to address the littoral issues, the overall Pacific issues and Mideast against this backdrop?

And Dr. Erickson, if you could start?

DR. ERICKSON: Yes, sir. Thank you for those important questions.

I think the bottom line is that in the future, the U.S. is going to have the Navy that U.S. taxpayers are convinced that the U.S. should have. In that regard, it's essential for taxpayers to understand what U.S. interests are and what are some of the ways of realizing those interests.

I think prioritization is also essential. It's necessary to ask: what are the areas of investment with the most efficient, disproportionate payoff? There are many answers to that question, but I would particularly highlight undersea warfare. U.S. submarine and other operations are extremely advanced and, relative to some other areas, face far fewer countermeasures and potential impediments to their operations.

So in a difficult budget environment in which tough choices need to be made, I think we should look, for example, to undersea capabilities as a key area to preserve and build on our already existing proven strengths.

COMMISSIONER WESSEL: But also from a surface combatant and a policy matter, understanding you're speaking for yourself, do we have an adequate build in terms of surface combatants when you look at the projections over the next two to five years?

DR. ERICKSON: Well, sir, I focus on looking at the China side so unfortunately I can't give you the most authoritative answer to that. If I might, what I'd also add, though, is that there's another side to this equation, and it's China's future trajectory.

I think there are a lot of unknowns there. No question, China is already here to stay as a great power in East Asia with global implications. However, I think that some economic estimates may potentially exaggerate the future rate of growth of Chinese power. There are a lot of downside risks to China's economic development. At the same time, if you look at future indicators of U.S. power, there are many positives there. I think all this points to the need for the U.S. to proceed confidently, not make any overhasty adjustments vis-à-vis the bilateral arrangement and see how things shape up over time.

I think it will be a much stronger future for U.S. power and influence, and the possibility for cooperation using institutions as the U.S. would see them than some people are concerned about at this point.

COMMISSIONER WESSEL: Dr. Alterman.

DR. ALTERMAN: Let me be brief but not terse. I think there are three questions involved, and I think the answers are yet to be determined.

One, what is the U.S. role protecting the global commons? I don't think we've figured it out. Going forward, what role are we going to play? Going forward, what role is China going to play? That's question number two. Are they going to be a responsible international power trying to protect the international system? Or are they going to be an essentially mercantilist power looking after their own national interests?

The third question is what threat are you trying to build a navy to deal with? Are you trying to fight pirates? Are you trying to be ready to fight China if you have to?

They're very different sets of capabilities, very different sets of ships and everything else. I think we are, as I see it, as a country, we're trying to think about what threats our military will deal with. Will we be fighting conventional wars or not? The most likely conventional near peer is going to be a war against China. What would that take and how much can you offset the needs for that by creating additional special forces capabilities, unmanned capabilities, and the other kinds of things we're also developing? Those are policy questions that have to be decided by people more senior than us.

COMMISSIONER WESSEL: Thank you.

HEARING CO-CHAIR FIEDLER: Senator Talent.

HEARING CO-CHAIR TALENT: I thank all the witnesses. Great initial testimony.

One question, and I guess I'll address it to you, Dr. Alterman, but the others can comment. You mentioned that dealing in the Mideast is hard for China, and I think some issues probably are hard. I'm having a little trouble seeing what's so hard, though, about dealing responsibly with Iran and Syria.

I mean China's interests are oil specifically, markets, stability. Everybody who's testified here today has said that they don't really have any kind of enduring national ambitions in the Middle East, and you said the same thing, in contrast to Asia.

So what would be so hard about the Chinese just deciding, for example, that they're going to abstain in the Security Council on issues relating to Syria and Iranian sanctions? I know they get some oil from Iran, but there's other ways of dealing with that. And if, indeed, it's not that hard for them on those issues, then why aren't they doing it? That is a question that has come up in my mind.

What other interests are they advancing by not doing something? That seems to me very much in the interests that we all recognize them as having in the Middle East.

DR. ALTERMAN: Thank you very much for that question. I think it's a very important question. It's one that I've paid attention to, and I've spoken to Chinese scholars and read Chinese scholars.

I think the first thing that many Chinese strategists like about Iran is it keeps us focused on Iran and less focused on China. They like the fact that we had two carriers off the coast of Iran, which means we don't have two off the coast of China. There's an advantage to the fact that the United States can't fully pivot to Asia because it's busy, preoccupied with the Middle East. I think there are some people who are delighted with that aspect.

There are people who believe the principle of not having foreign powers involved in regional security issues is a great precedent to maintain, a great precedent to talk about. It would get the United States out of their hair in Asia, and they will fight that principle by arguing against the United States being involved in Iran. They also think that that sort of resonates well with local audiences, opening areas up for more Chinese influence.

I think the Chinese, in my experience, have doubted the international system. They say it's stacked in favor of powers that are friendly to the United States and hostile to China. They think that the "international system"--whatever it means, and they use air quotes that many people in Washington would also use--is not fair to China, and they don't see a need to protect that.

I think they like the idea that they have a source of energy that isn't going to restrain exports to China because the United States asks them to. So where I think China comes down on all of this is about maintaining a balance. They don't want Iran to go nuclear. They don't want there to be a conflict in the Gulf. They can't alienate Saudi Arabia, from which they get twice as much oil as they get from Iran.

But to the extent that Iran is an irritant, to the extent that Iran undermines, to the extent that Iran requires attention, to the extent that Iran supports their more global arguments of nonintervention, I think they feel that balancing some attention toward Iran, some favorable relationship with Iran, is helpful for their interests.

I think Syria is a much more marginal play for China. They don't like the idea of supporting rebellion. They like the idea of lining up with the Russians to some degree. They like the idea of supporting the status quo because China, after its revolutionary days, has really become very much a status quo power.

But I think China can be persuaded, and what China is really looking for in Syria is to get a sense where the wind is blowing. They were burned in Libya, where not only did they seem to be supporting the Gaddafi regime rhetorically, but they also were selling weapons and equipment to the Gaddafi regime after it was clear it was going down.

There were many statements afterward from the people who won the revolution and said we won't deal with the Chinese, and I think they were burned. If you look, they've been much more careful not being as clear in their policy toward Syria, because ultimately the most important strategic decision on their part, I think, and it explains certainly their policy throughout the Middle East, is, "We'll be with the winners, whoever the winners are. We'll find a way to be the winners."

HEARING CO-CHAIR TALENT: So with regard, and I won't go through all the rationales, with regard to the first one, though, that they want to keep us occupied in Iran. If we were to respond and maybe back channel, maybe don't do this publicly, but back channel to them--although I guess I'm suggesting it, but unfortunately I have no power--that if we can't trust them to cooperate even on subjects away from what they see as their sphere of influence. Even when it would be in their economic interests to do so, on a subject that's this important to us, that, in fact, we're now going to have to pay even more attention to Asia because if we can't trust them to do even this, then how can we trust them to cooperate in a reasonable and peaceful result in Asia?

In other words, if the reason they're doing this is to keep us occupied in Iran, if it results in us getting more occupied in Asia, isn't that a reason for them to start cooperating in Iran?

DR. ALTERMAN: Their argument is they do cooperate. All the actions of the P5 have been unanimous. They've demarched the Iranians every time the P5 has demarched Iranians. Their argument is that they're cooperative, but if you look at the scholarship, if you talk to people, I think the analysis is, "We're trying to maintain the right balance." Being 100 percent with the United States doesn't make sense to them. They're hostile to the idea of sanctions anyway as the strategy. They have a lot of, I think, intellectual, theoretical, strategic problems with our strategy, and the added benefit that it occupies us works for them.

But their argument is also that "When the chips are down, we're with you guys. We're not busting apart the consensus in the P5. We're with you on the P5."

HEARING CO-CHAIR FIEDLER: Commissioner Wortzel is next.

COMMISSIONER WORTZEL: I'd like from any or all of you a short explanation of your understanding of how China handled its economic relations and arms sales to Iran and Iraq during the Iran and Iraq War, and then your reviews on evidence you may have seen of tension between Saudi Arabia and China over China's activities in Iran. Will China upgrade the ballistic missiles it put in Saudi Arabia as Iran develops its own missile programs and moves toward nuclear weapons?

DR. WUTHNOW: Commissioner, I can't offer you a very good explanation for the exact question that you're asking. I would say with respect to China's current involvement with Iran in terms of arms sales, this is a key area where we need further research.

In particular, I would encourage the Commission to query the U.S. government about what they know and what they should know about the current status of China's selling of arms to Iran because, as the Department of Defense has noted, Iran is one of the key anti-access and area denial challenges in the Middle East. The question of whether or not China is supporting, enabling or facilitating that challenge in the Middle East I think is one that deserves much greater study than exists in the public domain.

DR. ALTERMAN: I think for the Iran-Iraq War, of course, in the 1980s, China was not a net oil importer, and this was a commercial effort to develop their domestic arms industry. I think it's extraordinarily different from their relationship with Saudi Arabia now, which is fundamentally a strategic relationship. Saudi Arabia sells them 20 percent of their imported oil, sometimes a little bit more. It's twice as much as Iran does, as I said.

They are keenly aware of this balance. They are also keenly aware that Saudi Arabia is a very close ally of the United States, and they don't want to be reliant on Saudi Arabia. They don't want to alienate Saudi Arabia, and they're trying to strike that balance. But, again, I think China would love not to get involved in any of this. They'd love to have the relationship they had in the '80s, where they just trade with whoever has money.

But they don't have that luxury anymore, and it genuinely keeps them awake at night, because what they see is us shaping the battlefield. They see us with key relationships. They see us with legions of diplomats and soldiers who can monitor everything that's happening in the air, on the land, and on the sea and under the sea, and it makes them feel very vulnerable to everything we do in precisely the area the world on which they are most reliant.

COMMISSIONER WORTZEL: Anybody want to touch on these missiles and how China may or has to respond as Iran develops its own missile programs and any nuclear weapons that may come?

DR. ALTERMAN: Honestly, I think a lot of that would depend on what the attitude of the GCC governments is toward the United States. We've recently had two large weapon sales from the United States to GCC states intended to be directed toward deterring the Iranians. The missile sale deal in, I believe it was 1988, was very much directed at the United States and the United States' unwillingness to supply Saudi Arabia.

I don't think the Saudis right now would want to tweak the United States in that way, and I think the Chinese would not try to force a sale. I think that, in my mind, the decision point would be driven by the demand side rather than the supply side.

HEARING CO-CHAIR FIEDLER: Commissioner Shea.

VICE CHAIRMAN SHEA: Thank you very much for your very interesting testimony.

Dr. Alterman, you say in your first paragraph, you say that Chinese growth is dependent on energy that China cannot secure alone, and it relies on the goodwill of a country, the U.S., it often sees to be its principal potential foe, to help provide that security.

And then, Dr. Erickson, in your testimony, you talk about how the Gulf of Aden activities have enhanced Chinese naval operational experience, and I know in China SignPost--I go on there periodically--you write on Chinese naval developments as well. Over time, maybe in the next ten years, are we going to see greater--and in light of the fact that the U.S. reliance on oil from the Middle East is declining and Chinese reliance on oil from the Middle East is going to continue to explode--are we going to see greater Chinese military naval activity in the region to protect its own economic interests and potential basing?

DR. ALTERMAN: If I can start, the Chinese attitude has been changing remarkably quickly in a very, very short period of time. The evidence I give to you for this is in the Gulf of Aden, the U.S. Navy helped set up something called SHADE, standing for Shared Awareness and Deconfliction. And they hosted a monthly meeting with all the foreign navies that were operating there to try to make sure that everybody knew what was happening and they weren't banging into each other. The Chinese first said, "We're not going to go."

And then the Chinese started going. And then the U.S. Navy said, "You know what, I think we got it, we're going to stop the meetings." And the Chinese said, "Please don't stop." This is really in a period of about three or four years. They went from a period of, "We're not going to go because you're just going to spy on us, and you're going to try to find out what our capabilities are, and we don't want to have anything to do with it," to "Please don't stop the meetings because they're very helpful." So I think this is a rapidly changing attitude.

I wonder very much whether China feels the need to protect the global commons the way we do, whether they feel a need to project their navy to protect commerce the way we have done? And if we do less of it and they're not doing more of it, what does that mean for commerce?

I'm not an expert on China, and I'd be interested in Dr. Erickson's view, but it seems to me that China doesn't really see its navy the way we see our navy, guaranteeing the freedom of the high seas, freedom broadly.

VICE CHAIRMAN SHEA: It could see its navy as guaranteeing a secure supply of energy resources coming into the country?

DR. ALTERMAN: But I don't believe they've done that yet, and I don't know what would. I don't know whether that would be driven by a sense of capability. Now they have the capability to have a choice, whether they should build with a desire to create a doctrine where the navy would be used for that? And this is a question for Dr. Erickson really.

DR. ERICKSON: Well, Commissioner, you raise a very important area of questions because there is no question that things have been changing rapidly. China is developing dynamically. We're seeing China get into new areas in the security realm where China really didn't have a presence before. This raises a whole host of questions about what will be the trajectory of Chinese presence and capabilities, including in the greater Middle Eastern region.

There will be, I think, an increasingly robust logistics support infrastructure to enable that. If you look at a lot of Chinese military writings describing the Gulf of Aden operations, the earlier ones focused, I think, more on how to make the initial operations viable. There were a lot of hurdles they had to overcome, a lot of things they could only learn by doing--even just in terms of ensuring a supply of potable water on the ships.

Now, as things move forward, there's more of a concern and a focus, I think, on how to keep this, how to make this efficient, how to keep it sustainable from a cost perspective, because these deployments are incredibly expensive even for a country with the economic dynamism of China. So in my written testimony, I've included two appendices detailing where the task forces of the antipiracy mission have stopped, which ports they've called on, and also what are some potential ports, not just in the Middle East, but also in the greater Indian Ocean region for China's Navy to use. And I think we are going to see developments in those areas.

There is a lot of Chinese investment, at least on the more commercial side. I think the nuance here, though, is that China is likely to take more of what we would describe as a "places, not bases," approach.

Already, they have enough on their hands staying within some version of their stated policy of noninterference. There are enough contradictions to handle there ideologically. I think they're also very wary of getting overextended politically; but, nevertheless, there will be gradual development, more replenishment.

I would name Port Salalah in Oman as already a de facto "place" that China's Navy is relying on heavily. We may see Djibouti, as well, increasingly assume this role.

At the same time, though, I want to echo some of the things that Dr. Alterman said. It's true that China is doing things across the board in naval and military development, but in this time of flux and change and uncertainty, we need to try to identify what are some of the key concentrations and dynamics. When I overlay everything that China is doing in terms of military development, I see a much more robust and much more challenging set of developments vis-à-vis the Near Seas.

I think China is building, although it's building a navy, it's building an even more potent and disruptive "anti-navy" to include land-based missiles through the Second Artillery Force that are primarily relevant vis-à-vis the Near Seas. So you're right to identify these things that are changing; but, again, I think we need to keep that larger perspective and look at China's overall interests and how they perceive them.

As long as China's island and maritime claims remain unresolved in the Near Seas, that's going to absorb a tremendous amount of strategic focus. There will be additional layers of emphasis farther and farther out; but of ever-diminishing operational intensity and degree of investment. As I said before, while these sort of Far Seas operations can have strategic shaping impacts, they can certainly increase China's influence in the region, they are extremely vulnerable to disruption and anything that gets even close to a sort of kinetic combat operations situation.

Whereas, in the Near Seas, these focused anti-navy capabilities in some respects, I think, could be increasingly challenging to respond to with adequate countermeasures if the U.S. and its allies and its friends don't keep a focus on maintaining those capabilities.

VICE CHAIRMAN SHEA: Thank you.

HEARING CO-CHAIR FIEDLER: Thank you very much. Commissioner Slane.

COMMISSIONER SLANE: Thank you all for being here. Very helpful.

As China continues to expand their naval resources, including their projected four new aircraft carriers, do you see a naval arms race developing between the United States and China, and if so, is this something that we should alert Congress to?

DR. ERICKSON: Well, China's deck aviation development has certainly received a lot of attention of late. I've been following this for a number of years now, and I was privileged recently to spend a little more than a week aboard USS *Nimitz* going from San Diego out past Hawaii, and I learned a lot more about carrier operations from seeing how the best do it.

And what I can tell you is: while China has certainly made a lot of progress in a short time with carrier operations, they are very, very far from the state-of-the-art, and they know it. This is not just in terms of various technologies and the limitations of the current Liaoning aircraft carrier platform inherent in that ski jump, but even more importantly in the various operational capacities, the so-called "tribal knowledge" of how you do all these specific operations that add up to this intricate, complex ballet of system-of-systems of air operations. It is exceedingly complex.

So I do not see China being anywhere close to being able to match the U.S. in terms of deck aviation operations; but, then again, I don't think that's their goal. I don't think they want to become a carrier-centric navy right away. I think, rather, that there is this focus on radiating ever outward from the Near Seas but still very focused--they're very focused on this land-based anti-navy component.

What I was alluding to before, and what I think you were touching on, as well, Commissioner, is the fact that Congress and the taxpayer need to be acutely aware of what China is doing that is different, that is potentially very potent, and that is very disruptive. I think that especially pertains to anti-access/area denial capabilities development, or what the Chinese call "counter-intervention"--just two sides of the same coin, depending on your perspective.

That's where the big things are happening, and that's where I think especially there needs to be significant awareness. Otherwise, things could change in a very short time. There could be a sort of problem of being caught flat-footed in terms of funding in a vulnerable period, and then a few years from now we'd end up in a situation we didn't necessarily anticipate and people would be asking how we got there.

Thank you, sir.

COMMISSIONER SLANE: Anyone else?

DR. WUTHNOW: Commissioner, if I can just dovetail off of what Professor Erickson said, you mentioned China's development for carrier battlegroups. This is a potential challenge, but as Dr. Erickson was saying, the other challenge that we really need to be aware of is China's counter-intervention capabilities.

But I would go even a step further and say that it's not just a question of the anti-ship ballistic missile. That is part of the challenge that is threatening to U.S. Naval forces in the Western Pacific, but beyond that, I think we need to pay attention to electronic warfare, to submarine warfare, and to other areas, as I understand them from public reporting.

I think that Congress has a role to make sure that the Department of the Navy and the Department of Defense adequately understand this challenge to U.S. carrier strike groups in the Western Pacific.

DR. ALTERMAN: I agree. Just to reinforce what Dr. Wuthnow said, to assume that China is trying to do what we do, when we have such a lead, I think is unlikely. What they are likely to try to do is pick a different task set, do it differently, because they see their goals and their strategy differently. Seeing this symmetrically the way we saw the U.S.-Soviet arms race during the Cold War is the wrong way to see it.

I think the risk for us is not thinking through what we think our global role should be and what we think the Chinese global role should be, and having seams open up between our understanding of what we are going to do and what we should do and what others should do, and what the Chinese are willing to do, not for themselves but for everybody else.

COMMISSIONER SLANE: I have another question, but I will wait for a second round.

HEARING CO-CHAIR FIEDLER: Thank you.

Commissioner Tobin.

COMMISSIONER TOBIN: Thank you, gentlemen, all of you.

I have a question for Dr. Erickson, and it is really a clarification and request for more specifics. Looking at your policy recommendations, you mentioned, and reiterated here today, that we should encourage reduction in China's free-riding in the Far Seas, and then you proceeded to say that it is not an overactive China but rather a selfish superpower. Can you give me specifics on what the policy recommendation would be to help me understand that tactically, I guess?

DR. ERICKSON: Thank you, Commissioner. This is right at the center of what I would recommend, namely, China is clearly rising across all dimensions of national power. The future trajectory is uncertain, but it is already reached a level where it is a very significant great power, and it will stay that way in some fashion. So the question for the U.S. is not whether or not China will be powerful, but in what way the U.S. can encourage and in selective cases play a role in actively shaping how China will act?

And a framework I would encourage U.S. policymakers to raise with their Chinese counterparts for thinking of this is the sense that a great power like China can get status and recognition in the international system in proportion to the public goods that it provides to that system.

This in many ways has explained U.S. power and influence in the international system over the past century, and I think the same applies to China. Applying, looking at this in specific areas, I think the Gulf of Aden antipiracy missions are an initial, rather positive, step on the whole for China to be taking.

China should be encouraged to use its navy, to use its military, to do more of these types of things that genuinely serve China's interests without harming those of other countries, and also provide a real, measurable collective benefit. It should be communicated to China that the more China does things like this, the more that it will be recognized as a constructive force for good in the international system.

Conversely, the more that China saves its military capabilities to pressure neighbors close to home should not be seen as a constructive attitude, and this should be communicated to the Chinese.

Thank you.

COMMISSIONER TOBIN: That was very clear. If we have a second round, I have further questions.

HEARING CO-CHAIR FIEDLER: Commissioner Brookes.

COMMISSIONER BROOKES: Thank you.

Let's see here. I have a bunch of questions. This is for Dr. Alterman. I will ask both questions, and then I will let you respond. They are for different people.

What are the vulnerabilities of the Chinese growing position in the Middle East, if there are any?

And for Dr. Wuthnow, what would the Chinese reaction be to a U.S. or Israeli strike on Iranian nuclear facilities?

DR. ALTERMAN: The Chinese feel infinite vulnerabilities in the Middle East, partly because they feel like they cannot influence what is happening, and the United States can. There was a theory bouncing around

China that the United States caused the Arab Spring in order to hurt China.

[Laughter.]

DR. ALTERMAN: It is not an idea I heard bouncing around Washington, but I have heard it bouncing around Beijing and other places, that this was all part of the United States because they can control everything. They control the governments, they understand, they have all these military people, they have their spies there, they have their diplomats, et cetera. This was all supposedly concocted by the United States to create turmoil and hurt China.

Taking it down a level, I think on individual bilateral relationships, they feel that the United States has powerful embassies with all kinds of staffing and understanding and Chinese embassies are often more thinly staffed.

The Chinese are developing cadres of very impressive young diplomats, oftentimes fluent in languages of the region, oftentimes entrepreneurial, in some cases, to my great shock, sarcastic. Young sarcastic Chinese diplomats are quite something to behold. I think it suggests that there is an awareness that China will have a very different style, and I have been struck when I have met with Chinese diplomats in the Middle East that oftentimes with every decade of youth, seem to be from a totally different country.

And I think to me this speaks to a growing awareness that China will have to deal with the world in a different way, and the implication that China will deal with the world in a different way as time goes on.

They see themselves militarily vulnerable. The Fifth Fleet is a tremendous force, not only in terms of firepower but in terms of intelligence gathering, in terms of knowing everything that is going on in the region. All the other kinds of intelligence that go on, I think, the Chinese find rather awe inspiring.

I think on a basic level, also, they feel that the United States holds the key to whether there is war or peace in the region, whether there is a war with Israel, whether there is a war with Iran, that the United States somehow controls this and will decide based on what it wants and whether it wants to help China or hurt China.

DR. WUTHNOW: Commissioner Brookes, thanks very much for your question.

It is difficult to estimate what China's response would be, not knowing what the circumstances of a U.S. or Israeli strike are. I think at a minimum we would expect some level of diplomatic condemnation or rhetorical opposition, but beyond that it is unclear what steps China could take to pronounce its opposition.

I think the important point is that many in China right now do not believe that either the U.S. or Israel is actually prepared to use military force. That makes it difficult to obtain China's acquiescence in the Security Council and other places because China does not feel the sense of urgency that it does with respect, arguably, to North Korea and other cases.

I think it is incumbent on China's interlocutors to make sure that Beijing understands that there is a level of seriousness both in Washington and in Tel Aviv about the use of military force.

DR. ALTERMAN: Just to underline this difference in perspective, I was talking to a Chinese diplomat in Algeria, and in the middle of the conversation, he looked, and he said, "How about you do security and we do business?" And I think there is a way in which we look at the Middle East and we start thinking in security terms. We talk about how many carriers we are moving and how many ships, and that is the way we are seeing it.

I think as the Chinese look at this region, they look at vulnerability. They are looking at commercial issues, they are looking at a whole other set of things and a whole other set of tools, and in a way that makes them feel vulnerable, but they are making do with what they have, and I think they see their strategy different. They see the tools of their strategy to be different, and they are in a position of vulnerability partly because they feel so globally vulnerable to the consequences of our decisions that they feel they cannot really influence.

COMMISSIONER BROOKES: Thank you.

HEARING CO-CHAIR FIEDLER: Commissioner Cleveland.

COMMISSIONER CLEVELAND: I think there would be some concern about the notions of free-riding if it did evolve to the U.S. doing security and China doing business. But I'm interested in your describing that they have different goals and strategies and see things differently than we do. And our understanding is not necessarily their understanding of what they are willing or capable of doing.

And I am wondering, in that context, if the term that has so far framed the discussion about our expectations with China, that being "responsible stakeholder," is not a dead letter, and if it is, what is taking its place? And if you were writing a memo to the Secretary now as Director of Policy Planning, for ten years out, what would be that characterization of the hope or expectation about their role and responsibilities in the world, and how would you make the case that that is how they are going to proceed and including your sarcastic diplomats?

So what is the right frame of reference for what they are willing to do, and what is it going to look like ten years out?

DR. ALTERMAN: Commissioner Cleveland, thank you.

You know I can't remember ever hearing one of my Chinese interlocutors use the phrase "responsible stakeholder." The way it seems to me, and I may have this wrong, is China often thinks in terms of its bilateral relationships, and we devote a lot of time to thinking about the international system and sort of international organizations, and we give a lot of thought not to the bilateral relationships independently but the bilateral relationships as they come down from the more international conventions, obligations, and treaties, those kinds of things.

I am not sure that China is in the process of change on that. I am not sure China feels a need to change. There are others who are much more expert on Chinese strategy. As I read people like Wang Jisi, they talk about which way China should look, and it continues to be very much based in China's national interests without thinking a lot about China's ability to shape the context.

And in my discussions with Chinese, I keep talking about how you do not appreciate your ability to help change the context. You have an effect on the environment in which things happen. You are not just a market maker. You can be a market maker by your actions, and sometimes your actions, for instance, with Iran, to my mind, undermine your commercial and security interests because China as a bad actor in the world increases the security premium on oil some people say $20 or $30 a barrel, which you are paying.

So to me, it does not make sense, but I do not see a broad awareness of the Chinese ability. I hear people talking about "harmonious relations." I hear people talking about the way they would like the world to be, but I do not hear people drawing the connection between Chinese actions and making the world that way. Whether that is going to come, or not, how the U.S. can help engender that view, how other parties can help engender that view, I think I leave that to the China experts. I have my hands full with the Middle East.

But I do make that observation that it feels like, as China looks at this region, they continue to look at the bilateral phase of this, and we continue to think in multilateral and in environmental terms as something we want to change, and they look at environmental terms as something that is there.

DR. ERICKSON: Commissioner, if I could add briefly, I think this is exactly the sort of thing that we need to be communicating to our Chinese counterparts. Certainly our saying certain things will not automatically change Chinese behavior on some specific issues, but, China cares deeply about the bilateral relationship with the U.S. and its status in the larger international community.

We can shape that to some extent, and using the framework of China being treated and accorded status in proportion to the positive public goods that it provides is a good way forward.

One positive step that we have seen in the maritime dimension just recently involves the Exclusive Economic Zone, the area that a coastal state can claim between 12 and 200 nautical miles. In the past, China had attempted a very exclusionary approach vis-à-vis military operations, trying to promote a view held in some form by probably no more than 26 of 160 plus nations, that the coastal state could exclude military, could restrict military activities in that zone.

We're finally seeing some encouraging signs that China's moving in the other direction towards the global system as its interests as a maritime power probably are moving things. In the latest Department of Defense China Report recently issued, we see documented, as well as in Admiral Locklear's testimony, that Chinese intelligence gathering ships have operated in the Exclusive Economic Zone of the U.S., the undisputed Exclusive Economic Zone off both Guam and Hawaii, and that these ships have also operated in the Indian Ocean.

Now, the U.S. as a matter of policy says that this is all fine. It is China that has been objecting to these types of things, but here we are seeing potentially a Chinese shift toward embracing the larger global system. I think as China's interests continue to evolve, with the right U.S. encouragement and support and judicious pressure, we can over time see some positive developments in that area.

COMMISSIONER BROOKES: Thank you.

HEARING CO-CHAIR FIEDLER: Thank you.

I have a couple of observations and questions because I am a little confused. I hear you describe a China that wants a risk-free exercise of international power. Oh, the Middle East is really complicated, we have to make very tough decisions, and some of those decisions are going to get us into trouble, and therefore, we would maybe like not to make those decisions.

Then you describe, Dr. Alterman, a conspiratorial view, being articulated by some unknown, that the United States in this complicated neighborhood has control over a place that nobody has control over and never did, which shows a fundamental misunderstanding.

We heard earlier this morning about this great Chinese desire for legitimacy as a world power. I do not understand. They seem to be really confused about how to act, and we seem to be hesitant to treat them as an equal because they are not, but they want to be treated as an equal, and they are very sensitive, overly sensitive, diplomatically and personally and politically to how we treat them.

That's a prescription for miscalculation in my view. In other words, there is a great danger in U.S. policy determination that we say, we got to treat them all right, you know they do not really get it, so we are going to kind of make their decisions for them? Do their thinking for them? Which we cannot do, that's wishful thinking on our part.

That, I would say, is your encourage--the notion that if we do positive things, they will do positive things; they will accept the international order contrary to all the evidence. You got them describing that perhaps their policy is to keep us occupied with Iran. That's in dealing with nuclear weapons. This is serious stuff.

So I am really confused by all of this. It seems that we are dealing with an unsophisticated power in very important matters that we would be better off if they are hesitant to make our decisions and do what we are going to do. Am I misunderstanding? Am I mischaracterizing their international profile here?

DR. ALTERMAN: Well, as I say, I am a little naive when it comes to Chinese strategy, but I can tell you what I have heard. One of the things I have always found puzzling is the longstanding Chinese desire to be a member of the Middle East Quartet and solve the Arab-Israeli conflict because I'm not sure why they would want that. There have been a number of Special Envoys who have left their jobs, but the Chinese seem persistently to seek this, I think because they want prestige.

I'm not sure what they think that prestige gets them. Maybe they think it gets them more consultation with the United States, more consideration of their issues. I am not really sure. They clearly think about us an awful lot because they think that we are the decision-makers who matter, and clearly the most important--and the most important influence on their national security. But when it comes to unsophisticated, they think we're unsophisticated because they think that our insistence on confrontation, our insistence on creating Manichean struggles, our insistence on "You're with us or you're against us," our insistence on relying on military tools, all those kinds of tools, they see as undermining our own interests and certainly undermining global security.

From what I can tell, they have a genuine philosophical difference with our understanding of how diplomacy does work and should work. They believe that they have a more sophisticated understanding, which is based on building common interests, on creating relationships that are durable, building out from bilateral ties rather than sort of relying on these multilateral frameworks.

So there is a part of it I understand, and there is a part of it I do not understand, and there is a part of it that I believe they think we do not understand, and I think that part that they think we do not understand is unlikely to go away. That is whatever happens, in response to Commissioner Cleveland's point, whatever happens in the future, ten years from now, China as a responsible stakeholder, all those kinds of things, it will be a less confrontational relationship with countries, especially those far away.

It may well be a more confrontational relationship with countries that are in what they believe to be their sphere of influence, but farther away, in this global sense that we are always thinking of, they may feel that our desire for confrontation, our desire for clear outcomes, undermines global security, and what they can do to the world is to enhance a willingness to accept ambiguity as the best that can be obtained at any given time.

DR. WUTHNOW: Commissioner, if I could follow up on that as well. I think part of the problem is that Chinese leaders and Chinese analysts may not have a very clear understanding of China's own interests in the Middle East and how those interests are affected by various types of policies and how those interests can be better safeguarded through international cooperation, especially with the United States.

I don't believe that the responsible stakeholder rhetoric and the entire program of naming and shaming has a good chance of being effective. Chinese interlocutors do not like to feel insulted in this way. I think the better approach is to help them understand how their interests are bound up in the international system. I think we have a responsibility to, based on our

148

understanding of how the region works, and to Iran and issues of this nature, I think we have a responsibility to help clarify for them how their interests are bound up, and how they may face cost to their own interests if they refuse to cooperate.

DR. ERICKSON: If I could just add, as well, Commissioner, there are certainly many aspects here that are somewhat confusing and nebulous. I think the difference in our national systems and our interests continue to create areas of misunderstanding. At the same time, I think some of the larger interests and areas in which our two nations differ are not necessarily that mysterious.

I think we need to focus on some of those differences of interest and see how we might approach those. Certainly, there are also some issues that stem from China's position and interests changing so rapidly. I think that sometimes explains some lag effects and some things that we find puzzling.

But if I were to try to put it simply, I think a lot of China's policies in the international arena boil down to trying to really focus energies in regions and areas of the greatest interest and the greatest payoff: in economic development and in territorial and maritime disputes close in, while minimizing risks and minimizing the international burden that they have to assume farther away, say in the Middle East.

I think that there is a way in the bilateral U.S.-China relationship that we can try to make it clear to China over time that we do not welcome an approach that focuses on building up military capabilities vis-à-vis the Near Seas but then expects to free-ride on U.S. capabilities farther away, and I do think we have some national levers over time that we can bring to bear on that.

Finally, though, we need a positive side to this story as well because China is big and influential in the international system, and there are many shared interests in which we could cooperate or that at least overlap. So we need to articulate a path to greater power status in a positive way for China, and that's where I advocate emphasizing that to the extent that China provides more public goods to the international system, it should be accorded more status; whereas, to the extent to which it builds up power in more negative ways, that will be resisted.

And to the extent to which it attempts to sort of free-ride and just say, "our internal development should be enough to make you appreciative," well, the U.S. has its own internal development to do, and we don't use that as an excuse not to provide public goods to the international system.

So these are some ways in which I think we can try to move forward from what is a dynamic and sometimes complicated set of affairs.

HEARING CO-CHAIR FIEDLER: Thank you.

We have three Commissioners who want to have a second round.

COMMISSIONER CLEVELAND: I am interested in keeping it going, in part because, Dr. Erickson, when you say that it should be a positive that there's an emphasis on their greater global power status, and that we should encourage it in terms of their participation and contribution of goods to the global commons, I guess I am not sure I really know what that means.

They have an important role in all the international financial institutions. They have a decisive role at the United Nations. I mean we are not talking about public flattery so what is the manifestation or how is that expressed or what is done to give content or meaning to what you suggest in terms of conferring this greater global status? And I welcome all of you speaking to it.

DR. ERICKSON: Thank you, Commissioner. I think this is a really important area to focus on.

And while you mentioned the wide range of international institutions and organizations in which China is an active participant, where we have seen less Chinese participation is in international military and security operations that can help safeguard and support the functioning of the international system in that regard.

Now, it's true that China has made significant contributions to U.N. peacekeeping over time, but beyond that, until the Gulf of Aden operations, there really wasn't much else that China was doing in that category. I think the U.S. can continue to place focus on this area and recognize China for its contributions there and suggest that China is strongly welcomed in that dimension and would be strongly welcomed to engage in analogous activities.

For example: using its navy and its other military capabilities in disaster relief in Southeast Asia and the Indian Ocean, areas like that, but again with the focus on providing these public goods, I think the U.S. view and the U.S. interaction really counts. The U.S. should not sell itself short in terms of influence and persuasion in this area. It won't be magic and simple, but over time, I think we can have an impact.

DR. ALTERMAN: And if I may just add a couple of thoughts. We're used to thinking about the interagency process on the U.S. side. We're not used to thinking about the interagency process on the Chinese side because it's so opaque.

But there are some suggestions that there actually is an active interagency process with different views, and the Ministry of Foreign Affairs is thought to be in the pocket of people who want a good relationship with the United States, and the PLA is thought to be more concerned and paranoid about U.S. intentions. And you have a whole set of commercial interests.

So it seems to me that just to enrich this discussion, there is not a single rational actor thinking about a Chinese strategy. We are used to thinking of this as a top down system, and I just wonder if as we think forward to ten or 15 or 20 years from now, whether the dynamics of trying to reach consensus among stakeholders in China are going to hold the key to making the kinds of decisions that we are talking about now in front of China.

I just wonder if what we are seeing is less coherent because there are so many different people coming to the table whose views are trying to be reconciled.

COMMISSIONER CLEVELAND: Thank you.

HEARING CO-CHAIR FIEDLER: Senator Talent.

HEARING CO-CHAIR TALENT: Let me just follow up on my earlier question. Is it possible that their activities in the Middle East are understandable in terms of the following theory about their motives, that what the Chinese, they have a very definite view of their own interests. I think everybody agrees on that. They want an international order where they are able to maneuver effectively for their own interests and enjoy the benefits of the international order without being effectively constrained by the norms.

They realize that this is going to bring them into conflict with the United States or likely to on two levels. One, our perception of our interests will bring them into conflict with theirs, and the second, the United States wants a norm-based international order; right?

And so they are balancing the desire to inhibit that order and keep the United States occupied against their desire for stability so they can get energy. And the different interagency type of disputes are basically over how much, not the goals, but over how much risk they are willing to take in terms of their operations in the short term? I mean is that an analysis that maybe explains this?

DR. ALTERMAN: I think it does, and what I think is most powerful is the word "balance." My understanding of the way the Chinese think about strategy in the Middle East is you have a whole series of incompatible extremes, and the question is what balance do you maintain between them, what element of risk are you willing to take, what level of conflict are you willing to have with the United States on what issues at what time, what's happening with Iranians, how close are we to war?

I think the more the Iranians seem aggressive, I think the farther the Chinese move away. The more conciliatory the Iranians seem, I think the closer the Chinese draw. I think it is a constant balancing act, and in many ways, it is a more supple policy than we often have because we often like to have the same policy, and then we copy/paste, copy/paste, copy/paste, and then one day it changes, and we all denied we ever changed the policy.

It seems to me that the Chinese policy is always changing, as they try to balance between their different goals.

HEARING CO-CHAIR TALENT: But a key thing for us to keep in mind is that they do not want an international system that is capable of effectively enforcing its norms against them.

This idea that we can educate them to the benefits of that kind of a system, they don't quite see it. I mean they have their view of their interests and who they are, a proud people, particularly with regard to Asia. I think they view themselves as the leading power in Asia, and historically they have some basis for that view.

But I just think we ought to be clear about what we are going to be able to convince them of and what we are not going to be able to convince them of.

DR. ALTERMAN: And international law, as I understand it, was created by American and British lawyers in the first half of the 20th century to meet precisely the kinds of capabilities that our countries have and serve the interests of an order that serves, and it has served the interests of American development for more than half a century.

HEARING CO-CHAIR TALENT: And this gets back to your original point, which I really think was good to start this hearing off since we are now coming to the end, Mr. Chairman, is that we have to decide what is important to us in the world.

I mean is this view of the international order important to us, and if so, why? Because if we are going to stick with it, we are going to come into conflict with the Chinese, not necessarily kinetic, but--there is a real inconsistency between that view, and it is going to manifest itself in all these areas of the world, and I think at this point, they are at least asking themselves the right questions, and we are not.

DR. WUTHNOW: Senator Talent, can I just briefly follow up on this? I think it is important to realize that the evolution of norms is a long-term historical process, especially for the Chinese.

For instance, in the 1970s, when China originally joined the U.N. Security Council, they subscribed to none of the prevailing norms. They frequently abstained. They launched vitriolic rhetoric. Twenty, 30 years later, we are at least at the stage where China occasionally votes in favor of norms, for instance, on Libya and referring Gaddafi to the ICC. This is something that was probably unimaginable 25 or 30 years ago.

So in the long sweep of history, 25 or 30 years from now, I think we will expect similar changes.

HEARING CO-CHAIR TALENT: We do not know what is going to happen internally in China either. I mean I am just saying given who we are, the leadership that we are now dealing with, I think what I described accurately describes where they are coming from. You're right. That could change.

We do not know what kind of governing system they are going to have 20 years from now.

HEARING CO-CHAIR FIEDLER: Let me just add something to this conversation, that earlier I think it was you who said, Dr. Wuthnow, that something we ought to tell the Chinese is that it is not in their interests. I think the Chinese fully know what is in their interests, that we do not have to be arrogant enough to tell them what is in their interests because they would be suspicious of that, as I would be, if they told me what was my interest.

I have never met people who did not know their interests. So to that discussion that we were having about keeping the United States occupied versus closing the Strait of Hormuz, I would say that--observe, without knowing, that they've made a decision, in your balancing, that, you know, we don't, we'd rather tweak the United States with Iran and we're less worried about the closing of the Straits of Hormuz because that oil problem is a real one. Okay.

And it is a short-term real one, too, because I don't think their strategic reserve is enough for their expanding economy. And so to your suppleness, I do not know how supple. I think it is conscious. I am not convinced how supple it is because one of the things that I seem to have learned over a lifetime is that superpower interests, especially as articulated by the United States, on very frequent occasion subordinates the interests of its citizenry to the exercise of that power.

You discussed mercantile supernational interests here. They have not learned how to subordinate their national interests on a temporary basis or even on a long-term basis or their citizens' interests because they are worried about their citizens overthrowing them, i.e., domestic stability, that they are not true exercisers yet.

I mean the only way you get exercise, just as any way you learn as a navy, is to do. I think you were talking about it. So I think the process of failure and of exercising of power, just hopefully that it does not result on a whole lot of conflict along the learning curve.

So I would like to end the hearing today on that note and thank you all very much for coming. We have had a lively afternoon, and I would like to thank Caitlin Campbell for her work in putting this hearing together and all you witnesses, and we will see others again at our next hearing on June 27.

Thank you very much.

[Whereupon, at 2:02 p.m., the hearing was adjourned.]

www.ingramcontent.com/pod-product-compliance
Lightning Source LLC
Chambersburg PA
CBHW081103290526
45795CB00006B/1975

* 9 7 8 1 4 9 2 9 8 2 4 8 7 *